# Contending with Globalization in World Englishes

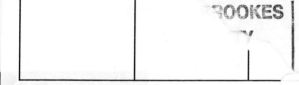

D1614868

## CRITICAL LANGUAGE AND LITERACY STUDIES

*Series Editors*: **Professor Vaidehi Ramanathan** (*University of California, USA*), **Professor Bonny Norton** (*University of British Columbia, Canada*), **Professor Alastair Pennycook** (*University of Technology, Sydney, Australia*)

Critical Language and Literacy Studies is an international series that encourages monographs directly addressing issues of power (its flows, inequities, distributions, trajectories) in a variety of language- and literacy-related realms. The aim with this series is twofold: (1) to cultivate scholarship that openly engages with social, political, and historical dimensions in language and literacy studies, and (2) to widen disciplinary horizons by encouraging new work on topics that have received little focus (see below for partial list of subject areas) and that use innovative theoretical frameworks.

Full details of all our other publications can be found on http://www.multilingual-matters.com, or by writing to Multilingual Matters, St Nicholas House, 31–34 High Street, Bristol BS1 2AW, UK.

**Other books in this series**

Collaborative Research in Multilingual Classrooms
*Corey Denos, Kelleen Toohey, Kathy Neilson and Bonnie Waterstone*
English as a Local Language: Post-colonial Identities and Multilingual Practices
*Christina Higgins*
The Idea of English in Japan: Ideology and the Evolution of a Global Language
*Philip Seargeant*
Language and HIV/AIDS
*Christina Higgins and Bonny Norton* (eds)
China and English: Globalization and the Dilemmas of Identity
*Joseph Lo Bianco, Jane Orton and Gao Yihong* (eds)
Bodies and Language: Health, Ailments, Disabilities
*Vaidehi Ramanathan*
Hybrid Identities and Adolescent Girls: Being 'Half' in Japan
*Laurel D. Kamada*
Decolonizing Literacy: Mexican Lives in the Era of Global Capitalism
*Gregorio Hernandez-Zamora*

CRITICAL LANGUAGE AND LITERACY STUDIES
*Series Editors*: Vaidehi Ramanathan, Bonny Norton
and Alastair Pennycook

# Contending with Globalization in World Englishes

Edited by
Mukul Saxena and Tope Omoniyi

MULTILINGUAL MATTERS
Bristol • Buffalo • Toronto

**Library of Congress Cataloging in Publication Data**
Contending with Globalization in World Englishes / Edited by Mukul Saxena and
Tope Omoniyi.
Includes bibliographical references and index.
1. English language—Globalization.   2. English language—Variation—
English-speaking countries.   3. English language—Variation—Foreign countries.
4. Intercultural communication.   I. Saxena, Mukul, 1956–   II. Omoniyi, Tope.
PE1073.C66 2010
427-dc22 2010014112

**British Library Cataloguing in Publication Data**
A catalogue entry for this book is available from the British Library.

ISBN-13: 978-1-84769-275-7 (hbk)
ISBN-13: 978-1-84769-274-0 (pbk)

**Multilingual Matters**
UK: St Nicholas House, 31–34 High Street, Bristol BS1 2AW, UK.
USA: UTP, 2250 Military Road, Tonawanda, NY 14150, USA.
Canada: UTP, 5201 Dufferin Street, North York, Ontario M3H 5T8, Canada.

Copyright © 2010 Mukul Saxena, Tope Omoniyi and the authors of individual
chapters.

All rights reserved. No part of this work may be reproduced in any form or by any
means without permission in writing from the publisher.

The policy of Multilingual Matters/Channel View Publications is to use papers that
are natural, renewable and recyclable products, made from wood grown in
sustainable forests. In the manufacturing process of our books, and to further support
our policy, preference is given to printers that have FSC and PEFC Chain of Custody
certification. The FSC and/or PEFC logos will appear on those books where full
certification has been granted to the printer concerned.

Typeset by Integra Software Services Pvt. Ltd, Pondicherry, India.
Printed and bound in Great Britain by Short Run Press Ltd

Even as I carried narratives of folks
And told tales to strangers about places
And things that are pieces of me
I listened and heard tales of other
Places and things that are pieces of them
Now I am a confluence of tongues
Merged narratives course through me
As I waltz, salsa and lion-dance in one breadth

# Contents

# List of Figures and Tables

## Figures

# Contributors

**Rakesh M. Bhatt** is Professor of Linguistics and SLATE (Second Language Acquisition and Teacher Education) at the University of Illinois, Urbana-Champaign. He specializes in sociolinguistics of language contact, in particular, issues of migration, minorities and multilingualism, code-switching, language ideology and world Englishes. He has published two books, *Verb Movement and the Syntax of Kashmiri* (1999, Kluwer Academic Press), and (co-authored) *World Englishes* (2008, Cambridge University Press). He is currently working on a book-length manuscript, under contract with Cambridge University Press, on the sociolinguistic patterns of subordination of Kashmiri language in Diaspora. He has published articles in the *Journal of Sociolinguistics, Annual Review of Anthropology, International Journal of the Sociology of Language, International Journal of Applied Linguistics, Lingua, World Englishes, Studies in Second Language Acquisition, Second Language Research, English Language and Linguistics* and other venues.

**Augustin Simo Bobda** is Professor of English Language and Linguistics and Head of Department of English at the Higher Teaching Training College (Ecole Normale Supérieure) of the University of Yaounde I. He is the author of over 70 publications on various aspects of English language and linguistics. He has mostly contributed to the knowledge of the status, functions, and features of African English, and the problems involved in using/learning/teaching English in non-native English communities. He has held research and teaching positions in many parts of Africa, Europe, America, and Asia, namely, at The University of Hong Kong where he was Visiting Professor in the School of English for several years.

**Dr Phyllis Ghim-Lian Chew** is Associate Professor/English Language and Literature, at the National Institute of Education, Nanyang Technological University. She has been invited to keynote at many conferences in ESL, gender studies and comparative religion both locally and abroad. Her research interests include general issues of pragmatics and sociolinguistics, metaphor and discourse and language ideologies on the social, cultural and religious level. She is also the project advisor for a series of textbooks for primary schools in Singapore entitled 'In-step' and the author of many books.

**Martin Dewey** is Lecturer in Applied Linguistics at King's College London, where he teaches Sociolinguistics, World Englishes and Teacher Education on undergraduate and postgraduate programmes, and supervises research students working in areas related to the globalization of English and English language teaching. He is currently engaged in researching the use of English as a lingua franca, investigating in particular implications for curriculum change in language pedagogy, and contemporary practice in teacher education. He has written numerous articles on English as a lingua franca, and is currently working on a forthcoming co-authored book on the subject (with Alessia Cogo, due to be published by Continuum 2010).

**Maria Georgieva**, PhD, is currently Associate Professor in the Department of British and American Studies, St Kliment Ohridski University of Sofia. Her research interests and publications are in the field of Applied Linguistics, Sociolinguistics, Intercultural Pragmatics, Communication Strategies and Canadian Studies. Author of monographs, articles and EFL textbooks for primary and secondary school. E-mail: mageorg@nlcv.net.

**Jennifer Jenkins** is Chair of English Language at the University of Southampton, where she teaches, and supervises research into, World/ Global Englishes and English as a Lingua Franca (ELF). Over the past two decades she has published numerous articles in these fields, as well as two monographs, *The Phonology of English as an International Language* (OUP, 2000) and *English as a Lingua Franca: Attitude and Identity* (OUP, 2007). She is also the author of a university course book, *World Englishes* (Routledge, 2009, 2nd edn), and co-editor, with Constant Leung, of *Reconfiguring Europe: The Contribution of Applied Linguistics* (Equinox, 2006) and, with Kumiko Murata, of *Global Englishes in Asian Contexts* (Palgrave, 2009).

**Paroo Nihalani** was Chair Professor of English Language and Applied Linguistics at the University of Brunei Darussalam (UBD) until July 2009. Before joining UBD in 2003, he worked at Central Institute of English and Foreign Languages (CIEFL) in India (1968–1982), National University of Singapore (1982–1997), Oita National University (1997–2001) and Chukyo University (2002–2003) in Japan. At the moment, he is working as a part-time Academic Consultant at the SIM University in Singapore. He has published eight books and contributed a large number of research articles to the journals of international repute. He has served as a member of Editorial Advisory Board of international Journals such as *RELC Journal*,

*Asian Englishes, Asian Quarterly.* He has held numerous visiting teaching/ research appointments in diverse linguistic, cultural and educational contexts such as USA (UCLA, Illinois-UC), Australia (Macquarie University), Scotland (Edinburgh University), Nigeria (University of Port Harcourt) and Norway (Institute of Phonetics, Trondheim), among several others.

**Tope Omoniyi** is Professor of Sociolinguistics in the School of Arts at Roehampton University, London (UK). His research interests straddle issues in language and identity, language in education, and language policy and planning in Europe and Africa. His scholarly articles and reviews have appeared in *TESOL Quarterly, International Journal of the Sociology of Language, Text, AILA Review, Language Policy, Language in Society, International Journal of World Englishes and Current Anthropology*. He is the author of the monograph *The Sociolinguistics of Borderlands: Two Nations, One Community* (AWP, 2004) and editor and co-editor of several volumes of essays.

**Alastair Pennycook** is interested in how we understand language in relation to globalization, colonial history, identity, popular culture and pedagogy. His many publications include *The Cultural Politics of English as an International Language* (Longman, 1994), *English and the Discourses of Colonialism* (Routledge, 1998), *Critical Applied Linguistics: A Critical Introduction* (Lawrence Erlbaum, 2001) and *Global Englishes and transcultural flows* (Routledge, 2007), as well as two recent edited books, *Disinventing and Reconstituting Languages* (with Sinfree Makoni; Multilingual Matters, 2007) and *Global Linguistic Flows: Hip Hop Cultures, Youth Identities, and the Politics of Language* (with Samy Alim and Awad Ibrahim; Routledge 2009). His new book *Language as a Local Practice* (Routledge) is due for publication in 2010. Alastair is Professor of Language Studies at the University of Technology Sydney.

**Kanavillil Rajagopalan** is Full Professor of Linguistics at the State University at Campinas (Unicamp), Brazil. He was born in India and pursued his studies in that country, as well as the UK, Brazil and the USA. He has published four books and upwards of 300 papers in journals and has contributed chapters to various edited volumes, encyclopedias, handbooks etc. His academic interests include the philosophy of language, linguistic pragmatics, postcolonial literature and the spread of this new linguistic phenomenon called 'World English'.

**Mukul Saxena** is working at the Centre for Applied Linguistics, University of Warwick, UK. Prior to Warwick, he worked in universities in Brunei Darussalam in Southeast Asia and in Lancaster and York, UK. His research interests in the combined fields of Socio-Applied Linguistics are Bilingual Discourse in English Classrooms, Multilingual Literacies, Language Maintenance & Shift, and World Englishes, with a particular focus on language, culture, identity and ideology. His ethnographic research in Britain and Brunei has been based in different research sites: in urban and rural settings, in community contexts as well as in educational settings, especially classrooms. He has published numerous articles in international journals and books.

**Farzad Sharifian** is an Associate Professor and the Director of the Language and Society Centre within the School of Languages, Cultures and Linguistics, Monash University, Australia. He is also the Convenor of the academic program of English as an International Language at Monash University. He has a wide range of research interests including cultural linguistics, pragmatics, English as an International Language, World Englishes, language and politics and intercultural communication. He is the editor (with Gary B. Palmer) of *Applied Cultural Linguistics* (2007, John Benjamins), the editor (with René Dirven, Ning Yu and Susanne Niemeier) of *Culture, Body and Language* (2008, Mouton de Gruyter) and the editor of *English as an International Language* (2009, Multilingual Matters). He has published numerous articles in many international journals.

# Preface

Flowing thickly through debates about World Englishes (WE), English as an international language (EIL), Global English (GE) or English as a lingua franca (ELF) are strains about urbanity, urban-ness and urban spaces that call attention to a network of connections that evoke the uneven overlays of globalism (Steger, 2005). Such intersections and our responses to them, where we struggle with the finer nuances of debates around these English language acronyms, make us pay heed to the shift that has occurred about our conceptualizations about spaces, geographic domains and the mapping of languages onto them. At stake here is the idea that spaces may now be less a matter of an actualized state of affairs than a matter of de-framings, where territories and our notions of them are forever fragmented and undone. This realm of flows, of which English teaching and learning is an integral part, is, as Manuel Castells (1996) points out, not just a space of dispersal with English emanating from particular sites (typically regarded as the 'inner' circle in the field). Rather, the flow is one of constant centralization and decentralization, in which command and control institutions in big cities (New York, London, Tokyo, Mumbai, etc.) spread out their networks to back offices in suburbs, at once opening up the possibility of the space of flows being a site for social practices without territorial contiguity.

The various pieces of this volume offer glimpses into this most complex canvas of networks. Whether it is Bulgaria, Iran, India, Gambia or Latin America, the pictures of how English is both appropriated and localized make us realize the dearth of information in the field about the ways in which modernity has historically evolved in the non-Western world, what urban constellations and articulations it has created (c.f. Chew, Sharifian, Bobda, Rajagopalan and Bhatt in this volume) and what such developments mean both for city cultures in general and for language policies in these geographic terrains in particular. More specifically, they contest our current discourses about hegemonic cultural globalization, and nudge us into realms where we see Englishes used and contested, understood and not, amid diverse experiences. Be they in call centres, or Japanese hip-hop, they are a part of a cacophony of voices, pinging off a range of spatial practices in all kinds of businesses, labour, leisure, politics and cultural events.

Like the urbanities of which English is a part, *English* is mangled and contaminated, and yet it enacts itself anew with each human interaction of which it is a part.

What this volume makes us confront through its glimpses around English debates is how modernity and its tropes collide with those of globalization. If Wallerstein's world systems theory (1989, 1998) gave us some key ways to study globalization (in sociology and economics particularly), the more recent resurgence of debates about modernity – where nation-states, in varying ways, seem to draw hard lines – offers another model to get at the cultural dimensions of globalization. Indeed, it is no accident that ever since the rise of 'globalization' as the master signifier of our times, the discourses of modernity and modernism have staged a remarkable comeback. Doyle and Winkiel (2005) offer the term 'geomodernisms' which for them signals a locational approach to modernism's engagement with cultural and political discourses of local modernity, a term that fits appropriately with the spatial transfusions around English on which this volume is predicated. Indeed, this term echoes other modernity-related phrases – modernity at large, late modernity, second modernity, liquid modernity and counter modernity – and underscores the simultaneous border-crossing and border-drawing that go on.

From such a point of view, ideas about a 'global culture' emerging from globalizing networks could be seen as somewhat premature. Indeed, the very term implies a unification that is scarcely possible given local and national histories, religious affiliations, customs, ceremonies and rituals. While the world-Englishes orientation, or the EIL viewpoint, or the ELF debates draw on such unifications either to contest native-speaking Englishes, or to address local uses of English amid other languages, or to view English as cutting across national boundaries, the various articulations are all still proceeding from the same terrains. However, anybody from or familiar with a non-Western space – indeed the editors of this volume and all the authors as well – can attest to the varying knots of internal variations in localized Englishes, the social stratifications around which English and other languages fall and ways in which we humans and the languages we use constellate around these issues. It is precisely because of such anxieties and tensions, uneven terrains and stony paths around these issues that Saxena and Omoniyi use the term 'contesting' in their title; it makes us take stock of the sweeping tropes by which 'less developed' countries are spoken of as being 'hurried along' into modernizing, or as being 'left out' by capitalistic flows.

So, how, then, are we to proceed with these various disciplinary cross-currents about English? Perhaps it is time to consider how our discipline 'speaks' about globalization and the knowledge-making apparatuses by which it does so, since this might nudge us to move beyond analytic or scalar levels that contain our thinking and permit us to seek contexts whereby some larger, broader questions about modernity, inequality and social justice can be posed (in ways that go beyond a simple aggregate of localities). Perhaps it is time to go beyond the plurality of Englishes (inherent in the world Englishes paradigm) to one that focuses on spatial diffusion, translations, appropriations, transnational connections and border-crossings that are not new per se, but have accelerated and intensified greatly in recent decades. Perhaps too it is time to view globalizing currents around cultures in ways that neither deny nor exaggerate the considerable impact of Western mass culture, technology and lifestyles across the world. Certainly, the various pieces in this volume prod us in this direction, whether it is questioning norms by which 'deviant English' gets judged (c.f. Bhatt, Nihalani, Dewey and Jenkins in this volume), or how miscommunications happen because particular terms and emotional states cannot be translated into English (c.f. Sharifian) or the ascension of English to a country's centre-stage amid tensions with other local languages (Rajagopalan, Georgieva, Bobda and Chew in this volume). The liberalizing of market economies, the outsourcing of jobs and the cross-currents of labour and capital seem to render much of our discipline's polarities around English – native/non-native, Western/non-western – defunct, leaving us at a point in the discipline to reconfigure our 'old' 'standards' (Milroy & Milroy, 1999), 'scales' (Blommaert, 2007) and assessments (Shohamy, 2001). What this new canvas is likely to look like, only time will tell; for now the various pieces in this volume point in that general direction. Overall, the volume makes us pay serious attention to how we 'waltz, salsa and lion-dance' all at once sometimes (as Omoniyi points out in his opening verse), while also pausing to remember the smaller steps to individual tunes in other moments.

Vaidehi Ramanathan, Bonny Norton, Alastair Pennycook
October 2009

## References

Blommaert, J. (2007) Sociolinguistic scales. *Intercultural Pragmatics* 4 (1), 1–19.
Castells, M. (1996) *The Rise of the Network Society* (Vol. 1). Oxford: Blackwell.
Doyle, L. and Winkiel, L. (2005) *Geomodernisms*. Indiana: Indiana University Press.
Milroy, J. and Milroy, L. (1999) *Authority in Language: Investigating Standard English*. New York: Routledge.

Shohamy, E. (2001) *The Power of Tests: A Critical Perspective on the Uses of Language Tests*. New York: Longman.
Steger, M. (2005) *Market Ideology Meets Terrorism*. Lanham, MD: Rowman and Littlefield.
Wallerstein, I. (1989) *The Modern World-System III: The Second Era of Great Expansion of the Capitalist World-Economy, 1730–1840s*. New York: Academic Press.
Wallerstein, I. (1998) *Utopistics: Or, Historical Choices of the Twenty-First Century*. New York: The New Press.

# Chapter 1
# *Introduction*

TOPE OMONIYI AND MUKUL SAXENA

> *What is interesting about the emerging body of writing associated*
> *with world Englishes is that it makes available a semiotic space for*
> *the articulation of the global imaginary and its formation within the*
> *phenomenology of the local*
> (Wimal Dissanayake, 2006: 556)

Globalization is perhaps one of the most troubled and complex concepts in the social sciences with each discipline proffering a definition and perspective it considers not only capable of effectively supporting but also reflective of its own theoretical and methodological frameworks. Stiglitz (2007: 295), in noting that 'few subjects have polarized people throughout the world as much as globalization', also remarks that globalization has had different interpretations in different places. In situations where themes of interdisciplinary relevance and application are concerned, such as language, it gets even more complex. More than any other language, the English language and world Englishes have been the subject of extensive scholarship. This is especially so when we consider that the cultural and political dynamics involving the English language in its multiple locations are varied and yet interconnected. Under the umbrella of globalization research, numerous and sometimes variant and even conflicting perspectives on what it is have emerged in economic, cultural, religious, political and other disciplinary analyses (see Hülsemeyer's (2003) edited volume from the perspective of international political economy).

For our purposes in this volume, we consider language not only to be crucial to the processes of globalization but to be its life force. Globalization is a social construct, a dense and universal network of exchange based on a structure of intensified relationships of interdependence (see Giddens, 1990; Robertson, 1992; Wallerstein, 1974 and 1979). Like all other social constructs globalization manifests as a patterned discourse, that is, it has specific communicative practices that characterise it. Globalization is not new but in its current manifestation or phase, it is powered by advancement in information and media technology.

Thus, irrespective of disciplinary specificities which enable us to recognise the different dimensions to globalization in, for example, the works of Amartya Sen (economics), Arjun Appadurai (sociocultural anthropology) and Anthony Giddens (cultural studies) among others, they are all anchored crucially in Information Age development. Participants in the globalization network are marked by difference and inequality and are therefore constantly (re)negotiating roles, relationships and interdependence.

In relation to world Englishes research then, we are concerned with the perspectives that globalization as a social process brings to bear on the forms, statuses and functions of the English language around the world. In exploring these, we are similarly probing the roles that the language plays in the process of globalization. The word 'contending' in the title is used cautiously and with an awareness of its connotation of negativity vis-à-vis globalization. The volume does not start from an assumption that globalization is problematic and therefore has to be contended with, but rather that it forces a re-examination of the traditional ways of explaining the place of English around the world. From the centrality of 'structure', 'relationship of interdependence', 'difference' and 'inequality' in our definition of globalization we are able to draw the connecting lines between 'English-speaking' and 'English-using' nations and peoples in a global network. We bring to the table the various contexts and debates from which we have drawn contributors to this volume but most importantly a critical look at the state of play in the field.[1]

To return to the question of contending with globalization, Kumaravadivelu (2008) devotes an entire chapter to processes of globalization in his book *Cultural Globalization and Language Education*. The opening to that chapter points us in the direction of a probable answer to our question:

'Hi, this is Sandy. How may I help you?'
When hundreds of thousands of North Americans and western Europeans dial a toll-free number to book airline tickets, check their bank account, solve a computer glitch, or seek investment advice, they may not be aware that they frequently are talking to customer representatives who are some six to eight thousand miles away, in India, working in the dead of night in quiet offices with clocks showing time in places like New York, Los Angeles, Frankfurt, and London. Nor are they likely to know that the helpful person who answers and identifies herself as 'Sandy' is in reality Lakshmi, a twenty-one-year-old who, after undergoing rigorous training to 'neutralize' her Indian accent, has

taken on a new workplace persona, including a pretend Western name and a pretend American or British accent.

Both 'Sandy' and the 'pretend' accents that Kumaravadivelu refers to are social constructions (Gergen, 1999) necessitated by the transnational dialogues and relationships created by globalization. In other words, in order to provide services to non-local customers via non-face-to-face interactions, Call Centre workers of necessity are trained into a new set of codes, dialects or languages deemed appropriate for efficient communicative exchange in their role as transnational consultants. Since much of the outsourcing originates from English-speaking Western nations coupled with the fact that a greater percentage of international business is conducted in English, it stands to reason that the codes and dialects are to do with the language. While Kumaravadivelu refers to 'pretend' accents with the connotation that they do not represent reality, we prefer to tag them no differently from any other performances accommodated by the theory of performativity as espoused by Butler (1997) and other critical thinkers. Indeed, the accents represent a kind of constructed reality of the contemporary globalization era, just as do the notion of English (Pennycook, Chapter 10, in this volume) or language itself (Le Page & Tabouret-Keller, 1985). Some of the perspectives on such language and globalization issues that have been explored elsewhere and in some of the contributions to this volume are discussed below.

## World Englishes from Colonisation to Globalization

A substantial portion of the traditional literature on world Englishes engages with the politics of colonisation to present descriptions and analyses of the linguistic ecology of former colonies. Whereas colonisation invokes a binary relationship between the colonisers and the colonised, globalization operates within a wider, more complex network of relationships of power and capital distribution, including linguistic and language power and capital. Thus, varieties of English or Englishes may be processed using either of these alternative paradigms. WE traditionally tracked the spread of English and its linguistic consequences in various locales (see Kachru, 1990; Melchers & Shaw, 2003). Constructing a historiography of language, however, does not engage sufficiently with the critical issues associated with language spread, particularly those that have to do with international and group relations. Braj Kachru's early account of the spread of English may be perceived as falling within the remit of a 'sociolinguistics of colonization' (cf. Omoniyi, in press).

It focused on analysis of the linguistic consequences of empire building thus offering a major ideological decentring perspective as an alternative to the mainstream centrist imperial narrative that is seemingly responsible for hierarchising global Englishes atop which sit native varieties of English. From an ideological standpoint, the world Englishes paradigm may be perceived as a rejection of and departure from the 'non-native Englishes' tag which has native English as reference point, and consequently acknowledging and legitimising English's multiple homes; after all, demographic evidence suggests that there is a larger population of users in these other homes.

The sociolinguistics of globalization (Blommaert, 2003) has prompted scholars of world Englishes to extend the frontiers of investigation beyond intra-state communicative regimes to look at English in inter-state and transnational relationships and communicative contexts. Kachru *et al.* (2006: 10) dedicate Part VII of *The Handbook of World Englishes* to globalization. It comprises three chapters that explore the presence of world Englishes in three cross-cultural and cross-linguistic domains of English language use: media, advertising and global commerce. Debates in English as an International Language (EIL) and English as a Lingua Franca (ELF) further exemplify that broadening of scope even if some regard both of these paradigms as one and the same thing.

Without prejudice to the four-diaspora delineation informed by the history of its spread in Kachru *et al.* (2006), we identify three broad diaspora Englishes that are relevant to our understanding of the interface between the sociolinguistics of colonisation and that of globalization. Diaspora Type 1 comprises speakers of neo-local diaspora Englishes who have relocated from an English-speaking homeland or nation. They include speakers of varieties of English identified with Canada, Australia and New Zealand. Here, English is the *de facto* language of establishment business whether or not this is expressly stated in any constitutional documents. It has displaced First Nation and/or Aboriginal languages, say, as in the case of Maori in New Zealand and Mohawk in northeastern United States and southern Canada.

The Englishes that have emerged out of colonial enterprise form Diaspora Type 2 and are found in the British Commonwealth, in other words, former British colonies like Nigeria, Kenya, Jamaica, India and Hong Kong among others, as well as in former colonies of the United States like the Philippines, Guam and Puerto Rico. English features in the language policy statement of these nations. In the case of the Philippines, for instance, English language was instituted as official language as part of the subjugation process in 1913.

The third category, Diaspora Type 3, comprises those that have evolved either as the consequence of or in response to global market-cum-political forces. This includes Japan, South Korea and China among others. In this context those who engage with the English-speaking world for commerce and popular culture purposes also engage culturally and represent a subculture in which English plays a significant role. The point to be stressed here is that in the era of globalization the notion of diaspora destabilises the Outer Circle category. Outer Circle is a sociolinguistic construct that was specific to territory. In its conceptualisation, however, the magic of globalization could not have envisaged the ramifications of open borders, human migration and transcultural flows facilitated by new media. These new developments have fashioned a new reality in which hybridisation, assimilation, integration and other forms of socialisation have seen Outer and Expanding Circle spaces as well as Outer and Expanding Circle speakers of English impacted in unanticipated ways. In the diaspora, we find reconstituted Outer Circle and Expanding Circle spaces on the fringes of Inner Circle spaces with interaction of varying intensities taking place between the cohorts. Little India, Little Jamaica, Little Lagos and other such constructs all of which together translate into the Multiculturalism Project in a place like the United Kingdom exemplify that phenomenon.

Of the three types presented above, Diaspora Type 3 leans most towards the so-called English homeland varieties of the United States and Britain in terms of attitudes and preferences. To cite an example, in China, the Department of Education in Shanghai implements a policy in Foreign Language teacher recruitment that requires prospective employees to have a native-speaker accent of English (*Shanghai Mail*, April 2007). Implicit in this is a reinforcement of the ideology that British and American accents of English belong to a higher ledge on a hierarchy of varieties of English. Kirkpatrick (2007: 6) describes this as prejudice and remarks that 'the idea that varieties of British English are somehow purer than later varieties is very difficult to support, however.' Arguably, the higher status accorded to British and American accents does not stem from the hegemony of colonisation but from their association with the new centres of the global economy. Jenkins (personal communication) suggests to the contrary that 'it's primarily because of a deep-seated belief that British/American accents are better . . . . This is the main reason that these accents/Englishes in general have become associated with the new centres of global economy.' Ironically, the rising appreciation of Diaspora Type 3 varieties seems to be directly proportional to the rising dominance of the economies in which they are based. In the example cited earlier (from Kumaravadivelu, 2008), the Call Centre accents may have emerged in the old colonial and post-colonial loci, but their reconstruction is produced for late 20th and 21st century globalization needs.

International labour mobility and migration are arguably features of globalization, thus by default language policy and employment policy are linked to globalization. A Reuters report (Beijing, 19 June 2007) headlined 'China demands its pilots speak better English' (www.reuters.com/article/oddlyEnoughNews/idUSKUA95049720070619) notes that less than a tenth of China's pilots meet industry standards of English proficiency. China's aviation authority insisting that its pilots must learn English to International Civil Aviation standards is a consequence of global interdependence. The motivation or propulsion in this case is internationalisation of the Chinese local space as well as a desire to register Chinese presence in the international airline community of practice which is run in English. This entails attitudes, preferences and hierarchies that are all anchored to globalization. We must add that liberalisation has led to some acknowledgement of diversity. Aviation regulations now have features that do not come from native British or American English. For example, the word 'three' must be pronounced 'tree'. The latest regulations have still more of this kind of thing and stipulate that British and American pilots also need to have accent training of this international variety.

Ironically, globalization has another kind of local tenor when the same attitude and preference issues play out among Inner Circle membership as we find in 20-year old British singer Joss Stone's reaction to the negative response to what the British press described as her 'fake American accent' at the 2008 Brit Awards:

> 'At the end of the day, I don't give a f**k if people have a problem with my accent. That's all I can say about it. The words I say do not change.
>
> 'If the way that it sounds is skew-whiff and you don't like it, don't listen. I'm not being a cruel person by sounding a different way.
>
> 'I made my album with a bunch of Americans. When people go to Australia for two weeks they come back sounding Australian – but the whole world doesn't turn round and say, "Well, f**k you." Which is basically what England had done.
>
> 'Obviously not everybody in England. But the big press people. They were just like, "You know what? We've decided we don't like you anymore." '

What comes across in this claim is the effect that collaboration and the diversity of daily communicative contexts that people experience may trigger convergence or shift to varying degrees. In Joss Stone's case, she had been working with Americans and therefore in her view her American accent was understandable. What is even more interesting here is the manner in which global networks and globalization privilege the American form; a probable reason for the treatment of globalization as a synonym for Americanisation (cf. Djelic, 2003). However, language use practices in global networks such as the fraud emails in transnational flights between continents (see Blommaert & Omoniyi, 2006) and the various crossings they entail call attention to the impossibility of holding up pre-articulated standards for literacy, English language use, or fluency over the acquisition of genres.

With reference to the Chinese examples above, so-called English language-medium international tests, especially professional ones such as IELTS, TOEFL, GRE, GMAT, and International Baccalaureate constitute a site of engagement with globalization. These tests are hinged to and framed by the usage culture of some native varieties and therefore run against the principal tenet of equality of nations and the experience of international mobility especially in the intellectual sector. This ironically perpetuates rather than negatively affects those involved in North–South labour mobility.

In contemporary times, the dialogues are no longer confined to managing Inner–Outer Circle relations. There are now Outer–Outer Circle and Outer–Expanding Circle dialogues too. These are exemplified by transnational and multilateral forums such as the Asia-Africa Summit, China-Africa Cooperation Forum and Organization of Petroleum Exporting Countries (OPEC) and regional groups like Economic Community of West African Countries (ECOWAS) and Asia-Pacific Economic Council (APEC) among others. The dynamics of these relationships fit into what development scholarship refers to as South–South dialogue. These new fora of international dialogue certainly constitute contexts within which world Englishes contend with globalization.

Another core argument here is that globalization privileges some languages more than others. This fact is closely linked to power and capital (Bourdieu, 1991) which derive partially from speaker population and the economy that support languages. A vast body of literature backs Colin Baker's (2007: vii) remark in his foreword to the volume of essays edited by Anwei Feng on bilingual education in China that 'the number of speakers of any language and its future status and power are not separate issues' and that 'English and Mandarin Chinese cannot be kept separate'. However, history also shows there are exceptions to the argument that there is a correlation between number of speakers and power with Apartheid South Africa an excellent example. Also, we cannot argue parity of power between one million native speakers of English in the United States and one million learners of English in China.

Besides, in a complex multilingual and multicultural world, discussions of language and globalization cannot be solely about the English language. Globalization entails some degree of competition between and for resources including language resources. It privileges the languages of special interest groups and global political elite. With particular reference to English, the forms of new Englishes are determined partially by forces and realities such as media (Martin, 2006: 583), advertising (Bhatia, 2006: 605) and global commerce (van Horn, 2006: 620) generated in contexts away from the traditional homes of these varieties.

## The Global is Rooted and Contained within a Local History

Whichever way one looks at it, that which we tag 'global' is the consequence of an identifiable local on a transnational flight. The factors facilitating such flights are indicative of the nature of global power relations. Different trajectories create or are the consequence of different power relations. In its destination, the local in flight settles into another local receptacle, an ecology into which it adapts and impacts. In essence then, globalization appropriately captures the transnational character and direction of flights as well as the power relations between the two locales – source and destination – which Appadurai (1996) refers to as 'translocality'. In the global economy, these are organised within the framework of free-market competition. The politics of these transactions is what engages globalization researchers in the various disciplines, particularly to do with issues of identity, distribution of goods and services, formation of capital (social, cultural and linguistic), access, exclusion/inclusion and inequality. With reference to world Englishes, the politics may be conceptualised in terms of a global exchange rate mechanism in which some linguistic currencies (languages, dialects and standard forms) enjoy the capital of distinction.

The reasons behind the choice of codes and, consequently, the seeming displacement of the local code in the south–south Business Process Outsourcing (BPO) transactions represent that politics and English language belong to the privileged group because of the control that native English-speaking nations have had on global politics and consequently on the global economy. The United Nations and the World Bank, two key institutions in world affairs, function in English alongside a few other languages. According to the UN Secretariat, the organisation uses 'six official languages in its intergovernmental meetings and documents,

Arabic, Chinese, English, French, Russian and Spanish; the Secretariat uses two working languages, English and French' (http://www.un.org/Depts/DGACM/faq_languages.htm). Similarly, the World Bank's annual report, a core publication of the world's fiscal engine room, is available in four languages on the organisation's website: English, French, Spanish and Arabic (see http://web.worldbank.org/WBSITE/EXTERNAL/EXTDEC/EXTRESEARCH/EXTWDRS/EXTWDR2007/0,menuPK:1489 865~pagePK:64167702~piPK:64167676~theSitePK:1489834,00.html). Of these, English has the widest global spread covering what Kachru called in his seminal research of the early to mid-1980s the Inner, Outer and Expanding Circle countries (Kachru, 1990). What this demonstrates is the relationship between language and power structures in the transnational political economy. It is understandable then that issues, controversies and conflicts in a complex global economy may be projected on to as well as partially emanate from language.

## World Englishes: A Community of Practice

In an article titled 'Across cultures, English is the word' in the *International Herald Tribune* (http://www.iht.com/articles/2007/04/09/asia/englede.php), Seth Mydans remarks that 'Riding the crest of globalization and technology, English dominates the world as no language ever has, and some linguists are now saying it may never be dethroned as the king of languages' (IHT, 10 April 2007). Mydans quotes Jean-Paul Nerriere, former vice president of IBM, United States, as arguing that in the long run, 'Globish' or World Standard English Language will emerge to displace British and American English at the top of the hierarchy. What comes across in Nerriere's argument is that non-native speakers constitute the majority of speakers, 'so our way of speaking English should be the official way of speaking English'; a structural adjustment concerned with positioning and power in the politics of language and identity, a subversion of the status quo ante.

The above-mentioned IHT article triggered a week-long discussion (24 April 2007–30 April 2007) among members of the Non-native English Speakers in TESOL (NNEST) Caucus. There were 49 responses in total and they covered issues such as what variety or varieties of English to teach and to whom, and professionals' response to remarks such as 'How come your English is so good?' and so on. What remains unresolved in such debates is a strategy for curtailing native speaker intuition even when desirability has been established based on *vox populi vox dei*; since there are more non-native than are native speakers of English. Because the 'international' tests listed earlier are set and managed by native speakers of English, it remains difficult to make a case for equal acceptance of *'stretching one's long hand'*, a Nigerian form, and *'stretching one's long arm'*, its native speaker equivalent. Perhaps the final frontier is already developing around world Englishes and popular culture, a relatively new-ish focus on the interface with globalization. The idea of a Global Hip-Hop Nation Language (see Alim, 2004) and the situatedness of transcultural flows in local histories (see Pennycook, 2007) bring new analytical tools to the party.

Other themes within the context of which World Englishes potentially contend with globalization include international relations and effect on local language policy, language rights, exploitation and neo-imperialism, language ecology – English cohabiting with indigenous languages, language globalization and post-colonial resistance, language and identity, language education, literacy and development. These themes allow questions to be raised around issues of serious concern. For instance, are local language policies affected by the global cultural-linguistic-economic hegemonies like English, and what is the nature of local linguistic acts of resistance to these dominant paradigms of global interactions? How does the local respond to the global? Or to the changes in the global? (cf. the report released by Demos, 'As You Like It: Catching up in an age of Global English' (http://education.guardian.co.uk/tefl/comment/story/0,,2033863,00.html).

The themes and questions raised above are not exhaustive but they certainly give a sense of the extensive forays that have been made in World Englishes within the frameworks of sociolinguistic and applied linguistic research. Of particular note is the manner in which these foci of research constitute the fora for examining, evaluating, negotiating and understanding social, political and economic structures both locally and globally. These raise issues of interest to language (in) education, literacy and development, and people such as conservationists and preservationists, language right activists and public intellectuals generally. In a seminal work that captures the intricacies of English as a medium of international communication, Andy Kirkpatrick (2007: 1) remarks that

> English has now become the language of international communication. Perhaps the most remarkable fact behind this increasing use of English is that the majority of English speakers are now multilingual people who have learned English and who use English to communicate with fellow multilinguals.

His focus on both the implications of different varieties of English for English language learning and teaching in a number of contexts and comparing 'international contexts in which English is used as a lingua franca' glorifies and documents the roles and contributions of multilingual and multicultural English language teachers as a constituency. The intended primary readership is of course English Language Teaching (ELT) professionals. In contrast, beyond learning and teaching, the essays in this volume cover a wider range of the contexts of English language usage worldwide, in particular tracking how varieties engage with the phenomenon of globalization. This breadth of coverage has not been previously achieved in a single volume and therefore represents a significant effort towards making a start.

Kirkpatrick (2007: 3) also notes that 'the model of English that should be used in classrooms . . . has been a subject of discussion for some time . . . . This debate has taken place alongside the dramatic increase in the pace of globalization and the expanding role of English as an International Language as well as the increased recognition of World Englishes and English as a Lingua Franca.' He references Jenkins' work on EIL (Jenkins, 2003). The issue that Kirkpatrick foregrounds as far as we are concerned is the immutability of English as a language as well as the undesirability-cum-indefensibility of pushing for 'a model' of 'Global English' if the latter is the consequence of globalization. But why are we sceptical?

If globalization is about restructuring in the world's political economy, the collapse of the three-worlds model – First, Second and Third Worlds – in 1989 with the fall of communism in Eastern Europe, the replacement one free-market world dominated by the United States raised the status of Global English.[2] The celebration of diversity obscures the asymmetrical relationship that exists between the varieties of English. Kirkpatrick (2007), for instance, remarks that prejudices against varieties 'are simply just that – prejudices'. But this reaches much deeper to a fundamental core if we consider the kinds of capital associated with language varieties. Some varieties belong to the privileged caucus of what we call *langues sans frontiere* while others are confined to provinces in nation-states (cf. Blommaert, 2009). Decisions as to which variety is allocated what kind of capital are made by the linguistic mainstream. The dilemma therefore that confronts global English is that what touches all ought equally to be decided by all at least within the liberal framework of the societies from which English derives.

But globalization discourses also state that by the mid-21st century China would be the world's largest and dominant economy. Part of the strategy of achieving that, it would seem, has been to first bend windwardly, gather sufficient momentum and then change the direction of flow. We see this consistently in China's policies. In the Reuters (19 June 2007) report cited earlier, China's Aviation Minister, Li Jian, noted that 'The requirement to raise pilot's English abilities comes from a formal decision by the International Civil Aviation Organisation' (ICAO). Like the United Nations and the World Bank, the ICAO runs in English. This affects 8000 pilots, the remaining 651 having already passed their English examination. This is also happening at the same time as China is making giant strides into economies where it previously had only a modest presence such as the Nigerian oil sector. The *People's Daily Online* (15 March 2006) reported that 'rapid growth of bilateral trade will put China in place to influence the value of the currency of South Africa.'

Developments such as those described above provide the rationale for diversification in foreign language education created by the introduction of Mandarin on University curricula as well as the setting up of 14 Confucius Institutes across Africa by China. The institutes are distributed between the beneficiaries as follows: Nigeria (2), Botswana (1), Cameroon (1), Egypt (2), Kenya (1), Madagascar (1), Rwanda (1), South Africa (3), Sudan (1) and Zimbabwe (1). These developments and patterns of international relations are complex and are governed by a new political economy of language and a new discursive practice. For instance, Fantu Cheru (2007: 12) describes what he sees as 'the Chinese onslaught on Africa' as 'recolonization by invitation' and thus represents it as replacement hegemony for European colonial dominance on the continent. This can be extrapolated to other parts of the world previously ruled by Europe where China's economic presence is currently being registered. We can glean some idea of that general politics from Mohan and Kale's (2007) report prepared for the Rockefeller Foundation on South–South globalization. The language dimensions of globalization are the theme of recent scholarship such as Djite (2007) and Rassool (2007). Contributors to *Languages in a Globalizing World*, a volume of essays edited by Jacques Maurais and Michael A. Morris (2003), have similarly explored the theme.

Some complementary paradigms are emerging within the framework of the 'Global English Project' (see, for instance, Jenkins, 2000; Seidlhofer, 2001). Some of these researchers have raised issues well beyond concerns about the patterns and history of the spread of English around the world which Kachru's 'Three Circles' framework was set up to explain. Critiques of the latter are contained in work by Bruthiaux (2003: 159), Canagarajah (1999: 180) and Pennycook (2003: 516–517). They put the spotlight on the sociolinguistic accompaniments of globalization. It is no longer enough to simply track the spread of English and the politics and/or ideologies that underlie it because the focus of that exercise is on differences and variations that spring from the nation-state framework. For some stakeholders, the notion of EIL or ELF appears to take on the challenge of forging recognition for a kind of English that is not bound to a specific nation-state but is at the same time a sub-set of those national varieties. What seems immediately problematic is who the standard bearers would be. Within the nation-state framework, corpus planning and status planning are carried out by local experts, and institutions such as the school and media become channels through which the resulting policies are visibly executed or disseminated. Seidlhofer (2009), in contrast, suggests that the problem is one of disposing of old ways of thinking about categories such as (English) language variety, speech community, categories and ways of analysing language behaviour.

In South–South relations that do not involve native speakers of English, non-native varieties appear to be more mutually tolerant or accommodating of one another. This is particularly relevant with reference to the growing incidence of labour migration intra-Asia, intra-Africa, Africa-Asia and vice versa. In some cases, these represent either English as a second language (ESL) to ESL/EFL (English as a foreign language) in the former and/or ESL to EFL exchanges in the latter. For example, state-controlled firms in China invest heavily in the railway, oil and gas sectors of the Nigerian economy thus bringing ESL and EFL together. According to the *International Herald Tribune* (12 March 2007), 'trade between China and Africa reached $55.5 billion, up more than 40 percent from 2005, according to data from China's Ministry of Commerce' (http://www.iht.com/articles/2007/03/12/business/oil.php). In contrast, in bilateral relations involving native and non-native English-speaking countries, the former's intuition may be a little less accommodating of 'deviant forms' such as long hand for long arm, and nook and corner for nook and crany. Thus, international communication remains a site of conflict. Native speaker intolerance and immigrant or L2 bravado in appropriating, indigenising and institutionalising English are at the centre of such conflict.

We have a diversity of contexts in which English co-exists with other languages around the world and each context has its own peculiar characteristics. For one, the dynamics of state policies, language needs and language choice in real time situations potentially yield different dimensions of language politics and how our experiences are shaped. The synonymisation of 'native varieties of English' with an exogenous ideal and standard to which people aspire in non-native English contexts does in a Whorfian sense perpetuate hegemony and inequality both of which contradict the tenets of liberal thought in late modernity. So, how does globalization's overt or covert threat to or management of diversity and multiplicity pose a challenge to World Englishes and how does/can the latter respond? There are tensions here that we believe need to be addressed in relation to globalization. It is against this backdrop then that contributors to this special volume of essays will consolidate and extend the debate in ways that they believe our understanding is facilitated by their individual projects. What follows next is a chapter-by-chapter synopsis. They fall into three parts. Chapters 2, 3, 4 and 5 are conceptual and global in orientation. Chapters 6, 7, 8 and 9 have a regional focus. Chapter 10 has a conceptual and local orientation and reflects upon as well as interrogates the framework of the four preceding chapters.

In Chapter 2, 'Globalization and International Intelligibility', after a critical examination of the impact of globalization on the educational patterns in general and English language teaching in particular, Paroo Nihalani focuses on intercultural communication in the global context, and examines the three much-debated major related issues of 'comprehensibility', 'intelligibility' and 'interpretability' from the perspectives of linguistics and social psychology. It presents arguments in favour of World Englishes, and against the ELF model, with the help of quantitative acoustic data from the Expanding Circle (Japanese English), the Outer Circle (Indian English, Malaysian English, Singapore English, Brunei English, Nigerian English, etc.) and the Inner Circle (British English, Scottish English and American English). It proposes a pragmatic model that is informed by the multi-dimensional view of intelligibility and, more importantly, multicultural interpretability in order to address the third major concern of language standardisation for global communication. The pragmatic model outlined is a hybrid, characterised by 'divergence' at the segmental level and 'convergence', in some ways, at the supra-segmental level, in order to harmonise the two seemingly opposing tendencies of 'national identity' on the one hand, and 'international intelligibility' on the other. Such a hybrid form of global pronunciation, it is suggested, will create a synergy that will bind all the three concentric circles (so-called diverse periphery and central communities) together, and will prove to be highly vibrant and truly international. The endocentric model, as proposed here, will promote respect for one's own social identity, one's own national identity, without sacrificing international intelligibility and multicultural interpretability, and truly epitomises the rhetoric 'unity in diversity'.

In Chapter 3, 'From Chaos to Order: Language Change, Lingua Francas and World Englishes', Phyllis Ghim-Lian Chew reconstructs the synchronic and diachronic dimensions of the nature of and the reasons for the emergence of lingua francas (LFs) at tribal, city, national and global levels. It argues that World Englishes (WEs)is best studied under the wider umbrella of evolving LFs. It presents an alternative way in understanding and appreciating WEs in the wake of globalization and its accompanying shifting priorities in many dimensions of modern life, including the emergence of the English language as the dominant LF. The supporting arguments are provided by a sociolinguistic case study of Fujian, China. The chapter concludes that at the heart of linguistic discussion in China today is no longer putonghua, the national LF but rather the emergent LF of the 'new world order', often referred to as 'the next LF'. It contends that the discussion of 'globalism' in China reflects more of a pragmatic attitude in the query 'How can one learn the LF of the age quickly so as to ensure everyone has an equal chance of living well?', rather than Seidlhofer's (2006) concern 'How can one promote a common language of the community while supporting equal rights for all community languages at the same time?'.

In Chapter 4, 'English as a Lingua Franca in the Global Context: Interconnectedness, Variation and Change', Martin Dewey and Jennifer Jenkins propose that consideration of current theory regarding the nature of globalization's impact on the social and political world order is of particular relevance to empirical work in the Outer Circle and Expanding Circle. Locating ELF in the transformation list perspective of globalization, it argues that far from a trend towards increased homogenisation, a fundamental consequence of interconnectedness (a defining feature of late modernity) is the blurring of distinctions between internal and external affairs, between the international and domestic and thus between the local and global, and that this blurring leads, on the contrary, to an increased hybridist of cultures. The chapter proposes that the transformationalist perspective shares much with the way ELF research approaches the use of English in LF settings, whether these settings occur in Inner, Outer or Expanding Circle contexts. It regards ELF interactional settings as sites where distinctions are blurred, and where there is considerable lingua-cultural intermixture. By reporting on other corpora and drawing on one of the authors' own corpus of naturally occurring talk in LF settings, the chapter presents empirical evidence which suggests that the use of English in ELF communication is a perfect example of the kind of transformation of cultural resources, here linguistic ones, that are currently occurring in a globalising world. By situating descriptions of ELF within a theoretical framework of globalization, it is able, especially in light of the continuing growth in discourse about both ELF and WE, to take account of the fuller context within which debate and analysis regarding the diffusion of English internationally are situated.

In Chapter 5, 'World Englishes, Globalization and the Politics of Conformity', Rakesh M. Bhatt points out that World Englishes, under the stewardship of Braj Kachru, has established itself as a paradigm of research in the study of English in the global context that focuses on English language variation and change over time and space. The stated agenda of WE, as part of the intellectual movement known as 'Liberation Linguistics', is to not only examine the forms of linguistic beliefs and practices that accent the socio-political dimensions of language variation – rooted in contexts of social injustice – but transform these contexts radically in the interest of the speakers of the 'other tongue'. In the (postmodern) era of globalization where the dominance of English is seen as displacing local linguistic practices, world Englishes studies have instead highlighted the forms of globalization that fertilise new forms of locality: spanning literary works of creative writers such as Raja Rao to artistic performances of hip-hop and to globalised identities of English accents of outsourcing. Yet, in spite of the advances in the field of world Englishes, controversies abound, both in terms of the empirical status of world Englishes (the *pro*fusion and the *con*fusion arguments of Quirk (1990)) and in terms of the theoretical conceptualisation of them (WE, ELF, EIL, etc.). These controversies, this chapter argues, follow from a political logic of conformity – outside, and within, the field of world Englishes – that at once *en*ables discourses of strategic essentialism (via branding, policing labels, imposing boundaries, sanctioning legitimacy, etc.) and *dis*ables discourses of transformation (of hybridity, heterogeneity and diversity). The chapter examines how, in the context of globalization, the politics of conformity, with its attendant enabling and disabling discourses, explains the contentious issues, the controversies, in the theory and practice of world Englishes.

In Chapter 6, 'EFL: From *You Sound Like Dickens* to International English', Maria Georgieva highlights that since the 1990s, the globalization processes in the *'Expanding circle'* present a much more complicated situation of the teaching, use, perceptions and affiliation with Englishes than the World English model can capture. The chapter focuses on the current growth of English into a tool for international communication viewed against the backdrop of dominant humanistic ideals for plurilingual Europe. On the basis of a small-scale survey of Bulgarian speakers' patterns of foreign language use, it discusses whether, and to what extent, the new *lingua franca* status of English has affected people's attitudes towards the language and the standards of its use as well as how English co-exists with the other languages spoken in the country. The results from the analysis show that although English has definitely established itself as the first foreign language in Bulgaria, most speakers from the examined group speak two or more foreign languages organised in diverse patterns of use in their private and professional life. Notwithstanding the fact that the domains of English use have multiplied and diversified in recent years, the language still has mainly instrumental functions. Moreover, Bulgarians tend to retain their affiliation to some of the established standards, namely, British or American English, and are not inclined to accept a new world standard established solely for the purposes of international communication and teaching, quite distinct from currently existing standard varieties.

In Chapter 7, 'Glocalization of English in World Englishes: An Emerging Variety among Persian Speakers of English', Farzad Sharifian focuses on the globalization and ensuing globalization of English within the paradigm of World Englishes. It contends that the paradigm has responded modestly to the rapid growth of new Englishes in the wake of increasing use of English for local and global purposes, including the use of the internet. As a case study, it explores how increasing numbers of Persian speakers are learning English. Their reasons for doing so range from using the internet and migration, to entertainment, trade and contact both within the country and with the diasporic community outside. The complex interaction between global and local forces is leading to what the author calls 'Persian English', resulting from a process of *glocalization* of English by Persian speakers. Analyses of 'Persian English' show how this *glocalization* is a reflection of various motives: a wish to become a global citizen, resistance to hegemony, the construction of certain sociocultural identities and the expression of what Sharifian calls 'cultural conceptualisations'. In light of these analyses, the chapter concludes with an appraisal of criticisms levelled against the World Englishes paradigm.

In Chapter 8, 'Local networks in the formation and development of West African English', Augustin Simo Bobda examines the various forms that English has taken across the world, and the circumstances leading to this phenomenon. It particularly focuses on the patterns of transplantation of English in West Africa (six countries of the former British Empire and American sphere of influence from the west to the east), from the 15th century to the present, and the modes of its diffusion throughout its history in the region. It identifies, in these local patterns of globalization, the networks that have developed from historical, geographic and other bonds between some countries in the region, a phenomenon which by no means precludes the existence of clear national and sub-national identities. Clear links are found between the period of transplantation, the modes of diffusion and the networks on the one hand, and the sociolinguistics of English and the structural features of the emerging varieties in the various settings. Particular countries have been involved in networking of one kind or another, creating some group identity, which has shaped the ecology of English in these particular sets of countries, while maintaining in most cases specific national and sub-national specific sociolinguistic and linguistic features. Common patterns of transplantation and diffusion of English in countries of West Africa have yielded the specific sociolinguistic and linguistic characteristics that West African English has, and which are different from the other world Englishes. The chapter predicts that in this era of globalization, greater population mobility will increasingly favour convergence and distinguishability at the structural level within the West African region, at the least.

In Chapter 9, 'The English Language, Globalization and Latin America: Possible Lessons from the "Outer Circle"', Kanavillil Rajagopalan discusses the political and ideological dimensions of the underlying relationships between globalization and World Englishes in Latin America as a whole and, more closely, in Brazil. It shows how, in Latin America, globalization is perceived as a homogenisation force representing the interests of the United States. Therefore, the national ideologies, politics, identities and the language policies in Latin America are constructed in opposition to the US ideological, material, cultural and linguistic incursions. In this context, (American) English is positioned as symbolic of 'linguistics imperialism'. Such an ideological stance creates a couple of paradoxes. First, the one language, one culture and one nation ideology inherent in the English-only movement in the United States is mirrored in the promotion of Portuguese in Brazil, having ramifications for the multilingualism. Second, the English is spreading phenomenally in the guise of British English (and culture) in opposition to the US English in Brazil and in Latin America as a whole. The chapter argues that, in the near future, English will cease to be a foreign language in the sense of Graddol (2006) and this will have important consequences for the way it is taught. It argues that from the point of view of language planning and curriculum development, there may be important lessons to be learned from experiences accumulated over the years in the so-called Outer Circle countries.

In Chapter 10, 'Rethinking Origins and Localization in Global Englishes', Alastair Pennycook, by drawing analogies with issues of localisation in hip-hop, argues that processes of localisation are more complex than a notion of languages or cultures spreading and taking on local forms; rather, we have to understand ways in which they are already local. Recent debates over the inapplicability of a World Englishes framework to current conditions of globalization, or concerns that a focus on ELF presents a new form of homogenisation, miss the point that what we need to react is not only to new conditions of postmodernity but also to the postmodern imperative to rethink language. This suggests the need to articulate a new sense of history and location, avoiding narratives of spread, transition, development and origins, and thinking instead in terms of multiple, heterogeneous and simultaneous histories that the dominant historical narrative has overlooked. If we question the linearity at the heart of modernist narratives about language origins and spread, we can start to see that global Englishes do not have one point but rather multiple, co-present, global origins. Just as hip-hop has always been Aboriginal, so has English. Such an understanding of global Englishes radically reshapes the ways in which we can understand global and local cultural and linguistic formations, and takes us beyond the current debates between monocentric and pluricentric models of English.

In the last chapter of the book, 'Final Reflections: Globalization and World Englishes', we, as editors, revisit the contributions to this volume and analyse and synthesise the arguments in terms of different approaches in WEs and locate them within different schools of thought in globalization debate. Our main focus is on what we think are the salient features of their interaction with each other in response to globalization. We relate these features to the central conceptual issues within the theoretical debate of globalization, and explore the way forward by raising questions which will point out the directions for future research in WEs. We present an agenda for WEs research which is decentred/deterritorialised and approaches the language/English issue in a holistic way capturing the diversity and the unity that is seen in global multilingualism and changing world order.

## Acknowledgment

We thank the series editors for their courage in accommodating this opening up of the world Englishes canon for interrogation.

## Notes

1. We acknowledge previous efforts in this area of scholarship. In addition to work by Kingsley Bolton and Margie Berns in the journal *World Englishes* (24.1, 22.3 and 22.4), a whole section is devoted to the subject in Kachru *et al.*, edited volume, *The Handbook of World Englishes* (Blackwell).
2. It is still not quite resolved whether or not an English-only official language policy is in place.

## References

Alim, H.S. (2004) Hip hop nation language. In E. Finegan and J.R. Rickford (eds) *Language in the USA: Themes for the Twenty-first Century* (pp. 387–409). Cambridge: Cambridge University Press.

Appadurai, A. (1990) Disjuncture and difference in the global cultural economy. In M. Featherstone (ed.) *Global Culture* (pp. 295–310). London: Sage.

Appadurai, A. (1996) *Modernity at Large: Cultural Dimensions of Globalization.* Minneapolis, MN: University of Minnesota Press.

Bhatia, T.K. (2006) World Englishes in global advertising. In B.B. Kachru *et al.* (eds) *The Handbook of World Englishes* (pp. 601–619). Oxford: Blackwell.

Baker, C. (2007) Foreword. In A. Feng (ed.) *Bilingual Education in China: Practices, Policies and Concepts* (pp. vii–viii). Clevedon: Multilingual Matters.

Blommaert, J. (2003) Commentary: A sociolinguistics of globalization. *Journal of Sociolinguistics* 7 (4), 607–623.

Blommaert, J. (2009) A market of accents. *Language Policy* 8, 243–259.

Blommaert, J. and Omoniyi, T. (2006) Email fraud: Language, technology, and the indexicals of globalization. *Social Semiotics* 16 (4), 573–605.

Bourdieu, P. (1991) *Language and Symbolic Power.* Cambridge: Polity Press.

Bruthiaux, P. (2003) Squaring the circles: Issues in modeling English worldwide. *International Journal of Applied Linguistics* 13 (2), 159–178.

Brutt-Griffler, J. (2002) *World English: A Study of its Development.* Clevedon: Multilingual Matters.

Butler, J. (1997) *Excitable Speech: A Politics of the Performative.* New York: Routledge.

Canagarajah, A.S. (1999) *Resisting Linguistic Imperialism in English Teaching.* Oxford: Oxford University Press.

Cheru, F. (2007) Decoding the evolving China-Africa relations. *News from the Nordic Africa Institute*, No. 3, 11–13.

Djelic, M-L. (2003) Globalization as soft Americanization: Illustrations from the Antitrust Story. *Stein Rokkan Center Seminar.* Bergen University, Bergen, Norway, 14 February 2003.

Djite, P.G. (2007) *The Sociolinguistics of Development in Africa.* Clevedon: Multilingual Matters.

Esteva, G. and Prakash, M.S. (2004) From global to local: Beyond neoliberalism to the international of hope'. In F.J. Lechner and J. Boli (eds) *The Globalization Reader* (2nd edn) (pp. 410–416). Oxford: Blackwell.

Gergen, K.J. (1999) *An Invitation to Social Construction.* London: Sage Publications.

Giddens, A. (1990) *The Consequences of Modernity.* Cambridge: Cambridge University Press.

Graddol, D. (2006) *English Next: Why Global English May Mean the End of 'English as a Foreign Language'.* London: The British Council.

Higgins, C. (2009) *English as a Local Language: Past-colonial Identities and Multilingual Practices.* Bristol: Multilingual Matters.

Hülsemeyer, A. (ed.) (2003) *Globalization in the Twenty-First Century: Convergence or Divergence.* NY: Palgrave Macmillan.

Jenkins, J. (2000) *The Phonology of English as an International Language.* Oxford: Oxford University Press.

Jenkins, J. (2007) *English as a Lingua Franca: Attitude and Identity.* Oxford: Oxford University Press.

Kachru, B. (1990) *The Alchemy of English: The Spread, Functions, and Models of Non-Native Englishes*. Urbana and Chicago: University of Illinois Press.

Kachru, B. (2005) *Asian Englishes: Beyond the Canon*. Hong Kong: Hong Kong University Press.

Kachru, B.B., Kachru, Y. and Nelson, C.L. (eds) (2006) *The Handbook of World Englishes*. Oxford: Blackwell.

Kumaravadivelu, B. (2008) *Cultural Globalization and Language Education*. New Haven and London: Yale University Press.

Kirkpatrick, A. (2007) *World Englishes: Implications for International Communication and English Language Teaching*. Cambridge: Cambridge University Press.

Le Page, R.B. and Tabouret-Keller, A. (1985) *Acts of Identity: Creole-based Approaches to Language and Ethnicity*. Cambridge: Cambridge University Press.

Martin, E.A. (2006) World Englishes in the media. In B. Kachru *et al.* (eds) (pp. 583–600).

Maurais, J. and Morris, M.A. (eds) (2003) English Trans. *Languages in a Globalising World*. Cambridge: Cambridge University Press.

Melchers, G. and Shaw, P. (2003) *World Englishes: An Introduction*. London: Routledge.

Mohan, G. and Kale, D. (2007) The invisible hand of South-South globalization: Chinese migrants in Africa. A Rockefeller Foundation Report. Milton Keynes: The Development Policy and Practice Department, The Open University.

Omoniyi, T. (2003) Local policies and global forces: Multiliteracy and Africa's indigenous languages. *Language Policy* 2 (2), 133–152.

Omoniyi, T. (2010) The sociolinguistics of colonization: A language shift perspective. In H. Igboanusi (ed.) Language Shift in West Africa. Special issue of *Sociolinguistic Studies*.

Pennycook, A. (1994) *The Cultural Politics of English as an International Language*. London: Longman.

Pennycook, A. (2003) Global Englishes, Rip Slyme, and performativity. *Journal of Sociolinguistics* 7 (4), 513–533.

Pennycook, A. (2007) *Global Englishes and Transcultural Flows*. London: Routledge.

Quirk, R. (1990) Language varieties and standard language. *English Today* 21, 3–10.

Rassool, N. (2007) *Global Issues in Language, Education and Development: Perspectives from Postcolonial Countries*. Clevedon: Multilingual Matters.

Robertson, R. (1992) *Globalization*. London: Sage.

Seidlhofer, B. (2001) Closing a conceptual gap: The case for a description of English as a lingua franca. *International Journal of Applied Linguistics* 11 (2), 133–158.

Seidlhofer, B. (2006) English as a Lingua Franca in Europe: Challenges for applied linguistics. *Annual Review of Applied Linguistics* 26, 3–34.

Seidlhofer, B. (2009) Common ground and different realities: World Englishes and English as a lingua franca. *World Englishes* 28 (2), 236–245.

Sen, A. (1999) *Development as Freedom*. Oxford: Oxford University Press.

Sen, A. (2004) How to judge globalism. In F.J. Lechner and J. Boli (eds) *The Globalization Reader* (pp. 16–21). Oxford: Wiley Blackwell.

Stiglitz, J.E. (2007) Globalism's discontents. In J.T. Roberts and A.B. Hite (eds) *The Globalization and Development Reader: Perspectives on Development and Global Change* (pp. 295–304). Oxford: Blackwell.

Van Horn, S.Y. (2006) World Englishes and global commerce. In B.B. Kachru *et al.* (eds) (pp. 620–642).
Wallerstein, I. (1979) *The Capitalist World-Economy*. Cambridge: Cambridge University Press.
Wallerstein, I. (1984) *The Politics of the World Economy: The States, the Movements and the Civilizations*. Cambridge: Cambridge University Press.

## Chapter 2

# Globalization and International Intelligibility

PAROO NIHALANI

## Introduction

One of the buzzwords of the 21st century is 'global connectivity'. Composed of three elements – (1) entrepreneurial energetic individuals, (2) the internet and (3) the English language – global connectivity serves not only to exchange information and ideas but also to create wealth. A poor Bangladeshi entrepreneur of textile-design software, with no means to borrow, was able through 'connectivity' to find clients in Washington State and Milan. Three years later, his business is roaring, and some 150 jobs have been created. As markets and geographic barriers become increasingly blurred and even irrelevant, globalization is no longer an objective but imperative. The last five centuries or so have seen a radical transformation of the existing world order and the subsequent creation of the modern Global era that has inescapable interrelationships in virtually all spheres of activity such as economics, trade and commerce, industry, international diplomacy, communications, transport and travel, defence matters, education (science and technology), entertainment and so forth. These global infrastructures in English have become the bases for the emergence of an *inextricably interconnected world* – a world we describe by the cliché: the 'global village'. The key word here is *interdependence*. The 21st century, scarcely begun, has already revealed some of itself in outline. Two safe assumptions are that it will be:

(1)  An online century, and
(2)  A predominantly English one.

With the dawn of the internet age and the trend towards globalization, proficiency in English is perceived as a crucial skill for survival. It is like a driver's licence or computer skills. It is no longer sufficient to be literate in one's own local language. A monolingual society is en route to extinction and total isolationism in the modern world. A self-taught

English-speaking 12-year old child from China's southern province of Sichuan says, 'If you can't speak English, it's like you're deaf and dumb.' At the new Toyota and Peugeot plant in the Czech Republic, English is the working language of the Japanese, French and Czech staff. A well-known Japanese company, wishing to negotiate with its Arabic customers, arranges all its meetings in English. English is thus acknowledged to be the main language of international communication. Governments, even linguistically protectionist ones, are starting to agree. In 2003, Malaysia decided to conduct its school-level mathematics and science curriculum in English. Professor Takashi Inoguchi of Tokyo University has cited Japan's shocking lack of mastery of English as one reason why Japan's financial Big Bang has not taken off in a big way. Recently, Professor Jean-Pierre Lehmann of International Political Economy at IMD and Founding Director of Evian Group, Lausanne (Switzerland), has remarked, 'Japan is, in virtually every respect, a closed, highly unglobalized society and economy. To globalize, it is not sufficient for Japan to open its markets, but also for Japanese to open their minds. A critical criterion of globalization is fluency in English, an area where Japan so pathetically lags' (Nishimura, 1999). Japan's linguistic barrier impedes it from 'connecting' to the outside world, especially in articulating views, positions and insights on itself. At the symposium held at Tokyo's Foreign Press Centre, the Japanese journalist Mr Funabashi observed that Japan's shyness of English is stunting its international stature, and the failure of its top people to master the language will mean an inability to engage the rest of the world, particularly the rest of Asia, on equal terms. Needless to say, the learning of English, a global language, is essential for Japan to have a bright future. Reports indicate that the Japanese Ministry of Education, Culture, Sports, Science and Technology (MEXT) is preparing soon to introduce compulsory English to the nation's 24,000 public elementary schools (Honna, 2006: 3). Well aware that economic competitiveness depends in part on the mastery of the international language of business, the former South Korean President Kim Dae Jung gave a stern warning to his own countrymen, 'We will not win in world competition unless South Korea masters the lingua franca of the Internet age. **LEARN ENGLISH OR FACE BEING LEFT BEHIND.**' Discerning parents therefore would admittedly like to give a bilingual edge to their children. Zhou Min, who hosts several English programmes at the Beijing Broadcasting Station, says some pregnant women speak English to their foetuses in order to give their children a 'head-start'. Along with computers and mass migration, English language has thus proved to be the turbine engine of globalization.

## Global Spread: Multiple International Identities

There has never been a language in recorded history to match present global spread and use of English (Kachru, 1986; Smith, 1983, 1992; Strevens, 1982; Quirk & Widdowson, 1985). The second half of the 20th century has witnessed an emergence of institutionalized varieties such as 'English as an African language' and 'English as an Asian language'. New Englishes are mushrooming all over the world, ranging from Englong (Tagalog-infused English spoken in the Philippines) to Hinglish (the mixture of Hindi and English in India), Singlish (spoken in Singapore), Japlish in Japan and Spanglish (spoken in Spain). Who is to say what is 'real' English in a world where native speakers of British and American English are in a minority? There has never before been a language that has been spoken by more people as a second language than a first, observes David Crystal (1997). The new-English speakers are not just passively absorbing the language; they are *shaping* it. India, Nigeria, Singapore, South Africa, the Caribbean and, long ago, America have taken the language of their overlord and made it uniquely and distinctively their own. And by doing so, they are changing the world's definition of what it means to speak English. Veteran actor John Kani told the BBC: 'We speak English with a Xhosa accent and a Xhosa attitude.' In the words of Kachru (1986), 'English has thus acquired, and is in the process of acquiring, multiple ownerships and multiple international identities.' The English language today has become a global product (an abstract entity like a phoneme) that has its various manifestations (allophones) available in different local flavours.

With the global spread of English, three most important related questions come to our mind:

(1) Variation.
(2) International Intelligibility.
(3) The pedagogical issue of an 'education target'.

With the demographic distribution of its speakers all over the world, *diversity* seems inevitable. It is at the phonological level that the New Varieties of English differ most from each other. The learner of English therefore is dealing with a language that offers a bewildering variety in its main transmission phase – its pronunciation. Language teachers, on the other hand, have pleaded for some kind of 'international uniformity', which has undoubtedly existed, to some extent, in grammar, lexis and its written form. Talking about 'Global norms', Strevens (1992: 39) has observed, 'Throughout the world, regardless of whether the norm is native-speaker or non-native-speaker variety, irrespective of whether English is a foreign or a second language, two components of English are taught and learned without variation: these are its *grammar* and its *core vocabulary*. There may be embellishments in the way of local vocabulary and expressions and there will certainly be great differences of pronunciation, but the grammar and vocabulary of English are taught and learned virtually without variation around the world. There is just one set of grammatical patterns and core vocabulary that is accepted everywhere throughout the English-using world, not just in one single locality.' He goes on to add that 'as long as teachers of English continue to teach the lexico-grammar of "educated English", the unity of the language will transcend its immense diversity.' Here, I am making a plea for a similar kind of core/unity of language in respect of pronunciation for global communication. People have invariably demonstrated some kind of tolerance in respect of phonology/pronunciation. In sociolinguistic circles, we do recognize the importance of 'variation'. Nativists argue that these innovations are to be regarded not as violations of the so-called prestigious norms of native varieties, but as a process by which English is acquiring various international identities and multiple ownerships (Kachru, 1986). One is a linguistic description that is worthy of the researcher's effort. In a classroom, however, we always match a compromise. For example, we have grammars of American English, British English, Cockney English, Scottish English and so forth. But for the purposes of textbook writing, we do not write in Cockney English; we resort to the Standard English, a kind of convergence towards an 'educated' variety of English that is intelligible across many varieties. Howsoever diverse as it may appear to be, there still has to be some kind of 'unity' in the so-called apparent 'diversity' that should enable it to function as an effective tool of international communication.

This chapter mainly addresses itself to the practical challenges involved in the learning and teaching of English in a world context, and to decide whether it is really necessary to attempt to engineer the use of a planned variety of English for global communication. A pragmatic model informed by the multi-dimensional view of intelligibility will be discussed in great detail as a solution that is guided by the philosophy that epitomizes the rhetoric 'unity in diversity'.

## Comprehensibility and intelligibility

Smith (1992) defines comprehensibility as 'word recognition', intelligibility as 'utterance comprehension' and interpretability as 'understanding the pragmatic meaning of the utterance'. The consonant system of English, as we all know, is relatively uniform throughout the English-speaking countries. Accents of English are mainly known to differ in terms of their vowel systems as well as in the phonetic realizations of vowel phonemes. Descriptions of vowel quality based on auditory perceptions are impressionistic and rather subjective. The use of the sound spectrograph in describing the vowels enables reliable and objective measurements of the vowels based on formant frequencies. The vowel chart given below is reconstructed on the basis of the mean frequencies of F1 and F2 (the distance between F2 and F1) computed for six tokens of all vowels for Japanese subjects (Nihalani, 2001) (see Figure 2.1 below).

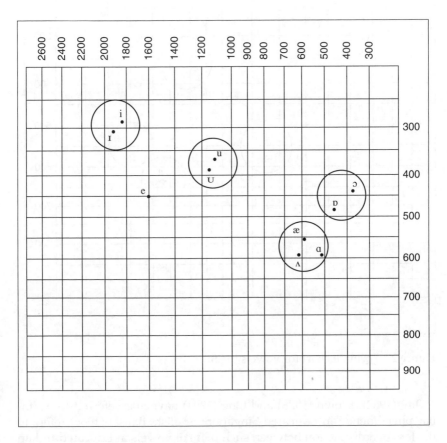

**Figure 2.1** Formant chart for vowels in JE

This acoustic study provides enough evidence that a Japanese English (JE) speaker fails to maintain sufficient perceptual distance between two vowels in each pair. A similar acoustic study undertaken on Standard Singapore English (SSE) points to a similar phenomenon of conflation of the same pairs of vowels (Nihalani, 1995). Given below (Figure 2.2) is a Formant chart for the vowels in SSE:

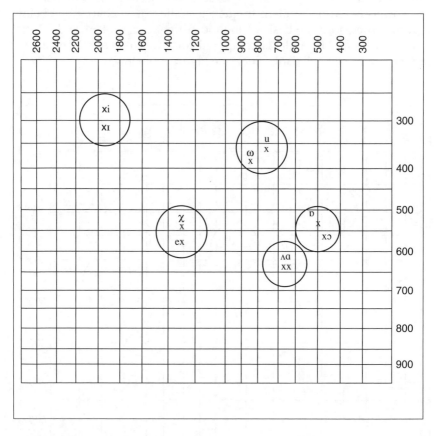

**Figure 2.2** Formant chart for vowels in SSE

Tay (1982), Brown (1988) and Ong (1994) have also referred to a similar phenomenon in Educated Singapore English. Bansal (1966) refers to the loss of a distinction between such pairs of vowels in Educated Indian English (EIE). Given below is the comparison of the vowel phonology of five different varieties of English from Kachru's three concentric circles (Figure 2.3):

| | SSE | EIE | JE | SCOTTISH | RP |
|---|---|---|---|---|---|
| bead | | | | i | i |
| bid | i | i | i | ɪ | ɪ |
| bed | ɛ | ɛ | e | e | e |
| bad | | | | | æ |
| | | | | ɑ | |
| bard | ɑ | a | ɑ | | ɑ |
| bud | | | | ʌ | ʌ |
| pot | | | | | ɒ |
| port | ɔ | ɔ | ɔ | ɔ | ɔ |
| pull | | | | | ʊ |
| pool | u | u | u | u | u |

**Figure 2.3** Vowel systems of Standard Englishes

## Conflation of pairs of vowels

A cursory look at the data above, based on acoustic investigation, clearly brings out the fact about the conflation of pairs of vowels such as /iː/ and /ɪ/, /uː/ and /ʊ/, /ɔː/ and /ɒ/ and, finally, /e/ and /æ/ in the varieties of English spoken in the 'Outer Circle' (including Nigeria, Pakistan, Brunei and Malaysia) and Japan, which belongs to the 'Expanding Circle'. The opposition of 'tense' versus 'lax' is systematically seen between these pairs in British Received Pronunciation (RP) where each of these pairs is reported to have a high functional load. Textbooks on English pronunciation, therefore, have repeatedly pointed out that if a speaker of non-inner circle English fails to maintain this distinction, it could cause a lack of comfortable mutual intelligibility when (s)he interacts with speakers of other varieties of English. Their view, I am afraid, sounds rather ethnocentric and displays intolerance of diversity that has been unfortunately perceived as a threat to the Western cannon. Such a view also presupposes a kind of superiority of experts' linguistic norms.

American speakers and Standard Scottish English speakers do not distinguish the vowels of *cot* and *caught*, and American speakers fail to distinguish between *bomb* and *balm*. Both Indian and American speakers of English distinguish between *caught* and *court*, but this distinction is lost in British English in the sense that these are homophones in RP. The two words *psalm* and *Sam* are homophones in Standard Scottish English. To illustrate my point further, here is an anecdote (Holmes, 2001: 124).

> A British visitor to New Zealand decided while he was in Auckland he would look up an old friend from his war days. He found the address, walked up the path and knocked on the door.
>
> 'Gidday', said the young man who opened the door. 'What can I do for you?'
>
> 'I've called to see me old mate Don Stone', said the visitor.
>
> 'Oh he's **dead** now mate,' said the young man.
>
> The visitor was about to express condolences when he was thumped on the back by Don Stone himself.

You will have rightly noted that the two words *dead* and *dad* are homophones in the New Zealand variety of English. If keeping the segmental distinction were the primary purpose of teaching spoken English, we would have to teach speakers of General American (GA) and RP speakers to keep the distinction they do not maintain in their varieties of English. Bansal (1969), Tiffen (1974) and Tay (1982) point out that the diphthongs /eɪ/ and /əʊ/ are realized as monophthongs in EIE, Nigerian English and SSE respectively. The same is true of JE. But is this not true for most North American varieties and Scottish English as well? I wonder why no segmental interference of any kind has ever been reported in respect of native varieties.

Let us try to read the following sentence aloud:

*Englsh bcms ncrsngly mprtnt s a mns f ntrntnl* cmmnctn

Most of us can effortlessly read the sentence from which all the vowels have been removed. Vowels are considered to be relatively less useful in distinguishing words than consonants. This clearly indicates that vowels are far less central in our concept of speech sounds than are consonants. The language of text messaging works exactly on a similar principle. It has been observed earlier that the consonant system of English is relatively uniform throughout the English-speaking countries.

We do not speak isolated sound segments. We use words in a social context, which serves to help with 'word recognition' that Smith (1992) calls 'comprehensibility'. Speakers of non-native varieties of English have been using their own vowel phonological systems for ages and they have been able to communicate with a fair amount of success across the national boundaries. Difficulties of comprehension are sometimes encountered especially when the parties talk quickly, but they are usually quickly resolved, and they seem to be diminishing, partly because the availability of international television via satellite is familiarizing everyone with the existence of other norms. In the context of the global spread of English and multilingualism, what one comes across, more often, is the 'conflation of pairs of vowels' rather than the 'tense/lax opposition'. One should therefore be raising a fundamental question as to why most of these non-native varieties share the phenomenon of the conflation of pairs of vowels. Further research perhaps needs to be done in this area in order to explore a common substratum that cuts across all these non-native varieties even though this phenomenon seems to be absent in the two varieties of GA and British RP. I cannot help but reflect here whether this linguistic feature of conflation, which is shared by most of the non-native varieties, will eventually constitute an integral part or the core of Global English for international communication.

## Allophonic features

Jenkins' study (2000) has admittedly been one of the most extensive and comprehensive investigations of the notion 'intelligibility' available in the literature so far. Jenkins (2000: 159) demonstrates, in general, a profound sympathetic understanding of the socio-psychological issues. In her discussion of the segmental features in the English as a Second Language (ESL) context, she refers to 'aspiration', 'allophonic vowel length' and the fortis/lenis consonantal distinction as an essential part of the core. Our experience in the Commonwealth will bear me out that the speakers of L2 varieties have been communicating fairly successfully without such allophonic features in their speech. This seems to me a rather over-rated/over-exaggerated claim on the part of Jenkins.

It has been asserted in the literature that the recognition takes place not always because of the phonemic distinctions but rather more significantly because of allophonic features (see O'Connor, 1973). For example, the distinction between the two words *pin* and *bin* is maintained not because of the presence or absence of [voice] feature. Perceptual studies have been cited to show that it is the [+aspiration] feature that distinguishes /p/ from /b/ at the beginning of a stressed syllable. Let us consider another example of a pair of words *seat* and *seed*. Once again, the distinction between [t] and [d] is maintained mainly because of the vowel length which gets comparatively reduced when followed by a voiceless consonant in word-final position. Thus 'there are many clues (allophonic features) to a particular distinction that are located right outside the segment with which the distinction is usually associated' (O'Connor, 1973: 133).

In this connection, Gleason (1961: 265) points out that 'the use of allophones is more important socially than it is linguistically'. Hayes (1968: 51) remarks, 'It is the mismanagement of allophonic differences that accounts for much of what we call a foreign accent. He who wants to avoid a foreign accent must use allophones in a way which is **normal in the language concerned**' (emphasis is mine). The foreignness in foreign accents is obviously ascribable to allophonic deviations. These allophonic features such as 'aspiration', 'allophonic vowel length' and so forth are normal in RP accent, and the L2 learners do not aspire to it any more. Attitudinal studies undertaken in India, Malaysia, Nigeria and Singapore at the undergraduate level have clearly revealed resentment against the native-like use of allophonic variants such as syllabicity, aspiration and dark [ɫ]. Non-native speakers have invariably expressed their fear of alienation from their peers, and the society in general.

Sounds of one language are known to differ from those of another because of the phonetic value of the segments along the same continuum. To take an example, the linguistic specification that distinguishes between [p] and [b] in English is that they are [−voice] and [+voice] respectively. The articulatory instruction that accompanies the feature [+voice] is 'vibrate the vocal cords'. In order to implement this instruction, a number of articulatory gestures have to be performed, such as keeping the vocal folds sufficiently lax, reducing the distance between the vocal folds, keeping the airflow through the glottis powerful enough to cause vibration and maintaining the difference between the sub-glottal and supra-glottal air pressure by lowering the larynx, allowing air to escape through a small velic opening, and/or expanding the walls of the pharynx. 'Vibrating the vocal folds', however, is the primary instruction that is associated with the linguistic feature [+voice], and the rest of the articulatory gestures are ways of implementing this instruction. Speakers of different language backgrounds choose different combinations of parameters for the implementation of voicing in stops. The phonetic implementation of these differences is as much important as those in the sound patterns. As phonologists, we tend to get involved in the description of the sound patterns so much so that we forget to point out that many of the sounds of English, for example, are not the same as the similarly specified sounds of, say, Hindi, Sindhi, French or Telugu. Let us consider sounds like the voiced stops in Sindhi and English, as an illustration. It is common practice to represent these two sounds with the same symbol [b] and they have the same set of feature specifications at the phonemic level. However, when one listens very carefully to the sounds produced by an Englishman and a Sindhi speaker, one would unhesitatingly say that they sound far from being alike; the phonological instruction to vibrate the vocal folds fails to apply pre-pausally and post-pausally during the closure period of voiced stops in languages like English; voiced stops in English are partially devoiced pre-pausally and post-pausally whereas these are fully voiced in Sindhi during the entire period of closure and are characterized by a slight nasalization (Nihalani, 1975). When a Sindhi speaker uses his own voiced sounds in English, he perhaps will not need to acquire the allophonic features of vowel length or fortis/lenis consonantal distinction, and the inner-circle speaker should not have any problems with his English speech. Further cross-linguistic research perhaps needs to be done in this area so as to explore how the sounds of one language differ from those of another because of the phonetic value of the segments along the same continuum.

Since in our proposed model, it is asserted that the national identity is characterized by the phonemic vowel system of the local variety, there is not much motivation for the learners to change their phonemic/phonetic segmental system; in fact, that helps them acquire their national flavour. Ironically, Jenkins' segmental core features for ESL context are heavily grounded in RP and, in many ways, provide further evidence of what Kachru (1992: 362) describes as 'the continuing grip ... on the profession of the traditional paradigm. What makes matters more complex is the fact that active interest groups want to maintain the status quo.' Roger Bowers, one of the senior most Executives of the British Council, aptly captures their ideology in the following words:

> ... we want to maintain the position of the English language as a world language so it can serve on the widest possible stage as the vehicle for our national values and heritage along with other English-speaking nations. And at an even more obvious level of self-interest, we need British ELT to continue to thrive – not only in terms of quantity of teachers employed, books sold, examinations taken, and departments funded, but also in the quality of academic and pedagogic development and research that a massive quantity of public and private sector demand is able to sustain. We have then a *vested* interest in maintaining the roles of English as a language, and of British ELT as a trade and a profession. (Quoted in Bamgbose *et al.*, 1995: 88)

## Educational Target: Standards and Models

Communication is one of the keywords that most often go with globalization. The term ordinarily conjures up the image of 'spoken interaction', even though the other two kinds of communication (the information related communication technology [ICT] and mass media communication technology [such as journalism, advertising, Radio, TV, etc.]) have significantly contributed to the process of globalzation in the modern capitalist economy. Recently, the University of Brunei Darussalam (UBD) carried out an in-depth study to identify the extent of employer satisfaction with the skills of UBD graduates who had entered the local labour market. Preliminary results (SMU Report 2008) conclusively indicate that

(i) UBD graduates are considered less 'employable' by employers as they tend to have significantly lower skills, competencies and attributes that are prerequisites for effective employment.
(ii) Employers appear to rate oral communication as the most important skills but it is here that UBD graduates tend to exhibit the greatest deficiencies.

Such findings remind us of a similar phenomenon in the eighties and nineties in Britain when the Thatcher government underwent a change in the perception of knowledge to be viewed operationally, in terms of competencies, and seeing education as 'training in skills' (Block & Cameron, 2002: 71). With globalization, this emphasis on skills has been increasingly marked. The new capitalism is dominated by forms of work in which the use of oral communication (mobile technology) and interpersonal communication (being pleasant, and attentive to customers and clients in face-to-face talk or on the telephone) is an integral part of almost every worker's function. Employers who are asked to specify their needs consistently stress that what matters to them is not the specialist subject knowledge new recruits bring with them from education, but rather the transferable or 'key' skills – among which oral communication skills are ranked as particularly important. As a result, the practice of instructing people in 'speaking' and 'listening' is gaining ground in educational institutions. In the fast-shrinking world of today where the spoken word reigns supreme, the 'speaking' skill will have to assume a prominent role in English language education, and there will be once again renewed energetic interest in the systematic teaching of phonetics in our English curriculum. Communication is emerging as the supreme value of language teaching for first language users as well as second language learners.

Once we are agreed upon the importance of speech in the new scenario of global economy, we are immediately involved in the pedagogical issues of 'standards' and 'models', and our concerns for international intelligibility are highly justified. The obvious question at this stage arises: What should be the 'educational target'? Is it convergence or divergence from the mainstream or a hybrid?

In principle, the pedagogical models for English are primarily what linguists have termed RP and GA. In practice though, it is always the teacher's model whatever be the model laid down on paper. In the Outer Circle countries where English is a second language, RP is the model described in textbooks and in theory is therefore the model for teaching. Textbooks aside, the reality is that the majority of those who speak English in Brunei, India, Malaysia, Nigeria, Pakistan, Singapore and some other countries in the Commonwealth have never been taught by native speakers, and those who have been taught by native speakers have not had necessarily RP speakers; there are just not enough to go round, not even in England. Any language model to be followed in instruction and learning has to be a living model. This does mean in effect that the teaching of English is significantly different from what the theory would lead one to believe. Abercrombie (1965: 14) observes that RP is an anachronism in present-day democratic society. In this connection, Gimson (1970) remarked that in the increasingly fluid structure of the British society the younger generation did not hold the high reverence that the older generation felt towards the RP. The so-called RP was indeed adopted 50 years ago by the BBC for use by its newsreaders and remains still valid as the foundation of a model for imitation abroad. RP, to my mind, is a dead horse in the 21st century, and I hate to beat the dead horse.

As an educational model, no purely imported standard can ever be practicable in countries where there is an extensive intra-national use of English. In our increasingly networked world, I believe there will be increasingly greater realization that native-speaker-like attainment is certainly NOT a basic criterion. The aim should be for foreign learners to acquire a form of pronunciation that is 'universally intelligible' and 'socially acceptable'. Let me quote here Larry Smith: 'Non-native speakers must develop a fluency in **educated** English but they do not have to have native-speaker pronunciation as their target. In contrast, they should be trained to be examples of educated speakers of Standard English, *identifiably from their own country* ... A good pronunciation is one that a variety of educated listeners find intelligible' (Smith, 1985: 5).

With the internet-oriented world, English is beginning to assume a new role as a global language for international communication. Globalization, however, has, by no means, eclipsed various countries' efforts to defend their national identities. National flavour is seen, nowadays, as a distinct advantage in speech, provided the 'national distinctiveness' doesn't interfere with 'international intelligibility'. These two tendencies are to be perceived as complementary rather than contradictory. It should not represent a kind of tension between 'nativists' and the 'purists', or a dilemma between 'national identity' and 'international intelligibility'. What I am recommending here is the emergence of home-grown varieties of English (called World Englishes) that are globally intelligible without sacrificing their own local (national) identity. This I prefer to call 'Borderless English' or, to use Pakir's term, '*Glocal* English': 'global yet rooted in the local contexts of its users' (Pakir, 1999: 108). Such a variety retains its own segmental features, particularly the vowel system, to characterize its national identity, and incorporates the larger units such as stress and pitch to render it internationally intelligible. These endocentric models will be the major codes of communication in the context of globalization. In the multicultural, multilingual and multi-ethnic world order, people are now getting more and more inclined to view 'diversity' in positive terms. Globalization has given new legitimacy to diversity that seems to have been validated and revitalized in the 21st century. Above all, such national varieties will be socially received well and shall present no psychological barriers for the learners of English.

## Speech: A Collaborative Enterprise

I consider RP or American Standard English as 'normative models' that limit themselves to the consideration of communicative intentions attributed to the speaker only. I would like to argue here in favour of a communicative model, which goes by the measure of success with which a transaction between the two participants, either individuals and/or groups, is negotiated. These two models have a set of rules prescribed for the speaker, whereas the two-way interactional model considers the listener as an active participant because it is after all up to the listener either to accept the speech act as a successful speech act or to reject it as more or less inappropriate. But only the observation of the hearer's answer can tell whether the speaker has succeeded in performing his/her speech act. Within the framework of Speech Act theory, an utterance is treated as an act performed by a speaker in a context with reference to an addressee. This pragmatic model focuses on strips of activity and speech acts as 'occurring in interaction'. Central to the understanding of communication as information transaction is the construct known as 'negotiation for meaning'. According to the Vygotskian perspective, meaning is inherently *relational* and is *socially constituted* through interaction and discourse. Speech, by definition, is a collaborative activity, where the listener is an equal partner. 'Intelligibility' has, unfortunately, emerged as the point of encounter between conventional meanings that are given by dictionaries. However, the individuals and groups elaborate on these conventional meanings through negotiation and discourse. The listener empathizes with the speaker (which I call 'mutuality of cognition' or 'reciprocity'). In passing, I would like to comment that spending time on teaching sound segments seems rather counter-productive in my opinion. We do not speak individual segments. These differences do not take us very far. We always speak in a social context, which helps the listener understand the meanings of even the homophones that are common in any variety of English. So learning to distinguish the individual sounds in isolation is not such a fruitful activity from the point of view of human interaction, and should be played down in our curriculum.

This brings me to the question of 'social acceptability'. In ESL context, a student is usually faced with certain kinds of problems: new sounds, new lexical items and new syntactic patterns. But even if a second language learner can pronounce his second language sounds correctly and put words together in a proper order, he still has to USE the language in a social context. He has to internalise the 'rules of the game', that is, he must know when to talk and when to keep silent, how loud to talk and with

*All about use*

what intonation, what constitutes a polite request and what a refusal, how to initiate a conversation and how to end one and so forth in order to make himself 'acceptable' in the society. It is just not enough to use speech as a tool of communication. The social purpose of language/speech has been emphasised in all linguistic theories. Speech is the noblest instrument that binds man to man, and thought to thought.

Speech is a mirror of the soul. As a man speaks, so is he. According to Ms Jessica Seet, a voice coach with the Art of Voice in Singapore, 'The human voice is an exquisite and expressive instrument which reveals your individuality and thoughts, and sometimes even your soul' (Seet, 2006). We can generalize, with a reasonable amount of accuracy, whether a person is pleasant, affectionate, polite and friendly, or aggressive, assertive and rude. A whole gamut of emotions and feelings is reflected in one's own speech. Psychological markers of personality and mood are often taken to reside in a speaker's tone of voice. The voice is the very emblem of the speaker, indelibly woven into the fabric of speech. Your voice is you. When you lift the receiver of your telephone, you are about to meet someone – to engage in a conversation just as if you were meeting face-to-face. *Speak pleasantly*! Your voice defines you in the ears of others just as much as your dress sense or hairstyle define you in their eyes. Millions of dollars are spent on cosmetics, clothes, courses for body and mind and books to shape up the image. Personnel directors cannot help but be influenced by the voice applying for a job. Entirely aside from appearance and manner, the voice can be a liability, or an asset. The tone of voice not only tells us a great deal about a person, it also arouses differing attitudes, varying from great respect to instant dislike. *The voice sets the key*.

Tone of voice is usually interpreted as a direct cue to attitudes and, therefore, is a piece of intended behaviour. Let us consider a social scenario where a five-year-old child accompanies his parents to the market. He is separated from his parents, and starts crying bitterly. There comes along a man with the honest intentions of helping him. He starts asking him questions:

What's your ⬲name?
Where do you ⬲live?
What is your telephone ⬲number?
Which school do you ⬲go to?

The child does not take any notice of him, but continues crying even more bitterly. Then comes along another gentleman who repeats exactly the same questions but with a low-rise intonation. The child jumps to him for help because he finds him more friendly, genuine and more reliable.

The child, undoubtedly, recognizes the words (comprehensibility) and understands the utterance meaning (intelligibility). The falling intonation patterns of the first speaker, however, clearly failed to arouse enough confidence in the mind of the child and convince him of the intentions of the first speaker, even though the dictionary meaning was absolutely clear. Intonation superimposes an additional layer of meaning (which I prefer to call 'pragmatic meaning') on the dictionary meaning.

A sequence of consonants and vowels is a good guide to the general dictionary meaning of the word but it is the intonation that gives its precision and a point. Perhaps it may not be so important for a foreign student to master all the individual sounds, but it is crucial that he masters the intonation that is known to encode inter-subjectivity between the speaker and the hearer. A beautifully articulated 'Good Morning' said with the wrong intonation 'characteristic of anger' may have more disastrous results than saying nothing at all. Intonation is one of the chief means by which a speaker gives exactness and subtlety of meaning. Intonation and tonal units serve to relate the segmental and syllabic material to the higher-order grammatical level and, most importantly, to the pragmatic level of interaction between the speaker and the hearer. Intonation is crucial to the art of communication.

## Conclusion

The key to international intelligibility, in fact, lies more in knowing how to move the voice according to accepted patterns of stress and melody than in making or recognizing correctly the component sounds. In this connection, Raschika *et al.* (2008) have recently observed, 'Although non-native accent can sometimes interfere with intelligibility, most second language research indicates that this does not necessarily act as a communication barrier. Evidence suggests that prosodic errors affect intelligibility far more than phonetic errors, i.e. errors in segmental production.' If we want to be understood and accepted internationally, we should learn to pay attention to the larger units of pronunciation (intonation and word stress). These units, called supra-segmentals, are relatively much more important than the smaller units of pronunciation (vowels and consonants) because they help us convey the meaning of an utterance, and also develop richer human relationships. I therefore recommend the 'top-down' approach in which the emphasis is shifted from the teaching of segments to the teaching of supra-segmental features. Instead of taking the learner systematically through each English vowel and consonant, perhaps one could concentrate on the *gross regional features*, and then quickly move on to features such as word accentuation and intonation. Admittedly, intonation IS a notoriously difficult area of phonetic investigation and the differences in intonation are harder to learn and teach. Since the implications are so serious, it is indeed a real challenge for the teaching community. Such an understanding will shift the focus from 'what is *convenient* for teachers to teach' to 'what is *effective* for learners to learn'. What is asserted here is that it is still realistically conceivable that a speech style could be constructed which includes the essential elements of stress and pitch that are most significant in the communication process, and it also retains its national segmental variations that help the speaker maintain a sense of national identity. This use of English in the expression of national identity is well stated in the words of Professor Tommy Koh, Singapore's Ambassador-at-large:

> ... when one is abroad, in a bus or train or aeroplane and when one overhears someone speaking, one can immediately say this is someone from Malaysia or Singapore. And I should hope that when I'm speaking abroad my countrymen will have no problem recognizing that I am a Singaporean. (Quoted in Tongue, 1974)

Dr Lee Siew Peng, a Singaporean living in Harrow (Britain), observes:

> ... despite my clearly Singaporean accent, I can address international audiences in English and still be comprehensible. That is what our younger Singaporeans should achieve.
> (*The Straits Times*, Forum, 26 June 2006)

I personally envisage that the preferred pronunciation model for global communication will be that of the fluent bilingual, perhaps a multilingual, 'non-native' speaker. This model will be based on the sound linguistic principles of phonetics and phonology of English as a 'Global language', reflecting the sociolinguistic maxim of 'variation' with strong support from the social psychology of language learning. Such a model

(i) will be well within the reach of learners under normal school and college conditions,
(ii) will not encounter any psychological barriers arising out of social inhibitions, and
(iii) will make the task of training teachers in the use of this model much easier. It will be a realistic situation for both students and teachers.

A shift towards this new paradigm is sociolinguistically realistic and pragmatically sound in the planning of courses in the transferable 'soft' skills of oral communication.

## Implications for the Classroom

The implications of this pragmatic approach to 'oral communication' in the global context can now be summarized as follows:

(a) It may be profitable for the learner to be exposed to many varieties of pronunciation, including native and, more importantly, non-native as well, in order to enrich his repertoire. Undoubtedly, one meets many varieties as one listens to radio, television and films. But exposure of this kind should also be *systematically incorporated in the learning programs.*

Unfortunately, listening is one skill that has received the least attention in our language teaching programs. Many people have great difficulty with listening because they have never been instructed in the 'active listening' skills. It has been pointed out that most people listen at a 25% level of efficiency. This is of a particular concern in the context of advanced mobile technology-based communication when the absence of visual cues makes it more important to demonstrate listening. Structured listening comprehension tasks may therefore form a part of the language teaching programme.

(b) We might want to abandon the teaching of Phonetics of English per se. At the moment, both trainers and trainees are grid-locked within the narrow borders of RP or GA, and anything deviating from the two systems is perceived as an error. Training in General Phonetics will raise awareness and a kind of sensitivity, among learners, towards the total repertoire of human articulatory possibilities. A sound grounding in General Phonetics will create more space and help learners broaden their perceptual skills, which I may call 'multi-dimensional view of intelligibility'. A sound training in General Phonetics will better equip learners to appreciate a whole range of L2 sounds that they might encounter in the speech of the international community of interlocutors, and also help learners of English acquire greater flexibility, empathy and tolerance for diversity. Most importantly, it will be the trained phonetician who will be the expert; a native speaker shall hold no canon or be a gatekeeper anymore.

(c) Students may be given training in some of the supra-segmental features (such as nuclear stress, word groups and pitch movement) that constitute a core as outlined in my presentation. Such a core will hopefully contribute to developing richer human relationships, making our language learning more relevant and socially more meaningful. There are universal norms for relating yourself to other people through talk. For example, speaking positively is better than criticizing; negotiating is better than arguing; sharing your feelings is better than remaining silent and withdrawn. It is the intonation that convincingly helps to characterize human diplomacy through these universal norms.

In summary, the pragmatic model outlined here will be a *hybrid*; it will be characterized by 'divergence' at the segmental level and 'convergence', in some ways, at the supra-segmental level, and shall serve to harmonize the two seemingly opposing tendencies of 'national identity' on the one hand, and 'international intelligibility' on the other. Such a hybrid form of global pronunciation will create a *synergy* that will bind all the three concentric circles (so-called diverse periphery and central communities) together, and will certainly prove to be highly vibrant and truly international. English today is not a monolithic entity. The awareness that English today is a multinational and multicultural language brings in its wake the spirit of 'tolerance'. The endocentric model, as proposed here, will help promote respect for one's own social identity, one's own national identity, without sacrificing international intelligibility and multicultural interpretability. There is no paradox in such a pragmatic approach, which truly represents the rhetoric 'unity in diversity'.

## References

Abercrombie, D. (1965) *Studies in Phonetics and Linguistics*. London: Longman.
Bamgbose, A., Banjo, A. and Thomas, A. (eds) (1995) *New Englishes: A West African Perspective*. Ibadan: Mosuro Publishers.
Bansal, R.K. (1966) The intelligibility of Indian English. Unpublished PhD dissertation, University of London.
Bansal, R.K. (1969) *The Intelligibility of Indian English*. Hyderabad: Central Institute of English and Foreign Languages.
Block, D. and Cameron, D. (2002) *Globalization and Language Teaching*. London: Routledge.
Bowers, R. (1995) You can never plan the future by the past: Where do we go with English? In A. Bamgbose, A. Banjo and A. Thomas (eds) *New Englishes: A West African Perspective* (pp. 87–96). Ibadan: Mosuro Publishers.
Brown, A. (1988) Vowel differences between Received Pronunciation and the English of Malaysia and Singapore: Which ones really matter? In J. Foley (ed.) *New Englishes: The Case of Singapore* (pp. 129–147). Singapore: Singapore University Press.

Crystal, D. (1997) *English as a Global Language*. Cambridge: Cambridge University Press.
Gimson, A.C. (1970) *An Introduction to the Pronunciation of English*. London: Edward Arnold.
Gleason, H.A. (1961) *An Introduction to Descriptive Linguistics*. New York: Harcourt Brace & Jovanovich.
Hayes, A. (1968) *Language Laboratory Facilities*. London: Longman.
Holmes, Janet (2001) *An Introduction to Sociolinguistics* (2nd edn). London: Pearson Education
Honna, N. (2006) Editorial. *Asian Englishes* 9 (1), 3.
Jenkins, J. (2000) *Phonology of English as an International Language*. Oxford: Oxford University Press.
Kachru, B.B. (1985) Standards, codification and sociolinguistic realism: The English language in the Outer Circle. In R. Quirk and H. Widdowson (eds) *English in the World*. Cambridge: Cambridge University Press.
Kachru, B.B. (1986) The power and politics of English. *World Englishes* 5 (2–3), 121–140.
Kachru, B.B. (1990) World Englishes and applied linguistics. *World Englishes* 9, 3–20.
Kachru, B.B. (1992) (ed.) *The Other Tongue: English across Cultures*. Urbana and Chicago: University of Illinois Press.
Lee Siew Peng (2006) *The Straits Times*, Forum, 26 June 2006. Singapore: Singapore Press Holdings.
Nihalani, P. (1975) Velopharyngeal opening in the formation of voiced stops in Sindhi. *Phonetica* 32, 98–102.
Nihalani, P. (1995) Phonology of non-native accents of English: Evidence from Singapore English. In *Proceedings of Thirteenth International Congress of Phonetic Sciences*, Volume 3 (pp. 504–507). Stockholm, Sweden.
Nihalani, P. (1999) Vowel phonology of Asian Englishes: Towards a characterization of International English. In *Proceedings of Fourteenth International Congress of Phonetic Sciences*, Volume 1 (pp. 97–100). San Francisco, USA.
Nihalani, P. (2001) Phonology of non-native accents: Evidence from three concentric circles. In E. Thumboo (ed.) *The Three Circles of English* (pp. 67–76). Singapore: Unipress.
Nishimura, N. (1999) Review of Gaishikei Toshiginko no Genba (The Front Line of Foreign Investment Banks), *Daily Yomiuri*, Business Section, 16 November 1999.
O'Connor, J.D. (1973) *Phonetics*. Harmondworth: Penguin.
Ong Hwee Ping (1994) An acoustic analysis of vowels in Singapore English. Unpublished Honours thesis, Department of English, National University of Singapore.
Pakir, A. (1999) Applied Linguistics in Asia: Pathways, Patterns, Predictions. In S.M. Gass and S. Makoni (eds) *World Applied Englishes* (AILA Review Vol. 17). Amsterdam: John Benjamins.
Peng, Lee Siew (2006) *The Straits Times*, Forum, 26 June 2006. Singapore: Singapore Press Holdings.
Quirk, R. and Widdowson, H. (eds) (1985) *English in the World*. Cambridge: Cambridge University Press.

Raschika, C., Butterfint, Z. and Song, L. (2008) Intonation and Prosody as markers of Intercultural Identity. Paper presented at 41st BAAL Symposium, University of Swansea.

Seet, J. (2006) *The Straits Times*, Forum, 28 June 2006. Singapore: Singapore Press Holdings.

Smith, L.E. (ed.) (1983) *Readings in English as an International Language*. London: Pergamon.

Smith, L.E. (1985) EIL versus ESL/EFL: What's the difference and what difference does the difference make? *English Teaching Forum* 23 (4), 2–6.

Smith, L.E. (1992) Spread of English and issues of intelligibility. In B.B. Kachru (ed.) *The Other Tongue: English across Cultures* (pp. 75–90). Urbana and Chicago: University of Illinois Press.

Strevens, P. (1982) World English and the World's Englishes, or whose language is it, anyway? *Journal of the Royal Society of Arts* 5311, 418–431.

Strevens, P. (1983) What is 'Standard English'. In L.E. Smith (ed.) *Readings in English as an International Language* (pp. 87–93). London: Pergamon.

Strevens, P. (1992) English as an International language: Directions in the 1990s. In B.B. Kachru (ed.) *The Other Tongue: English across Cultures* (pp. 27–47). Urbana and Chicago: University of Illinois Press.

Tay, M. (1982) The phonology of educated Singaporean English. *English World-Wide* 3 (2), 135–145.

Thumboo, E. (2001) (ed.) *The Three Circles of English*. Singapore: Unipress.

Tiffen, B. (1974) The intelligibility of Nigerian English. Unpublished PhD dissertation, University of London.

Tongue, R.K. (1974) *The English of Singapore and Malaysia*. Singapore: Eastern Universities Press.

## Chapter 3

# From Chaos to Order: Language Change, Lingua Francas and World Englishes

PHYLLIS GHIM-LIAN CHEW

## Introduction

Kachru's (1985) 'expanding circles' model has been important and successful in helping our thinking on the sociolinguistics of the global spread of English. It broke new ground by raising worldwide awareness of the existence of dynamic varieties of World Englishes (WEs). There is the norm-providing inner circle (i.e. the traditional bases of English) where English is spoken as a native language, the norm-developing outer circle where it is the second language, and the norm-dependent expanding circle where it is a foreign language (Kachru, 1985: 12). However, it has attracted criticisms pertaining to its relevance in an increasingly globalized world where identities are no longer pre-given or tied to nationalist policies (Pennycook, 2003). The model also appears to favour the inner circles as the 'original' owners and Higgins (2003), for example, has argued that non-native speakers do orient towards English in very similar ways to speakers from the inner circle, even if they do not claim ownership of the language. Bruthiaux (2003) criticizes the model as over representative of a political agenda while Nayar (1997) points to the referential fuzziness within English as a second language (ESL) and English as a foreign language (EFL) which hinders its practicality as an effective and relevant model. Seidlhofer (2001) laments that the model is unable to inform and explain the bulk of communication between increasingly large numbers of non-native speakers in the world today.

However, critics have generally been handier with the broom than the trowel and have not replaced these 'deficiencies' with a comprehensive model capable of matching important innovations which have taken place in the world. Bruthiaux (2003) suggested a departure from a focus on nation-states in favour of a sociolinguistic focus on English in the light of globalization but does not elaborate on how precisely this is to be undertaken. While globalization is intimately involved with the spread of WEs, one problem is that it is often discussed as if it were a recent phenomenon relating primarily to the development of world financial markets and technological advances in information and travel. For example, Giddens (1999: 10) argues that globalization is in many respects not only new but also revolutionary. Fortunately, Mignolo (2000: 236) has a longer perspective – tracing it back to the 16th century with the beginning of transatlantic exploration and the consolidation of western hegemony. However, both have characteristically viewed time within a history of European and American imperialism and run the danger of not acknowledging the diversity of global forces and locations of globalization: there have been other influential empires and global forces during this period, such as the roles played by Chinese, Russian and Japanese empires, or Islam (cf. Rodrik, 2007). Globalization is in reality a part of a long historical process; only the manner and speed in which it is taking place is unprecedented (cf. Modelski, 2008).

Not discounting what critics have said with regard to Kachru's model, its primary limitation, in my opinion, is the fact that it is situated in a point-moment of time, making it static, flat and too narrowly based. The unprecedented functional range and social penetration globally acquired by English demands fresh theoretical and descriptive perspectives. I believe that WEs is best studied under the wider umbrella of evolving lingua francas (LFs). The macroscope, not just the microscope, becomes crucial here, for it allows the inclusion of not just the synchronic but also the diachronic perspective and allows the distant and near past to inform the future. The first step towards understanding linguistic phenomenon in a wider frame is to free ourselves from our own historical time and cultural perspective. Another step in our analysis is the discarding of national boundaries, as these although important currently are basically impermanent and arbitrary. We should focus instead on dialectal, proficiency and functional ranges based on a sociolinguistic description of context and informed by cross-disciplinary discourses such as politics, economics and anthropology. A study of culture, rather than national boundaries, will include the set of values, customs and institutions, and commodities that most significantly characterize a community's identity, that is, the 'spirit' or 'genius' that distinguishes it from others. It also includes the inner values of the society interacting with its outer ones, that of behaviours, customs and institutions, and of all these, language will be the primary pillar of culture, the greatest socializing source since a common speech serves as a 'peculiarly potent symbol of social solidarity' (Sapir, 1949: 15).

Language, like all things, is never static despite the tendency by the Greek philosophers to view it as such. According to Aristotle, movement and change apply only to the attributes, and never to the substance of objects. In this bounded static view, an ideal and unchanging substance is the ultimate reality that underlies all outward manifestations of change. Therefore, the substantive stratum of existence which is postulated by Aristotle – stable, permanent and unmoving – is regarded as primary, while change and relationships are the secondary phenomena of reality. In contrast, in the Chinese worldview, all things either make progress or lose ground and everything moves forward or backward. Nothing is without motion and movement is important to existence since all material things progress to a certain point and then begin to decline. Movement is essential to existence: nothing that has life is without motion and the response of Aristotle is non-existent in nature. Hence, languages' unceasing companion is change and together they affect socio-cultural-political structures and these structures, in turn, influence and affect language change.

Highlighting change is forefronting reality. If reality is infinitely complex, and if particular forms of language used correspond to a specific stage in the historical development of a society, then it follows that each system of Truth or the ensuring debate on language standards can only be partial, limited and relative. A relative view is also more suited to a circular, rather than linear way of viewing time. While the Western worldview tends to divide the world into two opposing parts such as 'matter and form' and 'reality and reason', the Chinese worldview, for example, is a circular one. The Biography of Feng Yi, written in the East Han Dynasty, narrates, 'What is lost at sunrise can be regained at sunset' (cited in Zuo, 2001: 4). When a language is lost, that loss can be made up in other ways as time rotates. Hence, while the West emphasizes the synchronic opposition between loss and gain, the Chinese worldview combines the two through a diachronic perspective and encloses the opposition.

Phenomena such as language variation, loss, shift, revival, maintenance, and so on are intricately connected and form part of the wider circle of language change. To understand this well is to reopen the topic on linguistic evolution, which has, since the rise of Nazism and Fascism and their emphasis on the superiority of certain languages and races, been a politically incorrect one. 'Language change' rather than 'evolution' and 'progress' has been the preferred term not least because evolution is first and foremost a biological process with which language may or may not have parallels, and also because 'progress' is such a controversial notion. Nevertheless, we should not be afraid of 'progress' because biological evolution is difficult for the human eye to perceive since it is very difficult or impossible to detect in a short period. Also, progress is very difficult to define and measure and is likely to be discerned only in the very long term. On the other hand, it would be very strange to say we have seen no progress in communication in the last million years of human evolution since those times when ancestors common to modern humans and our nearest cousins, the chimpanzees, lived. It would be strange if language sprung up from nothing in this period and reached immediately its present degree of sophistication (Croft, 2000). Indeed, the theory of lexical diffusion has been recognized as the most important innovation in the study of language change (Labov, 1994). Lexical diffusion is the phenomenon whereby an individual tends to homogenize its linguistic behaviour with respect to similar parts of the lexicon. This phenomenon is typical of cultural evolution, and language is a central cultural phenomenon. The diffusion among related words occurs because of the tendency of the brain to use rules as much as possible in producing language, resulting in considerable standardization. The major advantage must be the economy of labour but in our present limited understanding of the brain, it is best not to say anything more.

Since evolution moves at a seemingly snail's pace, a longitudinal stand and diachronic perspective will enable us to 'stand back' and survey the landscape. Of course, it is impossible for a human being to jump clear of their situation in time-space and look at events with the eye of a hypothetical God (i.e. it is difficult for a human being to be objective since they see all things only from their perspectives). However, there are advantages of bringing together and finding linguistic patterns across world orders, cultures, classes and races, which are not often thought to be strictly compatible. A study of analogies, if kept within bounds, is a useful guide, not merely to understand the linguistic practices of the past but also that of the present and the future. The discovery of patterns can raise questions, build links, generate predictions and allow a bifocal vision, that is, the ability to see the parts as well as the whole.

Such a perspective that enfolds inclusion and integration as well as dissection and separation is incompatible with both extreme individualism and structuralism. For the former, society is a fictitious entity; only the individual is real; and, social institutions are only the reflections of a static human nature. Social development is accomplished by a strategy of changing individual ethics and ideology and the agent of social historical change is individual consciousness, values and ideas. Structuralist theory, on the contrary, regards individuals as the passive embodiments of social relation and the structure of society. Like the grammar of language which predetermines the speech acts of individuals and is not created by their speech, individual acts are embodiments of the structure of society without the conscious knowledge of the individual actor. The moderate path is preferred – one which takes into account cultural, ideological and political factors as important agents of change but which is opposed to the fatalistic determinism of structuralism which implies individual resignation. This allows for active participation and interference of human beings in the dynamics of history and for an active, critical and theoretical outlook. In other words, the universal rhythms of the rise, flowering and decline of languages and LFs are not necessarily predetermined but are often due to the particular language's response to meeting new sets of challenges in liminal periods when one worldview replaces another. Languages and LFs are more likely to die from suicide rather than murder (Aitchison, 1992).

## From Chaos to Order: A Model of Language Change, LFs and WEs

Cultural heterogeneity is usually associated with conflict but it can also be associated with unity. Indeed, heterogeneity tends to even out historically through diffusion, creating a kind of integration and bonding. This integration of diverse peoples generates other new kinds of heterogeneity, resulting in a 'unity amidst diversity'. In this manner, historical and linguistic changes move from chaos to order: in the direction of increasing complexity and integration of more and more diverse elements. Languages which arrive on the scene later are laid layer-by-layer on earlier ones. Generally, it may be argued that languages evolve either vertically through the forces of evolution or horizontally through social contact (Cavalli-Sforza, 1994). In Figure 3.1, social change is depicted as a spiral moving relentlessly onwards enclosing broader levels as time progresses. To understand this better, we may divide this momentum into broad historical periods, which within themselves contain various sub-periods. The analogy of a telescope may be helpful here (see Figure 3.2). From the telescopic small end, one can peer into bigger and bigger concentric circles – such as looking into a future time; and from the telescopic large end, one looks into smaller and smaller circles – such as looking backwards into time.[1]

Historical developments begin with the birth of the family, the advent of tribal society, the birth of city-states and, eventually, the nation and global state. Accompanying this movement to increasingly complex world orders are associated LFs that will enable each dimension to achieve variation in human thought, language, religion and culture through

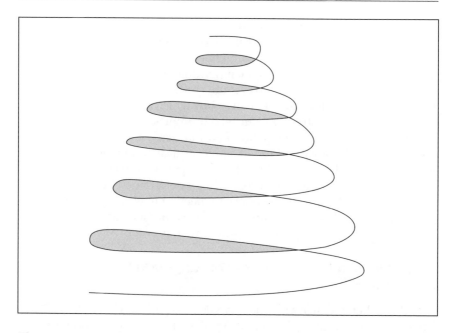

**Figure 3.1** A model of evolving world orders and their respective periods of liminalities (shaded areas show the periods of liminality)

communication strategies among diverse peoples. In other words, however paradoxical it may seem, the rise of LFs in different stages of humankind actually protects minority cultural rights in the longer term because it ensures a greater probability for the survival and 'progress' of the human species.

We will start with the world order of the family. As migrating families move geographically further apart because of increasing population and land pressures, the once familial language will inevitably diverge into various sub-languages. Hence, all human varieties of language can be traced back to some proto languages, and if we were to dissect a language and put it under a microscope, we would find it infinitely diversified. There is one form of cleavage and stratification along social and cultural lines, which leads to the infinite gradations of standard tongue, vernacular, slang, and so forth. There is also a local geographical division which extends not just to regions but to countries, towns and villages. An existing language is often a compromise among several forms of speech from these vertical and horizontal dimensions. Languages are constantly coming into contact with each other and sounds, words and phrases are

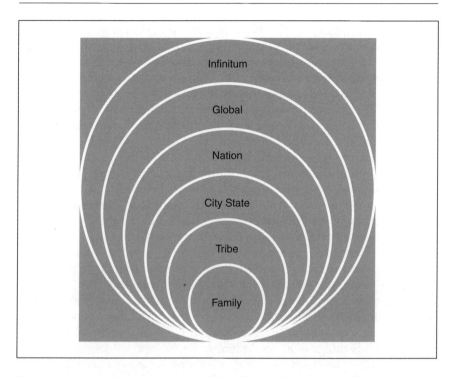

**Figure 3.2** A model of evolving world orders and their respective periods of liminalities (indicated in the white bands)

copied or 'borrowed' from one language to another in various degrees of code-switching and mixing. Spanish, French and Italian, for example, are all direct descendants of Latin and in a sense the same language. Of course, the further back the borrowing takes place, the more difficult it is to separate the horizontal (geographical) results from the vertical (evolutionary) ones.

In time, thousands of families are spread out over a wider area. In the family, it was very simple: everyone has their own idiolect but there might be discerned a preferred idiolect, a 'proto-LF' – belonging perhaps to the patriarch or the most articulate member of the group which most aspired to emulate (Deutscher, 2005). When distances were large, the passage of time ensured that the language evolved to suit the specific needs of that particular family, soon making this proto-LF unintelligible to other families around them, whose own languages have also evolved around their own special needs. Large families grow to become tribes or clans, which are organized largely on the basis of kinship and lineage and usually sharing a common culture and language. Such groupings allow a finer division of labour and protection, the fruits of which are advantageous to all. Early tribes were nomadic and we know little about the culture of pre-agricultural societies other than that tribes were the dominant form of organized life in foraging societies nearly 26,000 years ago. However, we know more about the advanced agricultural societies that emerged in the valleys of the Nile, the Tigris-Euphrates, the Yangtze and the Huang-ho by 3500 BC. Different tribes need a LF to communicate between themselves over issues such as agricultural, hunting and fishing rights. Usually the tribe which is the most powerful will have its language used as the LF. For example, the tribes in Arabia before the coming of Islam were a mixture of nomads, cultivators and traders grouped by a tightly knit system where kinship was the determining factor in a man's life. There were constant quarrels between the tribes; violence, particularly in relation to blood feuds, was endemic; and, generally, there was much brutality. Tribes were known to frequently engage in warfare over scarce land and resources and slavery was widespread. Eventually, the intense competition among them led them to the logical conclusion that one 'super-tribe' should predominate so that their diverse competitive energies would be better used to the advantage of all (cf. Manning, 2005).

'Super tribes' founded the early city-states, which are usually part of larger areas, such as those of ancient Greece, namely, Athens, Sparta and Corinth (Orreiux & Pantel, 1999). They are communities naturally organized around a monarch who ruled by sheer physical prowess or some form of divine dispensation. King Menes (2300 BC), for example, who established the Egyptian monarchy, united tribal settlements in both the upper and lower Nile regions over an area of 600 miles long. His language became the LF of the region since it was best able to sponsor education, military service, trade and a common religion – in short, leading to the eventual interdependence and integration of the various tribes of Egypt (Barfield, 1993). The languages of the subjugated tribe(s) would be implicitly ranked according to the tribe's social, cultural and military standing prevailing then. The amount of power one tribe has over the other tribes within a city-state would often be manifested by the mechanisms and means by which linguistic forms are sanctioned and what language(s) are deemed to be legitimate in varying settings. In time, some tribal languages would be lost as their once fierce loyalties become gradually assimilated under the city-state.

Always there are three operational layers, the past, present and future, each of which is associated with a LF. In other words, if one was the 'average' Joe of a city-state, one would most likely be trilingual: using the tribal mother tongue at home and other intimate settings, the tribal LF for use within the tribe and the 'city' tongue, the 'current' and prestigious LF of the time. If one were a slave from a subjugated tribe, one would probably speak the 'less valued' tribal tongue. Yet, if one were the leader of the slaves and the intermediary between the ruler and the ruled, one is likely to attempt to speak the LF of the city-state, although, haltingly, and possibly a disenfranchised variety. There will be others who might have to speak more than the three languages (especially if they had migrated from another city-state) and yet others who will only speak one language because the LF of the time coincided with their 'home' tongue, as well as their 'tribal' and 'city' tongue. If the state is strong and centralized, the LF will progressively become very powerful which means that in time, all the other subjugated tribal tongues will eventually disappear or sink gradually down the social scale, to become patois (see Figure 3.3).

As city-states flourished, they also became increasingly competitive: for example, the earliest cultivations in Egypt and Mesopotamia consisted of small city-states, which had no borders and were often in armed conflict with one another (Hansen, 2000). Sometimes, the conflict is temporarily resolved, when contending states split into two different ones – with one migrating further down the coast or river. For a more permanent solution, a 'super' city state will emerge with time to unite all the contending cities to form a 'nation' held together not so much by culture or race but by a feeling of oneness, solidarity and self-determination. For example,

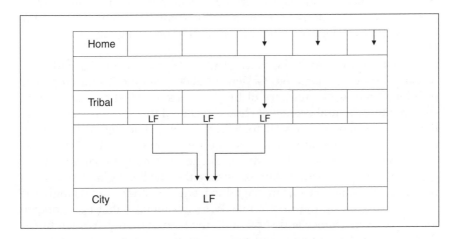

**Figure 3.3** Evolving lingua francas: A tribe to city-state scenario

the Arab group of city-states was united by the Arabic language to form the Arab nation and to become the supreme world power. We know today that the Assyrians, Copts, Syrians, Chaldeans and Egyptians are not Arabs, but as they all began to study the LF (Arabic), it became their 'national' identity. Similarly, although there are many religious groups in Syria such as Orthodox, Mussulman, the Dorzi and Nestorians, who consider themselves Arabs as they all speak Arabic, in reality some of them are Greeks and Jews (Versteegh *et al.*, 2007).

In Europe and thanks to the French Revolution, language played a pivotal role in providing the state with the means of developing a national identity. The fusion of city-states into nation-states engendered a lot of structural and geographic reorganization of different groups of people. Once again, the citizenry of previous city-states, held together under the banner of nationhood, will attempt to speak the LF of the nation, albeit with distinct accents and dialects. There will be migrants from the interior areas of the nations who are likely only to speak in the LF of the previous world order, hence suffering a temporary loss of symbolic capital until the national LF is mastered. In nation building, new varieties of languages are often formed when groups of people speaking different languages come into contact for the first time. At such times, there may come into existence a simplified language system to cater for essential common needs. A pidgin is formed which may later become elaborate and grow into a language in its own right. While some languages are born or destroyed, some also 'commit suicide' in the process of nationhood, as when the speakers of the old language continue speaking it but gradually import forms and constructions from the socially dominant language, until the old one is no longer identifiable as a separate language (Aitchison, 1992).

In every world order, the greatest undertaking for any individual is to make himself understood. Godenzzi (2006) refers to it as a 'linguistic solution' – that is, the mastery of LFs becomes the most efficient way to survive the structural change. It should be noted that the speed of change is increasing geometrically. It took a very long time before the family evolved into a tribe and a shorter time for it to evolve into a city-state and an even shorter time for the world to become national and, then, global. The LF of a nation-state is usually the one belonging to the most powerful city-state that has managed to bring the others into its fold. The reasons for learning the LF are mostly instrumental – that is, a concern for efficiency, relevance and survival in the new economy. At such times, the operation of multilingualism and multiculturalism as each nation tries to hold the disparate city-states within its fold is clearly seen. Sometimes, the operation is successful while at other times it is not. For example, in several eastern European areas, there were strong minorities of Germans and Jews in the cities, surrounded by a sea of Slav people in the countryside; in Hungary, the landowners were usually Magyars (Hungarians) while the peasants were drawn from a variety of Slav backgrounds. A typical quarrel would be about the official language of government, because the chosen language would obviously give great advantage to those for whom it was the mother tongue (Hansen, 2000).

In the nation-state, the designated LF (like its predecessors in the various city-states) will find itself in the forefront of change. Neither are LFs ever stable, standardized varieties nor a politically neutral communicative tool. It is often changed by speakers bringing a wider repertoire of both linguistic and non-linguistic experiences from the other languages and cultures they possess. LFs are likely to undergo simplification and reduction in functions. As a result, pidginized and creolized forms may appear as more and more diverse people gravitate to learn it. Hence, great phonetic, morphosyntactic, lexical and discursive diversity characterizes its speakers. Being prone to borrowings, the LF will naturally develop its regional, social and occupational varieties just as any living language is expected to do. The standard (or powerful) variety of the LF will cut across these regional areas, in the same way as standard American English in America or standard Scottish English in Scotland.

As more and more nation-states came into existence, problems begin to surface. In 19th-century Europe, for example, the worst clashes came when people of different languages and cultures were living together and it was therefore not practical to draw boundaries embracing peoples of only one nation or culture. The conflict and quarrels between nations became so frequent that two world wars resulted when bands of nations aligned themselves ideologically on either side in an effort at supremacy. This state of perpetual unrest and extreme competitiveness motivated leaders to look for a 'new world order' that would channel national energies in a fairer and less destructive way – hence the birth of the 'super' nation-state, that is, the global state. The integration of nation-states under one global umbrella would, it is argued, be mutually beneficial since it would not only prevent mutually destructive wars but also allow people to share and learn from one another. It is argued that the growth of the number, size and influence of transnational and global corporations, combined with technological advances in travel and communications, has *in de facto* created the global state, even if politicians have not as yet realized this (cf. Bhagwati, 2004; Pieterse, 2004). Nevertheless, in this nascent global order, there is once again great controversy as to which language will have the right to be the LF to link the myriad peoples of the world.

While history may march towards greater inclusivity and evolution may push us forward towards increasing complexity and integration, it should be noted that it is possible to traverse backwards on the spiral – temporarily at least. For example, nationhood can also be degraded, if there is not care and sensitivity, into a negative force of excessive nationalism involving contempt, hatred and violence against peoples of other cultures. This would deter nations from coming together as a global state. Also, on other occasions, while the masses irretrievably move with the flow of our spiral, there will always be groups of people at each time span, who will prefer to stay in their existing spirals or world orders. Hence, the longer our historical time frame, the more the number of groups discerned which are left behind in their special time zone and living under previous world orders either out of necessity, choice or accident. For example, while the 18th and 19th century saw the rise of nations, there were still groups which continued to live in city-states and a number of them in tribal orders. Today, as many nations begin to globalize, there will be some who will retreat through political means and/or geographic seclusion.

## The Liminal Periods

Between each world order, such as the transition from tribes to city-states or city to nation-states, are the liminal periods, characterized by ambiguity, openness and indeterminacy. It is a period of transition and there have been many such periods in linguistic history (cf. Laughlin, 2005). Here, one's sense of identity dissolves to some extent, bringing about disorientation. We live today in one such frontier and at this historical bar, we are typically experiencing two concurrent, intensifying and opposing processes – globalization and localization. Today, anthropologists and sociolinguists, for example, Kontra *et al.* (1999) and Skutnabb-Kangas (2000), often perceive linguistic globalization as an evil which runs counter to the cultural interests of local, indigenous or minority language groups. However, other more pragmatic segments of society, such as capitalists, technologists, and scientists, will tend to gravitate towards the synergy and cooperativeness inherent in the era of globalization (Alsagoff, 2007). Amidst this controversial backdrop, the masses are faced with the problem of culturally orientating themselves as to where their loyalties lie. Two opposing macro-cultural orientations prevail – one representing a globalist perspective and the other a localist perspective, and each of these perspectives is associated with a cluster of referential ideologies relating to culture, capital and identity (Alsagoff, 2007).

Each luminal period will see a new LF rising to the fore in relation to others. This is neither an unusual nor a recent phenomenon. In 2000 BC, for example, Akkadian replaced Sumarian, although the speech community retained the latter language in certain learned use. Also, it is a familiar phenomenon for one language to serve as LF or language of special function (religious, commercial) over a large area of many languages, for example, Sanskrit, Greek, Latin, Arabic and French. Also, the beginning of each luminal period will see several contenders for LF status. For example, in the early 20th century, Spanish, Russian, Chinese, French and German were all contenders for global LFs. From a micro perspective, it is unjust for one language to take ascendancy over others but in a macro perspective, it is a recurring historical phenomenon as LFs are instruments of progress, driven mainly by instrumental goals; and people will be driven to the language or LF with the most economic, cultural and symbolic rewards.

The liminal period is one of great conflict, there being basically two groups of 'realists'. One is fundamentally Hobbesian in nature, who will assume an environment of hostility or suspicion towards arguments for a 'supra' organization above the existing one. In the tribal world order, they will argue that just like multi-tribes will never be united into city-states, multi-tribes will never speak the same language. Indeed, all kinds of ingenious arguments are postulated. For example, today, the French in resisting the 'imperialism of English' will argue that they are not anti-English, but simply resisting uniformity – and that is about safeguarding cultural and linguistic diversity (Wright, 2006: 42). Others argue that there may be 'something different' about English, because of the scale of language spread (Skutnabb-Kangas, 2000). In contrast, the other group of realists recognizes the possibilities of establishing an enduring peace which will lead to the advantages of economic and cultural cooperation. Brutt-Griffler (2002) looks at English language learners not as passive recipients but as active agents of appropriation of the language. Her interpretation of English as the preferred language at international level is rooted in the desire by whole speech communities across the world to acquire the language as part of their struggle to be freed from the colonial burden. As great a paradox as it may appear, she quite reasonably argues that colonized people have used the colonizer's language as a fundamental tool in their quest for freedom. McKay (2003) proposes learning English while devoting time and attention to the learner's own culture as a means of not subjugation, but empowerment.

Different emotions are evident in the pre- and post-liminal periods. At the pre-liminal period, people are totally against new LFs as they are suddenly confronted by social, economic and political changes. This is not surprising since their ideas of life have evolved through a mindless mechanistic process of osmosis and unquestioning adoption of norms, inducing a tendency to resist all kinds of change. Linguistic change, in particular, creates a conflict of identity. Questions such as 'Which is better: to belong to a loving family of 3 or to a loving extended family of 39?' 'Is it better to belong to one nation among competing nations or to a united world?' and 'In which conditions do we have the greater opportunity for our own personal development?' come to the fore.

By the post-liminal state, however, one LF will have clearly emerged as the 'victor' and this in turn attracts more people to learn it. Success breeds success especially as communication hinges on working more and more across existing borders. Using Kachru's (1985) descriptive parameters, one can discern a group of 'lucky' people whose mother tongue is the LF and who will be the envy of all; a second group near the centre who is bilingual in both mother tongues and various varieties of the LF some of which with institutionalized status; and a third group which is trying to learn the LF as a 'foreign' language. It is a time when speakers begin to ask from which bases do they operate in terms of their linguistic cultural identities – is it that of the incoming language, the outgoing language or the language currently spoken?

Historical bars are also periods of greatest contacts when family, commercial, cultural and other types of exchanges occur between populations that speak different languages. Such periods promote bilingualism and/or the emergence of mixed modalities and the growth of LFs. As LF(s) spreads, there will be varieties (dialects and accents) of LFs some of which are more 'correct' or 'acceptable' than others, depending on the extra-linguistic context (social-political priorities of that time). This will promote discussion of a 'standard' which is often defined by codification and standardization, in other words, the suppression of optional variability and one which is tied up with the development of a supra level of identity. The word 'standard' refers to norms or canons of generally accepted language usage just like standards of behaviour, standards of education and standards of government, and there may be many hierarchies of 'standards' depending on the exigencies of the time. Historically, a minority, usually the king, the courts, the civil services and the surrounding geographical areas, use the standard but it is sufficient to note here that today, the mass media appears to be the metaphorical 'king' whereby standards are set.

## Caveats

At this juncture, a caveat must be added to the discourse on evolving LFs. I do realize that while it is possible to extrapolate linguistic patterns on the basis of new system sciences, this does not mean that the extrapolation has the force of necessity in the real world (cf. Laszlo, 1987). A prediction of what will happen in the future is not a guarantee of its realization. This is because the evolutionary logic exhibited in history is the same as the logic in the sphere of nature, which has more to do with probability and not necessity. Therefore, although a global state is the next world order, it is not guaranteed. Neither can we be assured that it will appear in the short or long term (Skyttner, 2006).

Indeed, the short term may be beset by a reversal of our spiral. Deviations and fluctuations of all sorts are not unexpected as the historical process always manifests a high degree of randomness and chance in its unfolding. If short-term reversals and fluctuations that change our way here include nuclear or environmental catastrophes, the long-term future would also be affected. For example, if there is such a disaster, this would lead to a great reduction in human population and may trigger a dark age of isolated warring communities. If the degradation is not permanent, the surviving communities would eventually, after some time, become prosperous and grow populous again and would once again, after the temporary set back, set out towards the path of globalism through multiple processes of differentiation and integration. But if there were permanent damages to vital processes in the life-sustaining environment, and the globe becomes uninhabitable or habitable only to low population density, this will result in the disappearance of our spiralling model. However, this is by no way an anomaly in evolution since 99% of all the species that had one time inhabited this planet have now become extinct; a large proportion of the culturally specific human groups and their respective languages that arose in the history of humanity have likewise vanished (cf. Calvert, 1998). Only the geographic time scale of the die-out would be new.

## Case Study: People's Republic of China (PRC)

The PRC has been chosen to exemplify our study of language change, LFs and WEs as it can be said to be a microcosm of the world, being a multicultural, multireligious and multilingual nation – a territory more diverse than most other nations. Countless little traditions, for example, folklore, cuisine, festivals, clothing, and so forth, exist under the umbrella of a 'great tradition' (cf. CIESIN, 2008). Since antiquity, different regional dialects have co-existed with different LFs – which are varieties of Chinese used by dominant groups in various capitals, such as Beijing, Nanjing or Xian. For example, when the classics *Shu jing* (the book of history) was written, it was done in 'yayan' (elegant speech), the LF used during the Western Zhou (1100–771 BC).[2] In the Southern Song dynasty (1127–1279 AD), the vernacular which became the LF was based on the dialect of Jinling (today's Nanjing). When Dadu (today's Beijing) was designated as the capital by the Yuan emperor, the LF gradually shifted to Northern Mandarin. When these strong centralized regimes faltered and disintegrated every few centuries China would be carved into contending states and its linguistic fortunes reshuffled. China's linguistic history is therefore the story of a congeries of Chinese languages: some forgotten while others continue to command great political and cultural significance (Mair *et al.*, 2005).

There are 22 centrally governed provinces in China out of a total of 33, and it is ironic that there are more scholarly data on the languages of the smaller subgroups of Papua New Guinea than on the languages spoken in each of these provinces.[3] I have decided to do a linguistic survey of Fujian province[4] not least because there is a dearth of research on this area but also because it is the author's ancestral home where she has had many opportunities to travel and observe. Fujian borders Zhejiang to the north, Jiangxi to the west and Guangdong to the south, and Taiwan to the east, and has a population of 35 million.[5] Broadly, all the multifarious languages of Fujian can be put under the category of Min, one of the many Southern Chinese languages. Min can then be further subdivided into seven dialects – some of which are mutually unintelligible such as that of Minbei (the north, e.g. Fuzhou) and Minnan (the south, e.g. Hokkien).[6] Minnan will be our focus here and it can be further divided into sub-languages of the different regions in Fujian itself, some of which are not mutually intelligible (see Figures 3.4 and 3.5).[7] Because of their considerable dialectal variation, the classification of these sub-languages of Minnan has confounded linguists so this preliminary analysis will be necessarily superficial and occasionally anecdotal. The Chinese are also averse to discussing variety in the country and prefer the use of the term *fanyan* (dialects) to refer to Chinese multilingualism, despite the existence of mutual unintelligibility (De Bernardi, 1991). Clearly, the Fujian topography affords a rich and layered sociolinguistic study of languages (and LFs) in a backdrop of successive periods of language attrition, preservation and maintenance.

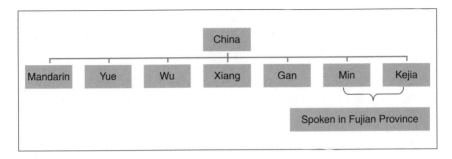

**Figure 3.4** The languages of China (Only Min and Kejia are spoken in Fujian province)

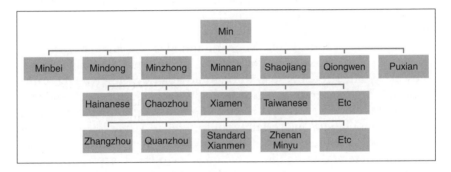

**Figure 3.5** The Minnan language tree

The first peoples in Fujian were families of Austronesians living along the Min River which subsequently evolved into tribes or clans (Ma, 2002). These tribes were relatively isolated from China proper even when it was first united under its first Emperor, Qin, in 221 BC. In time, they were forcefully held together by a powerful tribal king (as evidenced in the temples erected in Fujian to their first kings) who founded city-states in Fujian, such as Fuzhou, Nanping and Quanzhou (Xu, 1992). Their cultural isolation was shattered during the Han dynasty when huge forces were sent by sea in 11 BC to bring Fujian's little kingdoms under that of China proper. Nevertheless, as distances were vast, these city-states were left very much to themselves and behaved more like semi-independent tributary states with their own languages and cultures. Not surprisingly, it took quite some time before spoken Min became sinicized. For example, Forrest (1948) observes that the way plurality is shown in current Minnan pronouns may reflect influences from local aboriginal languages such as

Tai and Miao, which, like the Min languages, use separate forms for singular and plural pronouns. Other variants of ancient Chinese non-Han sounds have also been found in Minnan (Zhou, 2006).

For centuries, Fujian has always been the unwitting recipient of refugees from the north (Guo, 2002). Pursued by invaders from further north, the Wu people from the vicinity of present-day Shanghai made Fujian their home during the Jin dynasty (265–420 AD). These immigrants comprising of eight families[8] settled in Fujian, intermarried with the local people and adopted/modified their languages to their liking. Another large-scale migration happened in 317–22 CE when a huge population from the north followed en masse the court of Ji Yuandi to Nanjing and Zhongjian. Such mass migrations meant that Minnan was no longer calmly evolving vertically from parent to offspring but also horizontally through contact with external forces (Mountain *et al.*, 1992). As the northern migrants were always militarily more powerful, many features of their language were absorbed into Minnan, although the latter has its own unique cultural achievements. In such turbulent times, language change takes place either forcibly (e.g. through an edict by the invading army) or voluntarily (e.g. from a desire to enjoy the political, social and cultural capital of the new order). Such migrations fled to a mix of initially divergent populations and certainly contributed to a complexity of genetic and linguistic pictures. Archaeological evidence here points to Minnan acquiring more and more Sinitic features, including borrowings of specific words, sounds and, more rarely, grammatical rules (Mountain *et al.*, 1992).

However, those who resisted the linguistic change forced on them by Chinese emperors would find it more attractive to migrate further inland into the hills, and metaphorically backwards into our spiral, to the areas not originally occupied. Such migratory hordes would retain much of their original languages. Not surprisingly, there are still Min tribes, such as the *She*, which remain tribal in organizational structure until this day, linguistically fossilized by choice that was aided by difficult terrain which made contact with the outside barely possible (Wang, 1998). Yet other groups became stagnated at the city-state level, for example, the cities of Longyan and Zhangping in southwestern Fujian, where there still exists distinct sub varieties of Minnan language. In particularly harsh political conditions, such as during the Taiping rebellion where up to 90% of the inhabitants in some towns and cities of Fujian were reported killed, streams of migrants would migrate outside the province for better protection. Today, some Min enclaves can be found as far as the Zhoushan archipelago, a group of islands not far off the coast near Shanghai; the

Penghu islands in the Taiwan states; and the coastal enclaves on the Chinese mainland at several points to the southwest of Hong Kong or in Conghua, 50 kilometers north of Gangzhou (Chen, 2001). In their efforts to settle in new places, the Min migrants would willingly assimilate features of the native tongue to theirs, hence evolving new varieties of Min that would be further modified with each passing generation. For example, in Shangrao, Jianxi, and particularly in the city of Cangshan, only parts of the Minnan population can speak their original mother tongue. Simultaneously, as they left their fertile lands, such lands became available for people who lived in shacks coming down from the hills or other settlers from nearby provinces who would help fill the gap and who were regarded as relatively more 'desirable' by the invading army (Jiao, 2007). Their languages would then undergo a further process of assimilation and acculturalization. Fujian's fortunes peaked during the Song dynasty (960–1279 CE) when the region around Quanzhou became a major city of world significance (as recounted by Marco Polo) (Polo et al., 1986). From here, Chinese explorers reached as far as the east of Africa or even America (Menzies, 2004). Indeed, it was the staging and supply depot of Admiral Zheng He's naval expedition. Hence, the pre-eminence of Quanzhou also meant the rise of its native tongue to LF status. The people from the other cities of Fujian, such as Wuyushan, Sanming and Ningdei, flocked to its shores attracted by its culture and wealth. Their version of Minnan was variant and sometimes unintelligible, so they gravitated to the LF as the 'linguistic solution' to their economic and cultural aspirations. There were the people from further inland – Longyan, Guijiang and Zhangping – where the version of Minnan was more variant. An LF was needed not just to communicate with the people of Quanzhou but also among themselves. During such times, code-mixing, code-switching as well as different varieties of standard Quanzhou emerged.

Diglossia was practiced. On formal occasions, the Quanzhou and Nanjing languages functioned as official or 'H' languages while the local language was used for informal intimate and 'L' occasions in various locations respectively (cf. Brown, 2004). While the linguistic profile so far narrated has been that of an oral world,[9] the written script was a part of the 'H' group of languages which would distinguish a high official from a low one. Writing is preserved, otherwise Cantonese, Minnan, and so forth would all become foreign languages, unintelligible to Mandarin speakers. However, in writing Chinese characters, Minnan speakers also have a tendency to add a sizeable number of special characters unique only to Fujian province and sometimes used in informal writing (just like Cantonese). Despite the linguistic fluency of Quanzhou elites, Nanjing's (the symbolic centre of Chinese culture and language then) efforts to teach the officials in Quanzhou their dialectal pronunciation were of limited success. Minnan speech continues to be unintelligible to the northerners and in 1728, the Qing emperor, Yongzheng, issued a decree requiring all government officials to learn Mandarin (the northern LF) because of communication problems among government officials from different provinces (Li, 2006).

Amoy (present-day Xiamen) overtook Quanzhou in importance when the latter's harbour began to silt up. Migrants moved south to the port city of Amoy in the 19th century, hence making standard Amoy rather than standard Quanzhou (Chen, 2001), the LF of Fujian. Amoy at that time was one of the five treaty ports open to foreign commerce and a major centre for the export of tea and the import of opium. It was a city where many tongues co-existed (tribal, foreign and Chinese) and there was a prevalence of code-mixing and code-switching. People from various villages, towns, regions and cities in Fujian, for example, the Hakkas from Southwest Fujian or Shantou,[10] would learn Xiamen as a means of economic survival. It was a large port and traders used a number of LFs – standard Amoy and standard Nanjing for speakers from the near north, standard Cantonese for speakers from the near south to communicate with one another. Pidgin English was also spoken as Amoy city attracted many Europeans, Arabs and Jews. Despite the rise of standard Amoy, the people of Quanzhou still considered it as colloquial, unrefined and lacking of a past glory. Present-day Quanzhou dialect (also called Lungki dialect) differs slightly from standard Amoy in their nasal endings but they are still different (Erbaugh, 1995). Catholic missionaries, who first learnt Quanzhou, began to switch to Xiamen in order to compete with the Protestants who arrived later (Zhou, 1991).

In the 20th century, the Chinese nationalists, influenced by the European concept of nationhood, attempted to promote a national language as a means of communication both within and between provinces of China. Here, *putonghua* ('common speech'), originally a low-class variety of Mandarin from the north which came into general use at the end of the Qing dynasty, and had the connotation of being an adulterated form of the standard Guoyu ('national language') then spoken, was chosen as the base of the standard spoken norm (Chen, 1999). The idea of an LF was propelled further in 1958 when Premier Zhou En Lai initiated a decree to implement *putonghua* as the medium of instruction for all schools from first grade to university throughout China. Where Fujian was concerned, this was a radical move in view of the fact that *putonghua* and Minnan were mutually unintelligible. It also came at a time when most language teachers in the south were as unfamiliar with the Beijing speech as their students (cf. Guo, 2004). Nevertheless, persistent efforts to implement the language has paid off – today, in Fujian, it is possible to shop, buy a train ticket or ask street directions by using only *putonghua*, a far cry from the 1970s where many Minnan tongues were spoken. Code and style switching using Minnan languages and *putonghua* is common as people in Fujian go through their daily routines. While intra-regional migration in the 20th century has homogenized the Min tongues, there are still mutually unintelligible tongues, such as Minbei and Minnan. There has been some resistance to the imposition of *putonghua*, viewed as a language of northerners, cultural elites, hegemonic or dominating political parties, but these are less played out in the streets (humorously) than on local television. There are television programmes in local dialects (e.g. local opera) catering for the needs of those audiences who have difficulty understanding *putonghua*. However, Fujian television may use Minnan as a form of humorous contrast to the powerful north and occasionally to maintain the cultural hegemony of Fujian (Gunn, 2006). In this respect, Minnan is used as the signifier of the historical past, the intimate and domestic, the mundane, uncultured and philistine behaviour.

While nationhood has engendered the slow death of many original Minnan tongues in the past two generations, significantly, it has taken place without bloodshed and street protests probably because Minnan is not replaced but is just 'coated' with yet another layer. Hence, in the alleys and more intimate settings of Xiamen (or neighbouring Fuzhou and Guangzhou) most southerners still speak the same dialects as their grandparents speak. Further inland, in Fujian, there also remain well-defined communities within the larger sub-language groups, as the Fujian hills have protected their languages from being too quickly assimilated by the succession of Chinese LFs. But even there, the locutions of new ways of life will eventually reach the most intimate levels of language. In Fujian, as elsewhere in China, there is a very uneven pace of LF penetration, past and present. Just as standard Xiamen is spoken in varying accents in Fujian, so too is *putonghua* in China.

We should be careful not to view Minnan only in opposition to *putonghua* because *putonghua* itself has been contested and is always straining against its own division and multiplication in order to fulfil a mission to overcome the local cultural hegemonies and their contests for status (Guo, 2004). Movements to promote *putonghua* as an LF have also varied during this time and from place to place in the degree they have sought to dominate literature and mass media or elected to accommodate local languages (Gunn, 2006). Like English, *putonghua* itself is spoken in many different accents and dialects, some more prestigious than others. What began as a limited dialect has now become a conglomerate of mushrooming regional varieties, united only by the grammar and core vocabulary of the written script. In the past century, it absorbed many words from the surrounding languages so as to widen its function and there are, inevitably, progressive embellishments in the way of local vocabulary.

But at the heart of linguistic discussion in China today, there is no longer _putonghua_, the national LF, but rather the emergent LF of the 'new world order'. According to a report by _The Economist_ (12 April 2006), one-fifth of China's population is learning English, and at this rate it is estimated that the total English-speaking population will outnumber the native speakers in the rest of the world in two decades. There is a great impatience on the part of Fujianese to master what is considered '_the next LF_', hence the mushrooming of private schools offering to teach English in one way or other. At the end of 2005, 15 million students were enrolled in 77,000 non-state schools which is 8% of the 197 million Chinese children aged 5 to 14.[11] In Xiamen, as with other coastal cities of China, enrollment in private schools is way above the national average, as these cities are fuelled by the presence of foreigners and faster economic growth. In such environments, questions such as that posed by Seidlhofer (2006) 'How can one promote a common language of the community while supporting equal rights for all community languages at the same time?' should be more aptly replaced by 'How can one learn the LF of the age quickly so as to ensure everyone has an equal chance of living well?' This is the general pragmatic attitude in Xiamen today. Indeed, the Minnan peoples have an insatiable thirst for learning the LF at whatever competence level it may be. For this reason, Fujian holds the record as the historic homeland for the majority of overseas Chinese, and also enjoys the dubious reputation of being the major source of undocumented Chinese American aliens residing in the United States today.[12]

## Conclusion

Elsewhere (Chew, 1999, 2007) I have argued that an unfortunate aspect of the world debate on culture is the emphasis which some people place on the preservation of culture, almost with the same attitude that one has towards the preservation of museum pieces. While all kinds of loss, including language loss, is a situation deserving of empathy, sometimes sacrifices are necessary for the collective good in view of the inevitability of change. While the widespread use of English gave English-speaking nations a head start in the world arena, this will only be relevant initially. As more and more non-native speakers begin to learn English from an early age, they will naturally compete with traditional native speakers for the top literary and journalistic prizes. The mechanistic view that English is incorrigibly permeated with imperialism is rather stereotypical since it denies the dynamic and complex social potential of language change. A language must be at the service of the people who use it. Historically, the adoption of LFs has often not been viewed as a threat to the existing languages but as a key to a share of the period's symbolic power. Hence, the growth in the use of English should be seen more as part of a world-wide movement of 'globalism' rather than as an aspect of linguicism. Each new world order requires new ways of perception. Its auxiliary, the technological revolution in communication, also precludes the turning back to a more secluded and nationalistic lifestyle, although it is not possible to go backwards into the spiral.

The rise of the big blue marble has become the icon of the age, whether we realize it or not. It is the backdrop to television news, the logo for international conferences, sports events and for commercial enterprise. However, whenever there is change, there is resistance. Therefore, it is not surprising that we are also witnessing a worldwide increase in nationalistic and ethnic fervour. Poststructuralists are generally suspicious towards meta narrative. There is a tendency to reject universalism, although in science the more universal a theory the more truthful it is. These developments are the final efforts of various segments of humanity to establish and affirm their present respective boundaries. From a psychological perspective, this is an essential aspect of the development of human societies, as well as for a human individual. But humanity's journey from chaos to order, and always to greater complexity and integration, moves on and by some stroke of its own sheer good future, WEs seem to be bound up with our discussion of globalism. But English should not rest comfortably on its laurels as the fortunes of LFs rise and fall in the theatre of history with remarkable regularity.

## Notes

1. I am indebted to Dr Lubna Alsagoff for introducing me to the 'spiral', the analogy of the 'telescope' and the concept of 'liminalities'.
2. Chen (1999) believes that this LF was based on the Zhongzhou language, Henan, Central China.
3. Most of Fujian is administered by the People's Republic of China (PRC). However, the archipelagoes of Quemoy and Matsu are under the control of the Republic of China (ROC) based in Taiwan. The PRC side renders the

name of the province in Hanyu pinyin yielding 'Fujian' while the ROC renders the name of the province in Tongyong Pinyin, Wade-Giles and postal map spelling, resulting in 'Fuchien' and 'Fukien' respectively.

4. It must be noted that it is the areas around Fujian province rather than the province proper since boundaries were only established in the late Ming dynasty (1368–1644 CE).
5. Xu (1992) estimates, nevertheless, that there are 55 million speakers of Minnan all over the world.
6. The Min Nan, or Southern Min, is the largest Min language group. During the 10th century, the northern part of the Kingdom of Min in Fujian split off to form the Kingdom of Yin. The line between the Min Nan and Min Bei languages today very closely follows the border between those two kingdoms.
7. Hainanese is the most variant form of Minnan. The evolution of the initial consonants has left it no longer understandable to the Minnan speakers.
8. Namely, Lin, Huang, Chen, Zheng, Zan, Qiu, He and Hu.
9. If the Chinese writing system was phonemic, we would have been more aware of the vast amount of linguistic differences but because it is logographic non-alphabetic, it allows Chinese speakers to write down what they say when they do not understand each other.
10. People from Shantou spoke Chaozhou but would learn Standard Xiamen in order to take part in the Amoy economy just as they would learn Zhenan Miinyu in order to prosper in nearby Zhejiang.
11. Bloomberg news report 'Boom time for private education in China' *Straits Times*, 14 March 2007, p. 12.
12. Retrieved on 4 April 2007 from http://usinfo.state.gov/eap/east_asia_pacific/chinese_human_smuggling/originate.html.

## References

Aitchison, J. (1992) *Language Change: Progress or Decay* (2nd edn). Cambridge: Cambridge University Press.
Alsagoff, L. (2007) Singlish: Negotiating culture, capital and identity. In Y.B. Liu, V. Vaish and S. Gopinathan (eds) *Language, Capital and Culture: Critical Studies of Language in Education in Singapore* (pp. 25–46). Singapore: Centre for Research in Pedagogy and Practice, National Institute of Education.
Barfield, T.J. (1993) *The Nomadic Alernative*. Englewood Cliffs, NJ: Prentice Hall.
Bhagwati, J.N. (2004) *In Defence of Globalization*. New York: Oxford University Press.
Blum, S.D. and Lionel, M.J. (eds) (2002) *China Off Center. Mapping the Margins of the Middle Kingdom*. Honolulu: University of Hawaii Press.
Brown, B. (2004) *Mystic Quanzhou: City of Light*. Xiamen: Xiamen University Press.
Brutt-Griffler, J. (2002) *World Englishes: A Study of Its Development*. Clevedon: Multilingual Matters.
Bruthiaux, P. (2003) Squaring the circles: Issues in the modelling of English worldwide. *International Journal of Applied Linguistics* 13 (2), 159–178.

Cavalli-Sforza, L. (1994) An evolutionary view of linguistics. In M.Y. Chen and J.L. Tseng (eds) *In Honor of William S. Y. Yang Interdisciplinary Studies on Language and Language Change* (pp. 17–28). Taiwan: Pyramid Press.

Chen, P. (1999) *Modern Chinese. History and Sociolinguistics*. Cambridge: Cambridge University Press.

Chen, B.J. (2001) *Minnan fangyan·Zhangzhouhua yanjiu.* (Minnan Dialect·A Study of Zhangzhouhua) Beijing, China: Zhongguo wenlian chubanshe (陈碧加, 闽南方言·漳州话研究. 北京:中国文联出版社).

Chew, P.G.L. (1999) Linguistic imperialism, globalism and the English language. *AILA Review* 13, 37–47.

Chew, P.G.L. (2007) Remaking Singapore: Language, culture and identity in a globalized world. In A. Tsui and J. Tollefson (eds) *Language Policy, Culture and Identity in Asian Contexts* (pp. 65–85). Mahwah, NJ: Lawrence Erlbaum.

Calvert, L. (1998) *Language Wars and Linguistic Politics*. Oxford: Oxford University Press.

CIESIN (Center for International Earth Science Information Network) (2008) *Fujian Province Administrative Region GIS Data*. Retrieved on 19 June 2008 from http://sedac.ciesin.columbia.edu/china/admin/bnd90/bnd90data.html.

Coblin, W. (1999) Periodization in Northwest Chinese dialect history. *Journal of Chinese Linguistics* 107 (1), 104–120.

Croft, W. (2000) *Explaining Language Change: An Evolutionary Approach*. Harlow: Longman.

De Bernardi, J. (1991) Linguistic nationalism: The case of southern Min. In V.H. Mair (ed.) *Sino Platonic Papers, no. 25*. University of Pennsylvania.

Deutscher, G. (2005) *The Unfolding of Language: An Evolutionary Tour of Mankind's Greatest Invention*. New York: Metropolitan Books.

Dua, H.R. (1994) *Hegemony of English: Future of Developing Languages in the Third World*. Japan: Yashoda Publications.

Erbaugh, M.S. (1995) Southern Chinese dialects as a medium for reconciliation within Greater China. *Language in Society* 24, 79–94.

Forrest, R.A.D. (1948) *The Chinese Language*. London: Faber and Faber.

Giddens, A. (1999) *Runaway World. How Globalization Is Reshaping our Lives*. London: Profile Books.

Godenzzi, J.C. (2006) Spanish as a Lingua Franca. *Annual Review of Applied Linguistics* 26, 100–122.

Gunn, E.M. (2006) *Rendering the Regional. Local Languages in Contemporary Chinese Media*. Hawaii: University of Hawaii Press.

Guo, Longsheng (2004) The relationship between putonghua and Chinese dialects. In M. Zhou and H. Sun (eds) *Language Policy in the People's Republic of China Theory and Practice Since 1949*. Boston: Kluwer Academic Publishers.

Guo, X. (2002) *The Ideal Chinese Political Leader: A Historical and Political Perspective*. Westport, CT: Praeger.

Hansen, M.H. (ed.) (2000) *A Comparative Study of 30 City State Cultures; an Investigation*. A collection of revised papers contributed to a symposium held 5–9 January 1999 at the Copenhagen Polis Centre, with some additional contributions. Denmark: Kgl. Danske Videnskabernes Selskab.

Higgins, C. (2003) Ownership of English in the Outer circle: An alternative to the NS-NNS dichotomy. *TESOL Quarterly* 37 (4), 615–644.

Jiao, T. (2007) _Neolithic of Southeast China: Cultural Transformations and Regional Interactions_. New York: Cambria Press.

Kachru, B. (1985) Standard, codification, and sociolinguistic realism: The English language in the Outer Circle. In R. Quirk and H.G. Widdowson (eds) _English in the World: Teaching and Learning the Language of Literatures_. Cambridge: Cambridge University Press, 11–30.

Kontra, M., Phillipson, R., Skutnabb-Kangas, T. and Varady, T. (eds) (1999) _Language, A Right and Resource: Approaches to Linguistic Human Rights_. New York: Central European University Press.

Labov, W. (1994) _Principles of Linguistic Change_. Cambridge, MA: Blackwell.

Laughlin, R. (2005) _A Different Universe: Reinventing Physics from the Bottom Down_. New York: Basic Books.

Laszlo, E. (1987) _Evolution: The Grand Synthesis_. Boston: New Science Library.

Li, D.C.C. (2006) Chinese as a Lingua Franca in greater China. _Annual Review of Applied Linguistics_ 26, 149–176.

Ma, C.Q. (2002) _Min Tai fangyan de yuanliu yu shanbian_. (Origin and Evolution of the Dialects in Fujian and Taiwan) Fuzhou, China: Fujian renmin chubanshe (马重奇,闽台方言的源流与嬗变. 福州: 福建人民出版社).

Mair, V.H., Steinhardt, N.S. and Goldin, P. (2005) _Hawai'i Reader in Traditional Chinese Culture_. Honolulu: University of Hawaii Press.

Manning, P. (2005) _Migration in World History_. London: Routledge.

McKay, S. (2003) Towards an appropriate EIL pedagogy: Re-examining common ELT assumptions. _International Journal of Applied Linguistics_ 13 (1), 1–22.

Menzies, G. (2004) _1421: The Year China Discovered America_. New York, NY: Harper Perennial.

Mignolo, W. (2000) _Local Histories/Global Designs: Coloniality, Subaltern Knowledges, and Border Thinking_. Princeton, NJ: Princeton University Press.

Modelski, G., Devezas, T. and Thompson, W. (2008) _Globalization as Evolutionary Process: Modeling Global Change_. London, New York: Routledge.

Moser, L.J. (1985) _The Chinese Mosaic. The Peoples and Province of China_. London: Westview Press/Boulder and London.

Mountain, J.L., Wang W.S., Du, R., Yuan, Y.C. and Luca, L. (1992) Congruence of genetic and linguistic evolution in China. _Journal of Chinese Linguistics_ 20, 214–326.

Nayar, P.B. (1997) ESL/EFL dichotomy today: Language politics or pragmatics? _TESOL Quarterly_ 31 (1), 9–37.

Orreiux, C. and Pantel, P.S. (1999) _A History of Ancient Greece_. Malden, MA: Blackwell.

Pieterse, N. (2004) _Globalization and Culture: Global Mélange_. Oxford: Rowman and Littlefield Publishers.

Pennycook, A. (2003) Global Englishes, Rip Slyme, and performativity. _Journal of Sociolinguistics_ 7 (4), 513–515.

Polo, M., Cordier, H., Yule, H. and Yule, A.F. (1986) _The Book of Ser Marco Polo, The Venetia, Concerning the Kingdoms and the Marvels of the East_. New York: Airmont Publishing Company.

Rodrik, D. (2007) _One Economics, Many Recipes: Globalization, Institutions and Economic Growth_. Princeton: Princeton University Press.

Sapir, E. (1949) Culture, genuine and spurious. In D.G. Mandelbaum (ed.) *Selected Writings of Edward Sapir* (pp. 308–331). Berkeley: University of California Press. Republished 2003.

Scarre, C. and Fagan, B.M. (1997) *Ancient Civilizations.* New York: Longman.

Seidlhofer, B. (2001) Closing a conceptual gap: The case for a description of English as a Lingua Franca. *International Journal of Applied Linguistics* 11 (2), 133–156.

Seidlhofer, B. (2006) English as a Lingua Franca in Europe: Challenges for Applied Linguistics. *Annual Review of Applied Linguistics* 26, 3–34.

Skutnabb-Kangas, T. (2000) *Linguistic Genocide in Education or Worldwide Diversity and Human Rights.* London: Lawrence Erlbaum.

Skyttner, L. (2006) *General Systems Theory: Problems, Perspective, Practice.* Singapore: World Scientific Publishing Company.

Versteegh, K., Eid, M., Elgibali, A., Woidich, M. and Aaborski, A. (eds) (2007) *Encyclopedia of Arabic Language and Linguistics* (Vol. 3). Amsterdam: Brill.

Wang, Y. (1998) A study of migration policy in Ancient China. *Chinese Journal of Population Science* 7 (1), 27–38.

Wright, S. (2006) French as a Lingua Franca. *Annual Review of Applied Linguistics* 26, 35–60.

Xu, C. (1992) *Min nan bai hua zi.* Beijing: Yu wen chu ban she.

Zhou, C. (1991) Min *nan hua yup u tong hua.* Beijing: Yu wen chu ban she.

Zhou, Jixu (2006) The rise of agricultural civilization in China: The disparity between archeological disoversy and the documentary record and its explanation. In V.H. Mair (ed.) *Sino Platonic Papers, no. 173.* University of Pennsylvania.

Zuo, B. (2001) Lines and Circles. West and East. *English Today* 67 (17), 3–8.

藍雪霏., 閩台閩南語民歌研究 / 藍雪霏著. 福州市：福建人民出版社, 2003. 第1版. Min tai min nan yu min ge yan jiu / Lan xue fei zhu.

當代泉州音字彙. A dictionary of Quanzhou speech (1989) Xiamen: Xiamen Publishing Press.

## Chapter 4

# English as a Lingua Franca in the Global Context: Interconnectedness, Variation and Change

MARTIN DEWEY AND JENNIFER JENKINS

## Introduction

English as a Lingua Franca, the result of the recent massive expansion in English use across the countries where English has no institutionalized status (i.e. the expanding circle; Kachru, 1985), is the latest manifestation of the kind of language known as a 'lingua franca'. In essence a lingua franca in its original sense is a contact language used among people who come from different first language groups, and for this reason, it has normally been someone's second or subsequent language. The first lingua franca to be explicitly labelled as such was 'a variety that was spoken along the South-Eastern coast of the Mediterranean between approximately the 15th and the 19th century' (Knapp & Meierkord, 2002: 9), although earlier languages (known, for example, as 'auxiliary language', 'trade language' and the like) had performed lingua franca roles. Knapp and Meierkord (2002: 9) describe this first lingua franca 'proper' as being 'probably based on some Italian dialects' and including 'elements from Spanish, French, Portuguese, Arabic, Turkish, Greek and Persian', its hybrid nature being a defining feature of all the lingua francas that have followed.

English as a Lingua Franca (henceforth ELF) shares many of the characteristics of other lingua francas with one notable exception: the involvement of native speakers (NSs). The historical lingua francas had no NSs, but because of its global spread, ELF differs in this respect. For, as Seidlhofer points out, 'it has to be remembered that ELF interactions often also include interlocutors from the Inner and Outer Circles' (2004: 211–212), and as Jenkins has argued elsewhere, 'to put it another way, ELF does not stop being ELF if inner or outer circle members happen to be present' (2007: 2). By contrast with other lingua francas, then, ELF does indeed include NSs of both inner and outer circle Englishes.[1] However, these speakers' Englishes do not represent a linguistic reference point for ELF, and to participate effectively in ELF communication, NSs of English therefore need to observe ELF norms and employ ELF strategies such as accommodation in the same ways and to the same extent as do its non-native speakers (NNSs) in the expanding circle. In fact, the prevailing assumption among many inner circle English NSs that they speak a universally intelligible and appropriate English, coupled with their rampant monolingualism, is likely in the near future to seriously disadvantage them in their attempts at global communication (see Graddol, 2006; Jones & Bradwell, 2007), and although beyond the scope of this chapter, urgently needs to be addressed.

Empirical research into ELF began in the early 1990s and has accelerated dramatically during the first decade of the new millennium. The features being described and documented at a range of linguistic levels and across a number of domains and geographical contexts (see, e.g. Dewey, 2007a; Deterding & Kirkpatrick, 2006; Jenkins, 2000; Mauranen, 2006; Pitzl, 2005; Seidlhofer, 2004) have the potential to bring about a paradigm shift in the way the English of its NNSs is perceived. More specifically, ELF research is likely to facilitate a move away from perceptions of NNSs' English as by definition deficient where it differs from NS (usually, but not always, North American or British) English. Instead, ELF researchers are describing the English of proficient ELF speakers whose innovations (rather than 'errors') differ systematically from NS forms, are communicatively effective and are appropriate to lingua franca use (see Ammon, 2003) and are, therefore, entitled to linguistic legitimacy in the context of today's globalized world. ELF, then, its researchers argue, exists in its own right and should be explored and explained in its own terms rather than by comparison with some kind of British or North American yardstick, as is currently the situation.

As tends to be the case at times of paradigm changes, however, and especially those which involve language, the phenomenon of ELF has so far proved highly controversial among native and non-native speakers of English, World Englishes (WE) scholars, (applied) linguists and English Language Teaching (ELT) practitioners alike. It is arousing strong emotions and revealing deeply entrenched attitudes, the majority of which, nonetheless, are grounded in misconceptions of the very nature of ELF. Before we go on to explain how ELF deals with globalization, we therefore examine some of the negative and resistant stances that have been adopted vis-à-vis ELF and, in particular, the misconceptions involved.

## Misconceptions about English as a Lingua Franca

Negative responses to ELF are, broadly speaking, the result of two diametrically opposite positions: those WE scholars (many, but not all) who regard ELF research as promoting monocentricity; and, those theoretical and applied (and even some socio) linguists and ELT practitioners (again many, but not all) who see ELF research as promoting an unwieldy degree of diversity.

As an example of the first position, we focus on one particular instance: the call for papers for a recent volume on WE (Rubdy & Saraceni, 2006). In their rubric, the editors presented ELF as a concept that ignores the polymorphous character of the world's Englishes and attempts to prescribe a single model for all, thus denying the appropriateness of different varieties of English for different contexts of use. Seidlhofer, one of the scholars who responded to the call for papers, devoted her own chapter (Seidlhofer, 2006) to an attempt to set the record straight in this respect. In order to do so, she outlined and then responded to five misconceptions about ELF research: that it ignores the polymorphous nature of English around the world; that it denies tolerance for diversity and the appropriation of the English language by its speakers in different sociolinguistic contexts; that the aim of the description of ELF is to identify a set of rules that can be prescribed; that ELF researchers suggest there should be one monolithic variety of English; and that they believe this variety should be taught to all NNSs around the world.

Instead, Seidlhofer (2006) pointed out that the collection of ELF corpora is contributing to, rather than denying, the diversity of Englishes; that while there needs to be a degree of common ground (a number of 'core' features) among ELF users to facilitate mutual intelligibility, this leaves vast scope for regional variation; that far from attempting to prescribe, ELF researchers are attempting to counter the prevailing situation in which learners of English in the expanding circle have no choice but to learn standard British or American English – and thus that ELF increases rather than removes choice; that because of its potential to embrace local variation there is no such thing as a single variety called 'ELF'; and that there is no desire to teach ELF to all – that it should be learners themselves who decide locally, on the basis of sound information about the global role of English, which kind of English they would prefer to learn. Somewhat ironically, despite Seidlhofer's eloquent and detailed response to the points made about ELF in the call for papers, this was ignored in the published volume, and the 'accusations' were repeated not only in the editors' introduction but also in several of its contributors' chapters, and they continue to be reiterated by other WE scholars in other publications and fora altogether.

Turning to those who object to ELF for the opposite reason, that it promotes a policy of 'anything goes' and the acceptance of errors, we again find misconceptions. This time, though, they are the result of a deeply held belief that NNSs should not have any input into the determining of their own English norms, and lead to the assumption that any English forms produced by an NNS that do not conform to those used by NSs are, by definition, errors. So, whereas many World Englishes scholars accuse ELF of not 'allowing' any variation, those who dislike ELF for the opposite reason accuse it of 'allowing' too much variation. Underlying the objection of the latter is another misconception: that 'real', 'authentic', 'correct' English can only be that of particular NS groups. Thus, the Polish phonetician, Szpyra-Kozlowska, reports with evident approval a respondent in her study who states 'I don't want to learn some simplified version of English. I want to learn this language in all its richness and beauty' (2005: 173). The 'richness and beauty' in question refer to the NS accent, Received Pronunciation. By contrast, an ELF accent would, by default, be 'simplified'. Similarly, Sobkowiak (2005: 141) believes that an ELF approach to pronunciation 'will easily bring the ideal [Received Pronunciation] down into the gutter with no checkpoint along the way'. And very recently, a British linguist has described NNS English as 'a hotchpotch in which it does not matter how the words are spelt, whether or not singulars are distinguished from plurals, and which syllables are stressed in speech and which are not' (Harris, 2007: 12). Lingua franca hybridity resulting from language contact is, according to this perspective, then, no more than a 'hotchpotch'.

Equally disturbingly, Scheuer, another Polish phonetician, argues that ELF pronunciation models 'are about teaching foreigners only enough English – pronunciation-wise – to let them survive within the EIL [English as an International Language] community (i.e. be intelligible and get the message across), but those foreigners are then not taken seriously in professional exchanges, and often come across as unintelligent' (2005: 126). In other words, according to this perspective, despite the fact that NNSs of English form the majority in the EIL (i.e. ELF) community, should they not conform to an NS model, their ELF 'errors' will signal lack of intelligence. This is no different from the position taken by grammarians such as Quirk (e.g. 1990, 1995) and other prescriptivists such as Davies (e.g. Davies, 1999; Elder & Davies, 2006), who argue, for example, that it is 'a *trahison des clercs* for applied linguists to advocate a new or emerging or politically motivated variety of English as the standard of choice where it does not have the imprimateur of speech community acceptance' (Davies, 1999: 184–185).

This leads back to our earlier point about lingua francas and native speakers. The 'speech community' that Davies no doubt has in mind is the inner circle educated native speaking one and, in particular, that of Britain and North America. The point about ELF, however, is that inner circle speakers constitute a very small minority in the ELF-using community around the globe and, as we have already pointed out, ELF does not depend on them for its norms: rather, ELF norms are arising *sui generis*. According to an ELF perspective, then, both ELF norms and regional variations should be locally determined, and accommodation placed centre stage. For, as Canagarajah points out, '[a] general fluidity and mixing in languages, cultures, and identities is becoming a fact of life' partly because of 'the need to shuttle between communities in our postmodern society' (2005: xxiii). ELF, with its emphasis on hybridity, innovation and accommodation, is particularly well placed to cope with the new 'globalinguistic' (our word) situation of the 21st century, while the perspectives of those who misinterpret it would seem to be at the opposite end of the spectrum. We turn now to consider ELF within a globalization framework in greater detail, beginning with a review of some of the principal theoretical accounts of globalization, and going on to elaborate how one of these in particular aligns especially well with the position of ELF scholars regarding the internationalization of English.

## Globalization and ELF

The world is, it seems undoubtedly, an economically, politically and culturally interconnected, interdependent place. The latter half of the 20th century can be characterized as a period in which international exports increased exponentially[2] and, as a consequence, a period in which discussions surrounding the impact of this internationalization began to intensify. The continued and accelerated expansion of international trade has been attended by, and of course, further facilitated by, the establishment of numerous multilateral trade agreements. This has resulted in the emergence of more or less integrated trading blocks, some highly structured and consolidated such as the European Union (EU), others less established and still emerging such as Association of South-East Asian Nations (ASEAN), North American Free Trade Agreement (NAFTA) and the common market of the southern cone (MERCOSUR). These spaces inevitably provide more than the opportunity for the exchange and transfer of goods and services. While their principal purpose was in the first instance to liberalize trade, permitting free movement of goods via the elimination of customs duties and the adoption of common tariffs and policies in areas such as agriculture and industry, such coordination has also led to the enhancement of interaction (if not always integration) in all manner of communities of practice and walks of life at the local, regional and global levels. Thus, cultural goods and services, as well as the exchange of information, are all subject to the same processes of increased internationalization and global patterns of production and consumption.

Without doubt, the many and varied processes of globalization have major implications for the way we conceptualize, describe and try to make sense of language. There have thus far only been relatively few systematic attempts to consider at a theoretical level the relevance of globalization in applied linguistics. Perhaps most notable among those which have considered this, in addition to the current volume, is a special issue of *Journal of Sociolinguistics*, comprising a collection of papers which deal with various aspects of sociolinguistics, 'an organized sociolinguistic foray into globalization' (Coupland, 2003: 465). In this section, we therefore provide a still much needed, but necessarily brief account of attempts in the literature on globalization to theorize these phenomena. Our primary purpose is to evaluate ways in which broader socio-political debates can be relevant to an understanding of what is happening in the English language in the world today, especially with regard to ELF research and our still emerging understanding of the way English is currently being spoken as a means of intercultural lingua franca communication.

The literature on globalization is broad in its interdisciplinarity, typically combining history, political science, economics and cultural theory to conceptualize the global forces currently shaping the world. These themes have continually been present at various times and in various combinations in discussions of the international spread of English, though in much of the literature on globalization these have been more systematically integrated into a conceptual framework. Borrowing from this field, and thus relating the analytical frameworks constructed in political science, will no doubt be beneficial to any attempt to describe and explain ELF, a hugely socio-political phenomenon. Held *et al.*'s (1999) account of these many complex interrelated forces provides a very comprehensive analysis of the field. Widely acknowledged for its scope and depth in this area, Held *et al.*'s following description seems an ideal starting point for this discussion.

> Globalization may be thought of initially as the widening, deepening and speeding up of worldwide interconnectedness in all aspects of contemporary social life. (Held *et al.*, 1999: 2)

Acknowledgement of this globally constituted nature of much of the contemporary world inevitably involves consideration of language, discourse and communication. The current wider, deeper, accelerated interconnectedness has far-reaching implications with regard to the use of language, especially one which has been described so often as an (or *the*) international language, or perhaps unfortunately as a/the global language (e.g. Crystal, 2003).[3] The situation of English in the world in the early 21st century, where NNSs of the language are its majority users, is without historical precedent. Although of course there are and have been other international lingua francas (see our introduction), the case of English is fundamentally different for the extent of its spread and diversification worldwide. To reflect this diversity it has become preferable in many circumstances to talk of *Englishes*. This is as true in descriptions of English in the expanding circle as it is of descriptions in the inner and outer circles, a matter which will be taken up in depth in the following section where we consider some recent ELF data. For the moment, we return to the issue of theorizing globalization in relation to our own research.

A common argument in the debate about the cultural impact of globalization predicts a trend towards an increasingly homogenized world, in which globalization is equated with Americanization or a more general Westernization, or perhaps worse still is associated with what Robert Phillipson has described as 'McDonaldization' (Phillipson, 1999: 27). On the surface, the most visible expressions of globalization tend indeed to be the pervasive proliferation of multinational consumer brands, which are predominantly American. Brands such as Coca-Cola, cultural icons of Hollywood, popular music, and football, the Tom Cruises, Madonnas and David Beckhams of this world are public cultural symbols of a phenomenally widespread magnitude. While cultural interaction between societies has, throughout the history of human civilization, been complex in nature, the global extensity and volume of this in most contemporary societies is entirely unprecedented in scale. In relation to the various arguments about the nature of this phenomenon, Held *et al.* outline three broad theoretical positions, *hyperglobalizers*, *sceptics* and *transformationalists* (see Dewey, 2007b, for a more thorough discussion of each of these positions in relation to ELF research and the diffusion of English internationally).

The hyperglobalist hypothesis regards globalization as an epoch defining force, by which the traditional nation state has become redundant and inoperable and is ultimately superseded by new forms of social structure (see especially Ohmae, 1995). The emergence of a single, borderless global economy results in a decline in the authority of the nation state, and as a repercussion of this an increased cultural uniformity, where our societies appear ever more homogeneous in form.

In contrast, the sceptical hypothesis states that current levels of economic interdependence have historical precedent. Previous levels of heightened international interaction, such as those experienced during the colonial expansion of 19th-century European nations, have occurred at various periods in history. Thus, globalization is regarded as a myth, and current levels of economic integration have neither a profound nor a lasting effect on the structure and nature of societies, with little impact beyond economic activities (see e.g. Hirst, 1997). Sceptics argue that when compared to the Gold Standard era the world is less integrated than it was in the past, that there is no current increase in interdependence, and no restructuring of social or political world order.

The transformationalist perspective holds that globalization is the main driving force underlying rapid changes in the contemporary world, that we are currently experiencing a period of significant social, political and economic reshaping (e.g. Giddens, 1991, 2002). Those who subscribe to this view regard the processes of globalization, in common with the hyperglobalist perspective, as entirely without precedent, as a result of which societies across the globe are having to readjust to a transforming world. The impact and nature of these transformations are though very different when compared to the arguments of the hyperglobalizers. Far from this signaling a trend towards increased homogenization, a fundamental consequence of interconnectedness is a blurring of the distinctions between internal and external affairs, between the international and domestic and thus the local and global (see e.g. Rosenau, 1990, 1998) which leads on the contrary to an increased hybridity of cultures (see Appadurai & Stenou, 2000 on sustainable pluralism; see also Arizpe *et al.*, 2000).

In line with this perspective, we regard ELF interactional settings as sites where distinctions such as these are indeed blurred, and where there is considerable linguacultural intermixture. Speakers in ELF borrow from multifarious linguistic resources in the way they make use of English to achieve communicative goals. The heightened contact between communities results, in our view, not in a linguistic homogeneity, but in heterogeneity, as the English being spoken in these settings is not the English of the inner circle, but hybridized versions of the language that develop *in situ* as speakers accommodate towards the co-constructing of their discourse. This is similar in nature to the fusion of cultural forms that Omoniyi (2006) describes in his discussion of Nigerian hip-hop, a paper in which he addresses globalization from a WE perspective. The position we adopt regarding globalization is also comparable to many of the arguments presented in Pennycook (2006), especially in relation to his discussion of the involvement of English in what he describes as 'transcultural flows'. And although he does not mention ELF explicitly, Pennycook alludes to ELF type settings and phenomena when arguing that 'we need to understand how English is involved in global flows of culture and knowledge, [and] how English is used and appropriated by English users around the world' (2007: 19).

In short, enhanced interconnectedness is a particularly defining feature of late modernity, and must therefore be an element of attempts to provide a theoretical framework for describing and understanding the use of English, particularly in contexts where the language is being used for international communication. We turn now to a consideration of the nature of ELF spoken discourse. Drawing on a small-scale corpus of naturally occurring talk in lingua franca settings, we present empirical evidence that suggests very strongly that the use of English in ELF communication is a perfect example of the kind of transformations in cultural resources, here linguistic ones, which are currently occurring in a globalizing world.

## ELF Research and Lingua Franca Variability

There are a growing number of empirical studies in ELF, with emerging bodies of descriptive data that have specifically addressed the multi-faceted nature of English in the expanding circle. In addition, Seidlhofer's (2001) description of the 'conceptual gap' between applied linguistic discourse and current pedagogical practice in English language teaching presents a powerful argument for the need to go beyond a conceptualization of ELF to conduct large-scale systematic studies of how the language is used. This has now led to the establishment of several large-scale corpus projects, including ELFA (Mauranen, 2003) and VOICE (Seidlhofer, 2001) as well as a growing number of smaller scale, predominantly qualitative studies based on ELF corpora (e.g. Cogo, 2005; Cogo & Dewey, 2006; Dewey, 2007a). We report here on a number of findings of such a corpus, providing description and explanation of some of the patterns of use in lexis and grammar emerging from recent ELF corpus studies.

The ongoing emergence of empirical data in ELF is testament to the transformations that have taken place in the way English is conceived conceptually, the findings of which reveal some of the linguistic transformations currently and continually occurring in the way English is being spoken. By situating descriptions of ELF within a theoretical framework of globalization, we are able, especially in light of the continuing growth in discourse about both ELF and WE, to take account of the fuller context within which debate and analysis into the diffusion of English internationally are situated. Consideration of current theory regarding the nature of globalization's impact on the social and political world order is of particular relevance to empirical work in the outer circle and expanding circle. The transformationalist perspective discussed above shares much with the way ELF as a body of research approaches the use of English in lingua franca settings, whether these occur in inner, outer or expanding circle contexts. We believe that adopting this perspective to describe the work of empirical investigation into ELF also enables us to see how the conceptualization of English and the research undertaken by WE scholars shares common ground with current practice and thinking in ELF research.

Dewey (2007a) reports on a number of typical features in the lexicogrammar of ELF communication that appear to be emerging in naturally occurring ELF talk. Although, as iterated throughout this chapter, a defining aspect of ELF communication is its variability, there are indeed a number of areas in the linguistic systems of English which seem particularly predisposed to change in certain directions, and thus give rise to widespread systematic alterations to the lexis and grammar. In this section, we present a number of these findings, but rather than focus principally on the linguistic features themselves (a number of which are reported in Cogo & Dewey, 2006; and see also the similar linguistic innovations reported in Lowenberg, 2002; and Seidlhofer, 2004), we make more prominent in our discussion the underlying processes by which these innovations occur.

By describing the lexicogrammar of ELF from the point of view of these underlying processes and motivating forces that lead to innovation, we are better able to meet the task of theorizing ELF from a transformationalist take on globalization.[4] Focusing more on ELF processes, we are also thus better placed to avoid reifying features of ELF communication. This enables us to posit that what characterizes ELF interaction has perhaps more to do with the online performance, or enactment of linguistic resources and processes than with adhering to any predetermined set of norms (cf. Pennycook, 2007 for a critique of the habit of objectifying language). In turn, this may prove to be a useful way of countering some of those misconceptions we discuss above.

The motivating forces that lead to linguistic variation in ELF can in many cases be observed with a considerable degree of transparency. In other areas of change explanations have, for the moment at least, to be more speculative as there is not always the same level of transparency (as is undoubtedly also the case with language variation and change in inner and outer circle contexts), and because very often there may be more than one process in operation. Furthermore, such processes may even appear contradictory. In terms of these underlying motivations, innovative forms occur as the result of processes which can be described as *exploiting redundancy, enhancing prominence, increasing explicitness* and *reinforcement of proposition.*

The processes under discussion often result in a regularization of certain inconsistencies in the linguistic systems, changes which occur in the interest of efficiency and effectiveness of communication, and which are primarily reinforced via the accommodative behaviour of ELF speakers. To exemplify these processes, we now present a typical and representative stretch of ELF spoken discourse, highlighting certain commonly attested areas of innovation in order to illustrate and clarify the processes that underlie variation and change in lingua franca settings.[5] In considering the apparent underlying causes for each of the more frequent and salient features, our main objective is to give a more detailed explanation of the nature of the processes involved in their emergence, and to suggest how these are indicative of the kinds of changes taking place more broadly as a result of intercultural contact. As mentioned above, this includes in particular an enhanced role for accommodation in language change generally, and in ELF especially. In most cases, the nature of the processes involved is complex, and individual underlying motives are difficult to separate out. Most often there are multiple and interrelated motivations for the changes that have been recorded, but by attempting to classify these we feel we are better able to make sense of the way English is currently being employed as a lingua franca and is being significantly modified to facilitate its role as a medium as well as consequence of globalization.

The following is an extract from an ELF conversation among a group of postgraduate students at a university in London. The participants are here discussing their forthcoming reading week and the issue of locating appropriate library sources.[6]

1   **S1:**   what are you going to do next week (.) end?
2   **S2:**   next week holiday
3   **S4:**   next week?
4   **S1:**   no not holiday reading week
5   **S4:**   oh
6   **S2:**   camp in the library @@
7   **SS:**   @@@@
8   **S2:**   <@> I'm kidding <@> @@ no way @@ yeah
9   **S4:**   next week (..)
10  **S1:**   so you are not going (.) somewhere?
11  **S4:**   er unfortunately I am in travel industry and (.)
12  **S1:**   oh
13  **S4:**   world travel market exhibition is on next week so I have to work every day
14  **S5:**   ah mm (.) going to work
15  **S4:**   so I won't be able to to come (.) I know it's going to be very very very
16  busy
17  **S3:**   hm aha
18  **S5:**   oh that's (.)
19  **S4:**   and I won't be having time to read either @
20  **S5:**   yeah
21  **S4:**   so the next week after next
22  **S5:**   @@ (xxx) don't know (.) I haven't got any book to read @
23  **S4:**   no books?
24  **S2:**   yeah (.) there's no books in the library
25  **S4:**   no books?
26  **S2:**   yes because er (.) every book is on loan (.) I think
27  **S3:**   yeah
28  **S4:**   what is a good idea I think is to: get to any other library (.) you know like
29  any:
30  **S5:**   ah
31  **S4:**   library in any boroughs <1> er like </1> Hackney Westminster or
32  anywhere
33  **S5:**   <1> ah but </1> yeah they say there is one in Russell Square (.) it's really
34  good at like linguistic and er teaching
35  **S1:**   yeah but we – they can't borrow
36  **S3:**   they said that (.)
37  **S2:**   we can't borrow it from? (.)
38  **S5:**   <2> you can </2>
39  **S4:**   <2> yeah yes you can </2> take it for two weeks (.) one one month
40  **S5:**   they said – X said if you got the student card – the [name of university]
41  student they can lend you (.)
42  **S3:**   ah ah

This extract displays a number of typical characteristics of ELF talk. There are several examples where the speakers exploit redundancy, omitting non-essential items, such as can be seen in lines 35 and 41, where respectively *borrow* and *lend* are used without the object being explicitly stated. As it is clear from the rest of the discourse that the referent in each case is 'library books', then stating or restating this is deemed unimportant to the conversation and is therefore omitted through ellipsis. In addition there is use in line 24 of the invariant form *there's* (also widely attested in English as Native Language (ENL) corpora), which occurs in our data with either singular or plural referents, and is used in this case with the plural *books*. There is also widespread use of the zero article in contexts which ENL would require the definite article, as in lines 11 and 13. The overall frequency of definite articles found in Dewey (2007a) is comparable to that found in ENL corpora, suggesting that this is not an item simply being omitted, but rather a resource being deployed in different and innovative ways. The zero option is used in the above exchange as the definite article serves no communicative purpose – it is absent but by no means lost.

A principal aim of the research reported here has been to uphold the conceptual arguments made in ELF, namely, that English spoken as a lingua franca is not only a legitimate use of the language in its own right, and thus warrants proper systematic study, but that it is a particularly characteristic feature of the language in a globalizing world. The collection and analysis of our data need to be undertaken within newly defined frameworks and by means of newly emerging methods of analysis. This is fundamental to our approach, and necessarily so because of the unprecedented nature of the language use under investigation, a theme that should surely underlie any empirical treatment of ELF. In fact, with regard to the distinct nature of research into ELF, Seidlhofer *et al.* (2006) make the following crucial observation:

> Uncoupling the language from its native speakers and probing the nature of ELF is a special methodological challenge because most of the descriptive and analytic categories and approaches available have evolved through work on fairly stable codes in native-speaker communities, so these cannot automatically be assumed to be appropriate. (Seidlhofer *et al.*, 2006: 21)

This uncoupling of English from its 'native speakers' has been achieved to a far greater extent in the longer established research of outer circle English, and it is surely a vital objective that both research paradigms, WE and ELF, fundamentally share. Similarly, ELF research inevitably needs to make use of some of the previously established descriptive and analytic tools, but the application of these should in our view always be critically evaluated – and wherever possible existing frames of reference and analysis require adaptation to suit the situation with regard to ELF. Seidlhofer *et al.* (2006) go on to conclude that it is probably premature to consider to what extent ELF in Europe (the focus of their discussion) might be regarded as a variety. In fact, we can take the comments quoted above a little further and propose that the term 'variety' itself is perhaps one of those descriptive categories that might not be appropriate to a consideration of ELF at all. In all of the sociolinguistic studies which have made use of the term in the past, this has tended to be in more stable speech communities, both native and nativized. ELF is different for the more fluid nature of the communities of speakers that use it (though without doubt no community is not to some degree fluid), and the necessary flexibility displayed in the way the language is used. The data indicate very clearly that there are systematic features of innovative language use, and often these are shared across speakers of many different linguacultural backgrounds. The matter of whether or not we can describe these features in relation to notions of variety remains, however, an empirical question.

Some of the features attested in the corpus reported in Dewey (2007a), for example, zero article use in place of ENL indefinite article, as in *I want to be translator or interpreter in the future* (L1 Korean) may be more characteristic of a particular type of ELF, say in this case a Korean-influenced ELF, than lingua franca communication more generally. These features might also prove to be characteristic of say a Japanese-influenced ELF, and so on. Further in-depth investigations of ELF settings may also lead to the identification of variety features that are typical of regions, say an East Asian type of ELF or Euro English and so on. ELF speakers (just as ENL speakers and WE speakers do) have their own local and regional types of English, such as Italian English, Spanish English, Japanese English, the features of which become adjusted by means of processes such as accommodation when speakers participate in ELF communication. The features of lexicogrammar attested in the data reported here indicate there are emerging usages that are distinctive to ELF communication and that display some degree of stability. The processes underlying the occurrence of these features, however, are similar in kind to those that give rise to linguistic innovation in outer circle varieties. In contrast to WE on the other hand, it may be premature to describe lingua franca innovations that are indicative of ELF as a type of language variety in the conventional sense, but our evidence does show that there is at least an emerging agglomeration of language features that we can describe as characteristic of lingua franca communication, and which might in time prove codifiable.

Much further empirical study is of course essential, and especially from an ethnographically situated perspective (cf. Leung, 2005 for a reappraisal of Hymes's notion of the ethnography of language), to provide further qualitatively oriented descriptions, which can in time be cross-referenced with more quantitative investigations into lingua franca language use (cf. Seidlhofer *et al.*, 2006). It is also essential that researchers working in different ELF contexts share their findings, and that we continue to debate the emergence of ELF as a distinctly new type of language use and as a distinctly new field of language research, but one which has much in common with the approach of WE research (see Jenkins, 2006). In comparison with WE, ELF research is still very much in its infancy, and is beginning to become established, but in parallel with WE, ELF seeks to legitimize and make sense of the way English is being transformed by speakers outside the ancestral contexts of the language.

It is also important that we bear in mind that ELF is an especially characteristic phenomenon in the contemporary world. Ours is a world in which telecommunications and transport infrastructures have become in late modernity (for those who have access to the necessary resources) far more extensive than ever before, resulting in increased language and cultural contact at regional and international levels. The use of English as a lingua franca has become unparalleled, a phenomenon which thus far seems to be intensifying still further through the increasing volume of movement and communications between states and regions. This is no doubt especially so with the continued digitization of all media, with which comes the possibility of instantaneous communication across any distance. The continued collection and analysis of empirical data of English as used in ELF settings is essential if we are to properly understand how these phenomena impact on language use. It is also fundamentally important that we reflect on this kind of data in light of its consequences for the way language is conceptualized and described in applied linguistics, in much the same way the findings of WE have been already.

## Looking Ahead

The data presented above represent a selective sample of the findings reported in Dewey (2007a), a research project which provides description and systematic interpretation of some of the more prominent and frequent lexical and grammatical innovations as attested in the use of English in ELF settings. Among the objectives of this research, and of major importance to the debate surrounding ELF more generally, has been the discussion of our data within broader synchronic and diachronic frameworks. The research findings, and our discussion of the global and historical contexts in which the research was undertaken, will perhaps go some way in addressing many of the misconceptions about ELF discussed above and reported at length in Jenkins (2007).

By reviewing discussions about the spread of English internationally in light of theoretical positions on globalization, it is possible to align the primary commentators in debates surrounding the use of English globally with current views on the social and political world order as embodied by various means of conceptualizing globalization. We have argued that adopting what can be described as a 'transformationalist' perspective, wherein the contemporary world is best defined as a period of significant social, political and cultural transformations, is of most relevance to ELF researchers. The demographic changes in English language use (especially as described by Graddol, 1997, 2006), and the continued variability of English in lingua franca settings can be better understood in this light, that is, as fundamentally important transformations that are characteristic of late modernity.

In relation to the history of the language, the linguistic developments currently emerging in ELF interactions can be analyzed and interpreted in light of the historical evolution of the language more generally. The processes of change underlying the innovative use of English in lingua franca settings represent a continuation of a long-standing tendency towards shift in the lexis and grammar of the language – changes that have long been documented by sociolinguistics in the inner circle, and more recently by WE scholars' descriptions of English in the outer circle. That we are currently in an epoch of increased interconnection, in which communication takes place as much between communities as within them, means that these processes of shift are in many cases accelerated. The findings of ELF research as well as research findings in WE are perhaps both best conceptualized in relation to these phenomena.

In our research, we have approached ELF from a descriptive linguistics perspective, in order to carry out an investigation into the ways in which the language is varying in lingua franca communication. We also approach ELF research from a historical linguistics perspective, with a view to situating current developments in relation to previous moments in history. In its past English has experienced similar periods of heightened linguacultural contact, which often resulted in similarly accelerated periods of change. The data described above are presented as evidence that we currently find ourselves in a situation in which the language is developing in ways it has always developed, that is, in response to the purposes and experiences of those who use the language. Hitherto, these processes of variation and change have taken place in particular speech communities, leading to different ENL and nativized varieties of the language. What is different about the current situation is the unbounded nature of these phenomena – speakers from a multitude of linguacultural backgrounds regularly make use of the language in infinitely varied contexts and for unlimited functions. These include settings of language use that occur in all of the circle contexts. Lingua franca communication takes place to such an extent, and this naturally occurring phenomenon is so widespread that the ways in which ELF speakers innovate with the resources of the language have far-reaching implications for descriptive and historical accounts of English.

The research findings of WE are fundamentally important for our understanding of the linguistic development of English. New varieties of the language will continue to emerge in outer circle contexts as speakers continue to innovate with the set of linguistic resources we call English. As speakers appropriate the language to better suit their purpose, and thus modify the forms of the language, it is essential that descriptions and accounts of the nature of the language in these settings continue to be undertaken. Similarly, the research findings of ELF corpora, although still more in their early stages of development, shed much-needed light on the way in which the language is being transformed by those who use it in their largest numbers, that is, speakers of English who use the language primarily or even exclusively in lingua franca settings. The objective of describing and making sense of some of the commonalities of ELF interaction has been one of the driving forces of our research into ELF (e.g. the Lingua Franca Core, Jenkins, 2000, 2002; and descriptions of frequently used lexicogrammatical features, e.g. Dewey, 2007a). Our findings suggest that there are many central areas of linguistic commonality, or what Leung and Lewkowicz (2006: 228) have very aptly termed 'a constellation of language features'. We have found that there are certain phonological, lexical and grammatical features that can be regarded as particularly characteristic of successful lingua franca communication.

This is not at all incompatible with the sociolinguistic notion of variability in language. The objective of describing and making sense of areas of commonality does not by any means detract from the specificity of locally realized lingua franca talk. ELF research shows very clearly that variation in the way the resources of the language are used is in fact a particularly characteristic feature of communication in a lingua franca. Even more significant still, this is not incompatible with the perspective adopted by WE. It is our view that ELF research in fact complements the work of WE scholars; that far from contesting current research in outer circle contexts or denying the variability inherent in English, we approach the language from within a similar theoretical framework and from the same kind of empirical stance. ELF research upholds and celebrates linguistic diversity. It is not our aim to propose a uniform version of the language that might be termed 'Global English', or to imply that there are ways in which ELF speakers should or should not be using the language, including in relation to the adherence of L1 English norms. Rather, our purpose is to describe how the language is manipulated in innovative ways to suit the communicative needs of speakers who interact in complex multilingual communities of practice, in settings where the language is sufficiently stable to act as a lingua franca, yet sufficiently variable to fit the infinite purposes it serves.

## Notes

1. We do not use the term 'non-native speakers' to refer to members of the outer circle. An English speaker from India, for example, is in our view a native speaker of Indian English.
2. According to UNESCO (2000a), international trade between 1950 and 1997, measured in world exports as a percentage of world GDP, rose from 8% to 27%.
3. Crystal's (2003) use of the term 'global English' implies a certain uniformity, a single worldwide variety of the language consistent and stable in all international contexts. It is also worth noting that this world standard version would in Crystal's view be based on ENL norms, predominantly American English. This is in stark contrast to our approach.
4. See Held *et al.* (1999) on the virtues of adopting a more process oriented approach to globalization as opposed to the more commonplace practice of simply describing its impact.
5. See Dewey (2007b) for a fuller account of the processes involved.
6. In this conversation the speakers are L1 Mandarin (S1, S2, S3), L1 Russian (S4) and L1 Korean (S5). In the transcription conventions used: @ represents laughter, with each symbol representing approximately one syllable length; (.) represents pauses, where each full stop equals approximately one second; triangular brackets <1>, </1> denote simultaneous speech.

## References

Ammon, U. (2003) Global English and the non-native speaker: Overcoming disadvantage. In H. Tonkin and T. Reagan (eds) *Language in the Twenty-first Century* (pp. 23–24). Amsterdam: John Benjamins.
Appadurai, A. and Stenou, K. (2000) Sustainable pluralism and the future of belonging. In UNESCO (2000b) (pp. 111–127).
Arizpe, L., Jelin, E., Mohan Rao, J. and Streeten, P. (2000) Cultural diversity, conflict and pluralism. In UNESCO (2000b) (pp. 24–42).

Canagarajah, A.S. (2005) Introduction. In A.S. Canagarajah (ed.) *Reclaiming the Local in Language Policy and Practice*. Mahwah, NJ: Lawrence Erlbaum.

Cogo, A. (September 2005) The expression of identity in intercultural communication: The case of English as a lingua franca. Paper given at BAAL conference, Bristol.

Cogo, A. and Dewey, M. (2006) Efficiency in ELF communication: From pragmatic motives to lexico-grammatical innovation. *Nordic Journal of English Studies* 5 (2), 59–94.

Coupland, N. (2003) Introduction: Sociolinguistics and globalization. *Journal of Sociolinguistics* 7 (4), 465–472.

Crystal, D. (2003) *English as a Global Language* (2nd edn). Cambridge: Cambridge University Press.

Davies, A. (1999) Standard English: Discordant voices. *World Englishes* 18 (2), 171–186.

Deterding, D. and Kirkpatrick, A. (2006) Emerging South-East Asian Englishes and intelligibility. *World Englishes* 25 (3), 391–409.

Dewey, M. (2007a) English as a Lingua Franca: An empirical study of innovation in lexis and grammar. PhD thesis, King's College London.

Dewey, M. (2007b) English as a Lingua Franca and globalization: An interconnected perspective. *International Journal of Applied Linguistics* 17 (3), 332–354.

Elder, C. and Davies, A. (2006) Assessing English as a lingua franca. *Annual Review of Applied Linguistics* 26, 282–301.

Giddens, A. (1991) *Modernity and Self-identity*. Cambridge: Polity Press.

Giddens, A. (2002) *Runaway World: How Globalization Is Reshaping our Lives* (2nd edn). London: Profile Books.

Graddol, D. (1997) *The Future of English?* London: British Council.

Graddol, D. (2006) *English Next*. London: British Council.

Harris, R. (2007) Mother tongue twisted by drive for global gains. *The Times Higher*, 30 March 2007, p. 12.

Held, D., McGrew, A., Goldblatt, D. and Perraton, J. (1999) *Global Transformations: Politics, Economics and Culture*. Cambridge: Polity Press.

Hirst, P. (1997) The global economy: Myths and realities. *International Affairs* 73 (3), 409–425.

Jenkins, J. (2000) *The Phonology of English as an International Language*. Oxford: Oxford University Press.

Jenkins, J. (2002) A sociolinguistically based, empirically researched pronunciation syllabus for English as an international language. *Applied Linguistics* 23 (1), 83–103.

Jenkins, J. (2006) Current perspectives on teaching World Englishes and English as a Lingua Franca. *TESOL Quarterly* 40 (1), 157–181.

Jenkins, J. (2007) *English as a Lingua Franca: Attitude and Identity*. Oxford: Oxford University Press.

Jones, S. and Bradwell, P. (2007) *As You Like It. Catching up in an Age of Global English*. London: Demos.

Kachru, B.B. (1985) Standards, codification and sociolinguistic realism: The English language in the outer circle. In R. Quirk and H.G. Widdowson (eds) *English in the World: Teaching and Learning the Language and Literatures* (pp. 11–30). Cambridge: Cambridge University Press.

Knapp, K. and Meierkord, C. (eds) (2002) *Lingua Franca Communication*. Frankfurt am Main: Peter Lang.
Leung, C. (2005) Convivial communication: Recontextualizing communicative competence. *International Journal of Applied Linguistics* 15 (2), 119–144.
Leung, C. and Lewkowicz, J. (2006) Expanding horizons and unresolved conundrums: Language testing and assessment. *TESOL Quarterly* 40 (1), 211–234.
Lowenberg, P. (2002) Assessing English proficiency in the expanding circle. *World Englishes* 21 (3), 431–435.
Mauranen, A. (2003) The corpus of English as a Lingua Franca in academic settings. *TESOL Quarterly* 37 (3), 513–527.
Mauranen, A. (2006) Signaling and preventing misunderstanding in ELF communication. In C. Meierkord (ed.) *International Journal of the Sociology of Language*. 177, 123–150.
Ohmae, K. (1995) *The End of the Nation State: The Rise of Regional Economies*. New York: Free Press.
Omoniyi, T. (2006) Hip-Hop through the world Englishes lens: A response to globalization. *World Englishes* 25 (2), 195–208.
Pennycook, A. (2007) *Global Englishes and Transcultural Flows*. London: Routledge.
Phillipson, R. (1999) International languages and international human rights. In M. Kontra, R. Phillipson, T. Skutnabb-Kangas and T. Várady (eds) *Language: A Right and a Resource* (pp. 25–46). Budapest: Central European University Press.
Pitzl, M-L. (2005) Non-understanding in English as a Lingua Franca: Examples from a business context. *Vienna English Working Papers* 14, 50–71.
Quirk, R. (1990) Language varieties and standard language. *English Today* 21, 3–10.
Quirk, R. (1995) *Grammatical and Lexical Variance in English*. London: Longman.
Rosenau, J. (1990) *Turbulence in World Politics*. Brighton: Harvester Wheatsheaf.
Rosenau, J. (1998) Government and democracy in a globalizing world. In D. Archibugi, D. Held and M. Köhler (eds) *Re-imagining Political Community*. Cambridge: Polity Press.
Rubdy, R. and Saraceni, M. (eds) (2006) *English in the World: Global Rules, Global Roles*. London: Continuum.
Scheuer, S. (2005) Why native speakers are (still) relevant. In K. Dziubalska-Kolaczyk and J. Przedlacka (eds) *English Pronunciation Models: A Changing Scene* (pp. 111–130). Frankfurt am Main: Peter Lang.
Seidlhofer, B. (2001) Closing a conceptual gap: The case for a description of English as a lingua franca. *International Journal of Applied Linguistics* 11 (2), 133–158.
Seidlhofer, B. (2004) Research perspectives on teaching English as a Lingua Franca. *Annual Review of Applied Linguistics* 24, 209–239.
Seidlhofer, B. (2006) English as a Lingua Franca in the expanding circle: What it isn't. In R. Rubdy and M. Saraceni (eds) *English in the World: Global Rules, Global Roles* (pp. 40–50). London: Continuum.
Seidlhofer, B., Breiteneder, A. and Pitzl, M-L. (2006) English as a Lingua Franca in Europe: Challenges for applied linguistics. *Annual Review of Applied Linguistics* 26, 3–34.
Sobkowiak, W. (2005) Why not LFC? In K. Dziubalska-Kolaczyk and J. Przedlacka (eds) *English Pronunciation Models: A Changing Scene* (pp. 131–149). Frankfurt am Main: Peter Lang.

Szpyra-Kozlowska, J. (2005) Lingua Franca core, phonetic universals and the polish context. In K. Dziubalska-Kolaczyk and J. Przedlacka (eds) *English Pronunciation Models: A Changing Scene* (p. 151). Frankfurt am Main: Peter Lang.

UNESCO (2000a) *Culture, Trade and Globalization: Questions and Answers.* Paris: UNESCO Publishing.

UNESCO (2000b) *World Culture Report; Cultural Diversity, Conflict and Pluralism.* Paris: UNESCO Publishing.

# Chapter 5
# World Englishes, Globalization and the Politics of Conformity*

RAKESH M. BHATT

## Introduction

World Englishes, under the stewardship of Braj Kachru, has established itself as a paradigm of research in the study of English in the global context that focuses on English language variation and change over time and space. Its stated agenda, as part of the intellectual movement known as 'Liberation Linguistics', is not only to examine the forms of linguistic beliefs and practices that accent the socio-political dimensions of language variation – rooted in contexts of social injustice – but to transform these contexts radically in the interest of the speakers of the 'other tongue' (cf. Bhatt, 2001a). In the (post-modern) era of globalization in which the dominance of English is seen by some as displacing local linguistic practices (Phillipson, 1992; Skutnabb-Kangas, 2000),[1] world Englishes studies have instead highlighted the forms of globalization that fertilize new forms of locality: spanning literary works of creative writers such as Raja Rao (Kachru, 1998) to artistic performances of hip hop (cf. Lee & Y. Kachru, 2006) and to globalized identities of English accents of outsourcing (Cowie, 2007).

Yet, in spite of the advances in the field of world Englishes, controversies abound, both in terms of the empirical status of world Englishes (the profusion and the confusion arguments of Quirk, 1990) and in terms of the theoretical conceptualization of them (world Englishes, English as a Lingua Franca (ELF), English as an International Language (EIL), etc.). These controversies, I argue, follow from a political logic of conformity – outside and within the field of world Englishes – that at once enables discourses of strategic essentialism (via branding, policing labels, imposing boundaries, sanctioning legitimacy, etc.) and disables discourses of transformation (of hybridity, heterogeneity or diversity).

In the following sections, I first briefly examine the concept of globalization and its linguistic consequences. I then discuss how, in the context of globalization, the politics of conformity, with its attendant enabling and disabling discourses, explains the contentious issues and the controversies in the theory and practice of world Englishes. After that I discuss how the study of world Englishes can be integrated into a sociolinguistic theory of globalization. Finally, I conclude by offering some reflections on a politics of possibility: the idea that the interdependent global linguistic markets offer a competitive space for various local Englishes to invest their creative and communicative potential freely in anticipation of symbolic, and eventually economic, profit.

## Globalization: Concept and Consequences

Globalization, according to some scholars (cf. Giddens, 2000), represents a new, post-traditional order, forging new identities, institutions and ways of life. It is 'the way we live now', in a worldwide network of social relations, *seemingly* unfettered by the constraints of geography. And yet the situation is almost certainly more complex: while no one would deny that global flows of capital, of people(s) and of cultural products (e.g. media, language or music) have increased dramatically in their intensity and reach over recent years, it is hardly the case that national boundaries have evaporated, or that geography no longer matters. A quick moment of reflection will remind us of the effects of resurgent nationalism (e.g. in the former Yugoslavia), of heightened security at airports and other boundary-crossing points (e.g. the 'security fence' separating Israel and the West Bank, the US–Mexico border fence, etc.), of consolidating local ethno-linguistic solidarities (cf. Hoffman, 2000; Mcentee-Atalianis, 2004) and of the continuing political controversies around immigration in EU member countries and North America (cf. Crawford, 2000; Extra & Yagmur, 2004).

Given these different tropes of globalization, we need to ask the following questions for the study of linguistic globalization: (i) to what extent can we successfully draw, maintain and interpret linguistic boundaries, and (ii) to what extent are patterns of linguistic variation related to political-economic macroprocesses of valuation and domination. The study of world Englishes provides a powerful point of entry into these and other complexities of globalization, allowing for a nuanced understanding of transnational interactions between people(s) and – crucially – of the interdependence of cultures, economies and polities; all human interaction, after all, is mediated through language, with English occupying the lion's share of that mediation in a globalized world. Consequently, we notice how English not only challenges the constitution – the laws of linguistic conduct – of local communities and geographies but also shapes the global cultural politics of language and language use. In particular, we notice how English affects, and is affected by, the cultures it comes into contact with; its role in cross-cultural communication at the micro level of interaction that are shaped by global cultural politics and economic realities at the macro level.

In other words, the study of world Englishes in the context of globalization brings into sharp focus the relation between politics and culture, especially in post-colonial countries where information about power/status and identity – as well as economic calculations of efficiency and opportunity – are embedded in patterns of English language acquisition and use. Indeed, for many people around the world, access to – and participation in – global flows of (actual economic) capital is often predicated on the knowledge of English. However, the distribution and circulation of this knowledge, of English language acquisition and use, is restricted to the maintenance of power asymmetries mainly through the indulgence of academic discourses of conformity (cf. Bhatt, 2002). Yet, this power is often subverted, due mainly to the technologies of globalization, by local actors as they engage with and navigate in global networks, producing creative texts that are at once local and global. As such, this chapter deals with the ideological analysis of these two (simultaneous) aspects of linguistic globalization of English in terms of conformity, creativity and (re-)valuation.

## The Politics of Conformity and World Englishes

The politics of conformity draws attention to the role of language experts in the dichotomizing discourse of orientalism – the inherent superiority of the metropolitan bourgeoisie over primitive others. In the context of world Englishes, the dichotomy takes the form of the now familiar distinction: centre (English as a native language) and periphery (English as a second language). The study of the politics of conformity focuses on the scholarly ideologies about linguistic differentiation; in fact, it focuses on the social production of linguistic and disciplinary boundaries. The starting point of such an inquiry must include a social history of the production of difference that sheds light on contemporary practices of scholarship (cf. also Gal & Irvine, 1995) – a discursive reproduction of the past differences. As a guiding methodological principle in such a language-ideological inquiry, I follow the observations of Barthes (1972[1957]), who in a series of insightful essays argues that the function of ideologies is to present the contingent as self-evident. He notes (1972[1957]: 11)

The starting point for these reflections was usually a feeling of impatience at the sight of the 'naturalness' with which newspapers, art, and common sense constantly dress up a reality which, even though it is the one we live in, is undoubtedly determined by history. In short, in the account given of our contemporary circumstances, I resented seeing Nature and History confused at every turn, and I wanted to track down, in the decorative displays of what-goes-without-saying, the ideological abuse which, in my view, is hidden there.

Following Barthes' heuristic, I analyze expert discourses as a critical part of the politics of conformity: to demonstrate how History is portrayed as Nature, or how contingent affairs are portrayed, or *dressed up*, as predetermined, natural, essential and necessary. In the context of world Englishes, the expert discourses contribute to 'régimes of truth' (Foucault, 1980): the various forms of ideological control in which English linguistic beliefs and dispositions, values and practices are produced and distributed as fundamentally superior to the Other (local-native languages and cultures), which is tacitly rendered as backward and inferior. These 'régimes' also establish as fundamentally unquestionable the proposition that there HAS to be a single 'correct' standard of usage for the English language. In the remainder of this section, I explore these two aspects of the expert discourse in the ideological formation of linguistic differentiation.

Let me begin by presenting two excerpts as a quick illustration of the dichotomizing discourse of orientalism that will situate the discussion in the context of the politics of conformity. The first excerpt, (1) below (underlining added), is from the famous Thomas B. Macaulay's 'Minute on Indian Education' (2 February 1835)[2] and the second excerpt, (3) below, is from a recent scholarly piece by Robert D. King (2006). In the first excerpt, we see the sociolinguistic process of iconization at play (Irvine & Gal, 2000) that produces the ideological aspects of linguistic differentiation – the formation of the necessary contrast: the superiority of the English language and the primitive nature of the (local/indigenous) dialects.

(1) [8] All parties seem to be agreed on one point, that the dialects commonly spoken among the natives of this part of India, contain <u>neither literary nor scientific</u> information, and are, moreover, so <u>poor and rude</u> that, until they are enriched from some other quarter, it will not be easy to translate any valuable work into them. . . .

[9] . . . The whole question seems to me to be, which language is best worth knowing? . . .

[10] ... I have never found one among them [i.e. Oriental scholars] who could deny that <u>a single shelf of a good European library was worth the whole native literature of India and Arabia</u>. The intrinsic superiority of the Western literature is, indeed, fully admitted by those members of the committee who support the Oriental plan of education. ...

[11] ... It is, I believe, no exaggeration to say, that all historical information which has been collected from all the books written in <u>Sanskrit language is less valuable</u> than what may be found in the most partly abridgments used at preparatory schools in England. ...

[12] We have to educate a <u>people who cannot at present be educated by means of their mother tongue.</u> We must teach them some foreign language. The claims of our own language [English] it is hardly necessary to recapitulate.

[34] I feel with them that it is impossible for us, with our limited means, to attempt to educate the body of the people. We must at present do our best to form a class who may be interpreters between us and the millions whom we govern, – <u>a class of persons Indian in blood and colour, but English in tastes, in opinions, in morals and in intellect.</u>

The process of iconization works in a subtle and complicated manner in excerpt (1). Iconization, as one of the three semiotic process (the other two being *fractal recursivity* and *erasure*) used to construct ideologically constructed representations of linguistic difference (Irvine & Gal, 2000), involves the TRANSFORMATION of the sign relationship between linguistic features (or systems) and the social images with which they are linked (Irvine & Gal, 2000: 39). As Gal (1998: 328) notes, in the process of iconization, 'the ideological representation fuses some quality of the linguistic feature and a supposedly parallel quality of the social group and understands one as the cause or the inherent, essential, explanation of the other.'

In excerpt (1) above, the local dialects – the native languages of India – are presented in various polysemic forms of primitive: poor, worthless, uneducated and rude (cf. the underlined expressions in [8], [10], [11] and [12], respectively, of excerpt (1) above). The primitiveness of these 'dialects' is then easily mapped on to the native people, 'Indian in blood and colour', who must be educated in English to be able to acquire superior 'tastes, opinions, morals and intellect' [cf. underlined expressions in [34] of excerpt (1) above). Notions such as 'morally good', 'aesthetically pleasing', that is, evaluations about language, are used by the elites – the language-in-education policy makers in colonial India – to obtain the required complicity (Bourdieu, 1991: 113) of the dominated classes. In excerpt (1) then, we notice the process of iconization involving, on the one hand, colonial importation of European models of language and, on the other hand, a strategic representation of the non-European subject as the inferior Other.

Such productions of the inherent primitiveness of the Other – the dichotomizing discourse of orientalism – were quite pervasive in the practice of early to mid-19th-century scholarship, especially in the colonies. Charles Grant (1812–1813: 61–62), for instance, in his report ordered by the House of Commons on the state of society among the Asiatic subjects of Great Britain, particularly with respect to morals, and on the means of improving them, observes the following:

> (2) The true curse of darkness is the introduction of light. The Hindoos err, because they are ignorant and their errors have never been laid down before them. The communication of our light and knowledge to them would prove the best remedy for their disorders.

These 19th-century linguistic ideologies of European nation-states, discussed above, continue to inform and influence current intellectual practice in the field of World Englishes. Excerpt (3) below, from King (2006: 27–28), is a case in point. King, in excerpt (3), is discussing the function of 'Post-Empire English' in contemporary Indian linguistic ecology. What is noteworthy is that he uses the familiar rhetorical methods and ideological tools, used earlier by Macaulay in his Minute on Indian Education (see excerpt 1 above) to re-present an iconic linkage between categories of people (native-European) and their languages (primitive-advanced).

> (3) What remains however is infinitely more enduring, chaster, and nobler, more of a great thing, than lands or plants or possessions. What remains is the English language, **a gift** to the globe, a 'way of speaking, a mouth' to millions of people on this globe, often **to people who would not be able to express themselves if not for English**. One of the greatest and most underacknowledged gifts of the British Raj to India was English prose style. Not simply narrative prose … but the prose style of the polished English essay, of a Macaulay, of Samuel Johnson's Idler, of Edmund Burke or John Stuart Mill. This kind of graceful, spare, ironic prose was something altogether different from the forms of prose in indigenous literature. It was initially foreign to the 'cut' of any Indian language, from Sanskrit down to the meanest

vernacular. **But something about it kindled fire in the Indian mind.** (emphasis [underlining/boldface] added)

In excerpt (3), thus, we notice evidence of the reproduction of historical narratives of linguistic ideologies of differentiation in contemporary discourses, especially in the field of World Englishes. The presuppositions in this excerpt point to a particular alchemy of representations of social actors and their respective linguistic practices: the native people and their languages subordinated to – and symbolically dominated by – the noble, chaste, polished and graceful Western cultural product: English. The main argument of this narrative of language contact recalls the observation made by Charles Grant, (see (2) above), almost 200 years ago, and welds it to the contemporary logic of the linguistic politics of conformity. These contemporary practices of scholarship, following the ideological narratives of the past, carry on with the orientalist discourse constructing the local-native as unthinking and unimaginative, especially in the context of world Englishes (cf. the last sentence in excerpt (3)). Kachru (2001: 9) thus appropriately writes, 'The native mind is constructed as unthinking, without initiative and devoid of linguistic and literary vision . . .' The process of iconization entails the attribution of necessity to a connection between linguistic systems (native vernaculars-English language) and social groups (primitive-civilized) – the implication of necessity being reinforced by the iconicity of the ideological representation (Irvine & Gal, 2000).

The second aspect of the politics of conformity relates to the practices of scholarship – 'Expert Discourses' (see Bhatt, 2002, 2005) – in the global spread of English; its acquisition and use in what has often been called the new Englishes contexts (Kachru, 1977, 1994; Kandiah, 1998; Mufwene, 1994; Platt *et al.*, 1984; Pride, 1982). The expert discourses establish a single 'correct' standard of usage for the English language from which other usages are seen as DEVIATIONS. Here I begin by presenting an analysis of 'expert' texts that will yield an understanding of the bedrock axioms that characterize the formation of disciplinary boundaries: in our point of discussion, the boundaries (differences) between the study of English as a native language (ENL) and the study of English as a second language (ESL). It is worth noting here that some of the same processes operating in the creation of linguistic boundaries, discussed above, also appear in the construction of disciplinary boundaries (Gal & Irvine, 1995: 970).

The first set of texts is taken from Prator (1968) who was arguing against the 'doctrine' of establishing local models for Teaching of English as a Second Language (TESL). The local models of English that Prator was concerned with are the ones spoken 'in formerly British possessions such as India, Pakistan, Ceylon, Ghana, and Nigeria' (1968: 460). Although the merits of his paper have been thoroughly critiqued by Kachru (1976), Romaine (1997) and Bhatt (2002), the discussion below attempts to spell out the language ideologies that are intricately involved in creating linguistic and disciplinary boundaries between, as Prator puts it, 'mother tongue types of English' (e.g. British/American) and 'second language varieties of English' (e.g. post-colonial Englishes).

In excerpt (4) below, Prator (1968: 463) draws on the general naturalism argument, following, not surprisingly, the 19th-century linguistic ideology of European nation-states, which correlates one language with one culture:

(4) The British, American, and other mother-tongue types of English are each the unique linguistic component of the culture that produced them and are inseparable from the rest of that culture.

This position is then contrasted with ESL varieties (Prator, 1968: 465), which, he argues following Bloomfield, if allowed to continue to develop on their own will result in a pidgin or jargon, which is

(5) ...nobody's language but only a compromise between a foreign speaker's version, and so on, in which each party imperfectly reproduces the other's reproduction. (Bloomfield, 1933: 473)

Thus, linguistic varieties are interpreted within an ideological dimension of linguistic boundaries: ENL and ESL. The language-pidgin/jargon dichotomization with reference to ENL–ESL varieties of English attempted by Prator is established by means of the sociolinguistic process of fractal recursivity (Irvine & Gal, 2000), which involves the projection of an opposition made at one level onto some other level so that the distinction is seen to recur across categories of varying generality. Prator's distinction between ENL and ESL varieties of English is thus understood as a recursive projection of a wider distinction, at the interlanguage level between English and native Indian languages, discussed above.

Other experts have used the same logic of ideological distinction to activate the linguistic politics of conformity. Quirk (1990), for instance, positions himself with Prator by portraying English language variation in post-colonial contexts as confusion, and the fields of intellectual inquiry that use variation as an object of linguistic, social, cultural and cognitive description as mischievous and suspicious. An analysis of his arguments against English language variation shows the ways in which symbolic value (*à la* Bourdieu, 1991) is created and socially authorized by means of various sorts of rhetorical methods that assure the stable reproduction of linguistic and disciplinary asymmetries (cf. Bhatt, 2002). The dominant discourse produces an audience, context and text in which the reigning framework appears as normal and obvious. The process of normalization, of conformity, is put into place via fractal recursivity in the following manner. First, Quirk discusses Coppieters' work that shows that the difference in linguistic competence between French native speakers (FNS) and advanced non-native speakers (FNNS) is statistically significant (excerpt (6) below): the native speakers of French outperforming the non-native speakers in some, but not all, grammatical aspects.

(6) In a range of interesting and sophisticated elicitation tests, the success rate of the non-natives fell not merely *below* but *outside* the range of native success . . . [his emphasis]

The difference between FNS and FNNS, excerpt (6) above, is then claimed to recur more generally in other areas of foreign/second language teaching. It is thus through the process of fractal recursion that the differences between French native and non-native speakers are used to present differences between English native and non-native speakers. Quirk (1990: 8) uses the familiar rhetorical methods to claim the difference as deviance:

(7) No one should underestimate the *problem* of teaching English in such countries as India and Nigeria, where the English of the teachers themselves inevitably bears the stamp of *locally acquired deviations from the standard language*. [emphasis added]

Clearly, the problem is not really a linguistic one but rather a real problem of vested interests being poached upon. The real problem is disguised, predictably, by denigrating the Other, which as an ideological strategy of erasure glosses over the explicit empirical sociolinguistic realities of the new Englishes contexts of acquisition and use (cf. Bhatt, 2002; Sridhar, 1992). It is through the process of erasure – where language is imagined as homogenous, its internal variation disregarded – that a particular semiotic structure is established where a sacred Standard English-speaking 'core' appears to be surrounded by a profane 'periphery', exemplified in the following excerpt (8) from Quirk (1990: 4).

(8) . . . the interest in varieties of English has got out of hand and has started blinding both teachers and taught to the *central linguistic structure* from which the varieties might be seen as varying. [emphasis original]

The use of expressions such as *central linguistic structure* is ideologically strategic: it is used to refer to a monolithic model of British English to invoke erasure through selective disattention to (unruly) forms of linguistic variation and multilingualism within Britain and outside where English is used. The process of erasure thus permits a view of linguistic diversity, especially in the multilingual contexts of India and Nigeria, as pathological sociolinguistic chaos. Thus, writes Quirk (1990: 4),

(9) . . . there is a more serious issue that I would like to address, and that is the profusion and (I believe) *con*fusion of *types* of linguistic variety that are freely referred to in educational, linguistic, sociolinguistic, and literary critical discussion. [emphasis original]

Erasure is thus recursively applied first (8) to the British situation – constructing an opposition between Standard British English and local British English dialects – and then used to frame the discussion of the Other, the 'confusion' (9) and 'deviant' (7) varieties of English spoken natively in India and Nigeria. This deficit discourse (excerpts (7–9) above), serviced through an appeal to the politics of nostalgia, denies the newly emerging varieties their legitimacy. In fact, as Romaine (1997) notes, these discourses have been regularly recruited ever since the 18th century when the unity of English was broken by the establishment of new national standards (United States, Australia, New Zealand, South Africa, etc.). The emergence of new standard Englishes (Indian, Nigerian, Singaporean, etc.) threatens the stability of the previously established ideological opposition – standard/non-standard, native/non-native – and, therefore, these Other standard varieties are actively erased in expert discourses about world Englishes.

Not all is well and ideology-free – it never is! – within the world Englishes paradigm either. Part of the success of the process of the ideological representation of linguistic and disciplinary differentiation, discussed above, relies on the (unintended) complicity of world Englishes experts in the linguistic politics of conformity. Rather than confronting internal variation within each variety (Bhatt, 2000; Canagarajah, 1999; Ramanathan, 1999), world Englishes experts reify linguistic homogeneity in local contexts – via erasure – using iconic badges like Indian English, Nigerian English, Malaysian English, and so forth in their descriptions of local varieties of English. The erasure of variation 'within' is necessitated by the focus on nation-based models of English, as in the Concentric Circles Model (Kachru, 1985), which, as Bruthiaux (2003: 161) argues, 'conceals more than it reveals and runs the risk of being interpreted as license to dispense with analytic rigor'. A theoretical shift towards a demographic reduction, with a focus instead on the interactional patterns of different communities of practice and local networks, holds the possibility of describing the complexities of the sociolinguistics of English language use in an increasingly globalized world (cf. Canagarajah, 1999; Parakrama, 1995; Pennycook, 2003). This shift in perspective on world Englishes has important implications: (i) it renders the dichotomizing discourse – native/non-native, standard/non-standard – as theoretically uninteresting and invalid in the discussion of world Englishes (Bhatt, 2007; Mufwene, 1998; Singh, 2007); (ii) it displaces methodologies that use 'inner circle' English varieties as a theoretical reference point for grammatical descriptions of new Englishes (Bhatt, 2000); (iii) it opens up a space for a description of English as a lingua franca (Jenkins, 2006; Seidlhofer, 2001); and, finally, (iv) it affords a description of local linguistic acts of resistance, agency and appropriation that arise in response to the global hegemony of English in late-modernity (Bhatt, 2008; Coupland, 2003; Pennycook, 2003). What seems to me to be critically needed in the studies of world Englishes is engagement with the emerging field of the sociolinguistics of globalization (Blommaert, 2003; Coupland, 2003) in order for us to accomplish a comprehensive understanding of (a) the features of English that remain local and those that travel transnationally, and (b) the interdependence of English and local languages in creating new semiotic opportunities for the speakers in new English contexts. In the next section, I discuss the issues of world Englishes that arise in their engagement with globalization, focusing broadly on the local responses to the global linguistic hegemony of the English language – creating different and often new spaces of linguistic action.

## World Englishes and Globalization

Globalization is, by and large, understood as the intensification of worldwide social relations that link distant localities to proximate ones (Giddens, 1990). In fact, as I have argued elsewhere (Bhatt, 2008; cf. also Mesthrie & Bhatt, 2008), one of the defining features of globalization is the complex and multifaceted interaction of localism and globalism. In the context of world Englishes, this, of course, necessitates a methodological shift away from practices of discovering Englishes for the sole purpose of 'joining the communion with world Englishes', as, for instance, Proshina (2005: 437) offers in her introduction to Russian Englishes. Rather, the focus needs to be on the analysis of how certain features (identities, genres or systems) of local Englishes are re-shaped and re-negotiated under pressures of globalization, and to uncover social meanings of those features as they are activated in different global contexts. It is precisely in the interdependence of the global and the local that Coupland (2003: 466) correctly notes:

> The qualities of linguistically mediated social experience that define 'local' – inhabitation of social networks, social identities, senses of intimacy and community, differentials of power and control – all potentially carry an imprint from shifting global structures and relationships.

The interaction of global and local presents new theoretical challenges to the study of world Englishes, especially with regard to notions of space (geographic and social) and scales (global and local) (cf. Blommaert, 2005). A few examples should illustrate this point. The first example is an email – a specific speech form (Baron, 2003) – reproduced in its original form below in excerpt (10). The sender, UP (a pseudonym), is an assistant English teacher in a high school in a rural town of West Bengal, India.

> (10) dear,sir i am UP, a rural school teacher in India. I did my masters in Eng.lit.and B.ed.I am interested in reading about cultural globalisation. Residing in a rural area I dont have privelege to undergo such. Your course-syllabus2005 (language in globalisation) is very interesting for me as i found the content while searching on net.
>
> Please suggest me some that i can study (undergose any course) from my place that will also help me in future and matches my interest. My university teacher are not intersting in my outlook and i have very little knowledge. recntly i got a pc and looking for my area of interest. I would be thankful if you guide me on the way.
>     UP,assit teacher(eng.)
>     bhotepatty high school,jalpaiguri,westbengal,India

What we are dealing with here is the sociolinguistics of global 'mobility' of a specific genre, email, which involves the notion of scale, theorized in Blommaert (2003, 2007) as hierarchically ranked, power-invested, stratified spaces. The function of this local production and its translocal (e)valuation raise new, important questions for world Englishes study; for example, does the value, meaning and function travel along with the form (as in (10) above) transnationally?, how does the linguistic form (of literacy practices) of this email fit into local economies of resources?, how does such form translate into sociolinguistic inequalities between local writers and transnational readership – the issue of relative value-scale (or transnational–hierarchical space), and indexical frames of perception?

The putative answers to the questions raised above may be found in the 'language display' (Blommaert 2003: 618) in excerpt (10). English in the local, rural Indian context of (10) above is an 'expensive' resource that is used in the email to mobilize a request transnationally. The punitive reading of the text notwithstanding, the mobilization of the most valued resource, English, with the associated indexicalities of prestige, status and success in the local, rural economy of signs, becomes dysfunctional and loses its meaning when inserted in transnational networks of communication – a matter of differences, or movement, between indexically connected (micro and macro) scales. Consequently, as Blommaert (2003: 619) cautions us, 'a sociolinguistics of globalization should look into such processes of reallocation, the remapping of forms over function, for it may be central to the various forms of inequality that also characterizes globalization processes.' Sociolinguistic scales as an analytic tool can thus be recruited productively in the study of the distribution, spread and flow of different genres of world Englishes in a global context.

One of the most widely globalized genres of world Englishes that has drawn some attention recently is hip hop, especially with respect to language choices – English and local languages. The linguistic choices relate to the issues of identity politics and power struggles within the local contexts of the use of this global cultural product (cf. Berger & Carroll, 2003; Lee & Y. Kachru, 2006). Pennycook's (2003) discussion of Japanese rappers Rip Slyme's rap 'Bring Your Style', for instance, probes the larger questions of agency, identity and the politics of representation. Blending African American speech styles with the Japanese language, the rap artists accomplish two functional goals: (i) they manage to organize a genre that is simultaneously global – connecting with transnational social networks identified as hip hop culture – and local, expressive of Japanese language and culture; and, more importantly, (ii) they employ the language-blend locally as a form of 'resistance vernacular' (cf. Potter, 1995). Other, similar, creative articulations of world Englishes genre of hip hop appear in East African (Perullo & Fenn, 2003) and West African (and diaspora) hip hop (Omoniyi, 2006), and in East Asian hip hop (Condry, 2000; Lee, 2006). In these local genres of hip hop, one notices a semiotic process of social production of difference: the local (and translocal) African hip hop departs from the 'core' in its rejection of features that characterize the mainstream gangsta rap norms such as heavy sexualization, misogyny, politics and monolingualism (Omoniyi, 2006; cf. also Perullo & Fenn, 2003). The linguistic production of difference in this genre, on the other hand, relies heavily on the specific sociolinguistic choices that the artists make. The most dominant paradigm of difference is serviced by code-switching: the use of local languages in the global medium, English, extends the meaning potential of this genre to produce local indexicalities (cf. Omoniyi, 2006).

The inter-animation of local and global in the genre of hip hop is most clearly exemplified by the American-South Asian rap group Soul Tap whose latest production, 'Be Easy (Koi Naa)', a fusion of Punjabi (and some Malayalam) and English hip hop, was one of the three finalists with a shot at being featured in the Super Bowl XLII in Arizona, United States, on Sunday, 3 February 2008. The group is composed of rapper Alvin 'Nivla' Augustine, Punjabi folk singer Parag 'P. Oberoi' Oberoi, Sharad 'DJ Sharad' Bhavani and sound engineer Raj 'RVM Sounds' Makhija. In (11) below, I present a short excerpt of the beginning of the rap lyrics (see http://www.youtube.com/watch?v=64JGSpSSqnE). The italicized lyrics in (11) are in Punjabi, sung by the Punjabi folk singer Parag Oberoi and the English lyrics are sung by Alvin Augustine, both residents of New Jersey, United States.

(11) Be Easy (Koi Naa)

| Lines | Lyrics | Translation |
| --- | --- | --- |
| 1) | Ladies and gentlemen | |
| 2) | Get you're a** on the dance floor | |
| 3) | Soultap records proudly presents | |
| 4) | *o ki mEN chuuTh boleyaa* | 'Did I ever lie (to you)' |
| 5) | *Koi naa* (chorus) | 'Not at all' |
| 6) | *o ki mEn kufar toleyaa* | 'Did I commit a sin' |
| 7) | *Koi naa* (chorus) | 'Not at all' |
| 8) | *o ki mEn dil todeyaa* | 'Did I break a heart' |
| 9) | *Koi naa* (chorus) | 'Not at all' |
| 10) | *Bhai koi naa* (chorus) | 'Not at all' |
| | Repeat chorus | |
| 11) | Yeah, uh, yo | |
| 12) | Baby you workin' with some movers and shakers | |
| 13) | And music entrepreneurs | |
| 14) | So baby move it and shake it | |
| 15) | We got the track pumpin' | |
| 16) | Got your back bumpin' just a little bit | |
| 17) | Road, take a little hit | |
| 18) | Beef, better settle it | |
| 19) | 'Cause my persona | |
| 20) | I ain't here for no drama | |
| 21) | Just want some Sex on the Beach | |
| 22) | While you sippin' Bahama Mamas | |
| 23) | Maybe Piña Coladas | |

The rap music in (11) juxtaposes two linguistic communities, American and diaspora Indian, to demonstrate an articulation of interdependence in the new political economy of globalized signs. This Indian-fused bilingual East Coast rap accomplishes a number of sociolinguistic functions: (a) it re-presents and consolidates the previous efforts of Jay-Z and Panjabi MC's collaboration on the 'Beware of the Boys' track a few years ago, thus establishing and consolidating a particular *niche* – diaspora rap – in the genre of hip hop; (b) it allows the semiotization of unique indexicalities that points to the sociolinguistic consequences of demographic mobility and of modern social formations in the globalized context; (c) it shows accommodation of cultural specificities; (d) it demonstrates how members of diaspora population navigate and perform their dual identities; and, most importantly, (e) it illustrates, par excellence, effects of *disembedding* in the use of Punjabi language (lines 4–10), the 'lifting out' (Giddens, 1991, cf. also Coupland, 2003) of a song-dance sequence from an old Hindi (Bollywood) movie, *Jaagte Raho* ('Keep Awake') – a performance indexically linked to a powerful social critique of that time – and its re-articulation across time and space, assigning new sociolinguistic meanings to those items in re-contextualization, namely, laidback, leisure and good time. The notion of 'scales' thus becomes a useful analytical tool to unpack the various indexicalities and ideological representations bundled up in such genred performances.

Another globalized genre worth investigating is the online news, which demonstrates how world Englishes recreate, maintain or represent more faithfully local cultural practices and culturally embedded meanings via the process of code-switching. In excerpt (12) below, taken from *Times of India* news brief (www.timesofindia.com, 12 October 2001), we notice a strategic use of Hindi in English to create new semiotic opportunities for Indian English users (Bhatt, 2008).

(12) There have been several analyses of this phenomenon. First, there is the 'religious angle' which is to do with Indian society. In India a man feels guilty when fantasizing about another man's wife, unlike in the west. The *saat pheras* around the *agni* serves as a *lakshman rekha*.

The italicized Hindi phrases in (12) appear without any gloss. The switch to Hindi in the bilingual mode of this news-feature presentation realizes a significant pragmatic function, recalling the local-cultural practices of the past within the global medium of news reporting in English. The Hindi words in (12) – *saat pheras* ('seven circumnavigations during a wedding ceremony'), *agni* ('fire') and *lakshman rekha* ('a line that one never crosses') – are rooted in the most important historical narratives (Vedas) and the great Hindu epic (the *Ramayana*) of India. A full appreciation of the text therefore demands knowledge of the Sanskrit Vedic traditions and cultural-historical literacy of the indigenous people. The switch to Hindi thus produces an immediate, authentic and particularized interpretation of meaning among the bilingual readership of the Indian English newspaper. Such strategic uses of local languages in English reflect a new socio-ideological consciousness, a new way to negotiate and navigate between a global identity and local socio-historical practices (Bhatt, 2008).

As with hip hop, code-switching in the globalized genre of online world Englishes newspapers serves to communicate a kind of multiplicity that is highly contextual, a new habitus representing for its speakers a new, slightly altered representation of social order (Bhatt, 2008). The discursive mechanisms of globalization discussed above therefore demand a theoretical reorientation in the sociolinguistics of world Englishes, especially, a focus on the different ways in which English permeates local linguistic practices, reorganizes genres and creates new semiotic opportunities for its users – both locally and translocally.

## Conclusion: Towards a Politics of Possibility

The sociolinguistic phenomena of world Englishes in the era of globalization is becoming less predictable and more complicated. In order for us to understand the various complexes of sociolinguistic nuances of the acquisition and use of Englishes, we need to liberate the field of world Englishes from the orthodoxies of the past and instead connect it to a more general theory of the sociolinguistics of globalization, along the lines discussed above. The expert discourses on world Englishes in the past, and present, need to be constantly examined, using the theoretical framework developed above, to move the field forward from a politics of conformity – uncritical acceptance of received wisdom – to a politics of possibility, of growth, and of dialogue across intellectual (and even ideological) fault-lines.

The theoretical position defended in this chapter echoes Quirk's earlier position on world Englishes (1985: 3), more urgent now in the context of globalization: 'different standards for different occasions for different people – and each as "correct" as any other'. In the (late-)modern global system of capitalist economy based on market trade and commodification, the more linguistic capital the speakers of new Englishes possess, by virtue of creating their own intellectual and cultural property, the more they are able to exploit the system of differences to their advantage (Bhatt, 2001b). Globalization thus offers the critical space for local Englishes to secure the profit of 'distinction' as their speakers invest their creative and communicative potential freely in global linguistic markets in anticipation of cultural, economic, and eventually symbolic, profit. This fact, of course, is not lost on some 'inner circle' intellectuals who recognize the importance of changes in global English. Jones and Bradwell (2007: 12), in the much discussed 'Demos' report, note: 'Where we once directed the spread of English around the world, we are now just one of many shareholders in the asset that it represents.' In their model, English does not belong to a single nationality, but is, presumably, in the hands of different groups, all with their own stake in English, using the language to serve their own ends. This position on the globalization of world Englishes replaces the politics of conformity with a politics of possibility, as I have argued above.

In conclusion, I have argued that the study of world Englishes, if properly theorized, holds the key to the various understandings of the processes of linguistic globalization: the complexity and simultaneity of linguistic choices, the commodification of linguistic forms and functions, the worldwide patterns and stratifications of English language acquisition and use and the creative potential of bilingual English users.

## Notes

*My sincere thanks to Tope Omoniyi and Mukul Saxena for inviting, and encouraging, me to write this chapter. Many thanks to Agnes Bolonyai, Laura Rosulek and Antje Muntendam for their generous comments and suggestions on an earlier version of this chapter. My thanks also to the anonymous reviewer for her/his comments on this chapter. Finally, my thanks to Jill Ward for her editorial comments and assistance. The standard disclaimers, of course, apply.

1. There are several scholars who do not agree with Phillipson and Skutnabb-Kangas' views on language and globalization; see particularly, Bhatt (2005), Symposium on Linguistic Imperialism published in *World Englishes*, vol. 12, no. 3, pp. 335–373.
2. Information taken from the following URL: http://www.columbia.edu/itc/mealac/pritchett/00generallinks/macaulay/txt_minute_education_1835.html.

## References

Baron, N. (2003) Why email looks like speech: Proofreading, pedagogy and public face. In J. Aitchison and D. Lewis (eds) *New Media Language* (pp. 85–94). London: Routledge.

Barthes, R. (1972[1957]) *Mythologies* (Trans. A. Lavers). New York: The Noonday Press.

Berger, H. and Michael, T.C. (eds) (2003) *Global Pop, Local Languages*. Jackson, MS: University Press of Mississippi.

Bhatt, R.M. (2000) Optimal expressions in Indian English. *English Language and Linguistics* 4, 69–95.

Bhatt, R.M. (2001a) World Englishes. *Annual Review of Anthropology* 30, 527–550.
Bhatt, R.M. (2001b) Language economy, standardization, and world Englishes. In E. Thumboo (ed.) *The Three Circles of English* (pp. 401–422). Singapore: UniPress.
Bhatt, R.M. (2002) Experts, dialects, and discourse. *International Journal of Applied Linguistics* 12 (1), 74–109.
Bhatt, R.M. (2005) Expert discourses, local practices, and hybridity: The case of Indian Englishes. In S. Canagarajah (ed.) *Reclaiming the Local in Language Policy and Practice* (pp. 25–54). Mahwah, NJ: Lawrence Erlbaum.
Bhatt, R.M. (2007) On the native/non-native distinction. In R. Singh (ed.) *Annual Review of South Asian Languages and Linguistics* (pp. 55–71). Berlin: Mouton de Gruyter.
Bhatt, R.M. (2008) In other words: Language mixing, identity representations, and third space. *Journal of Sociolinguistics* 12 (2), 177–200.
Blommaert, J. (2003) Commentary: A sociolinguistics of globalization. *Journal of Sociolinguistics* 7 (4), 607–623.
Blommaert, J. (2005) *Discourse: A Critical Reader*. Cambridge: Cambridge University Press.
Blommaert, J. (2007) Sociolinguistic scales. *Intercultural Pragmatics* 4 (1), 1–19.
Bloomfield, L. (1933) *Language*. New York: Holt.
Bourdieu, P. (1991) *Language and Symbolic Power*. Cambridge, MA: Harvard University Press.
Bruthiaux, P. (2003) Squaring the circles: Issues in modeling English worldwide. *International Journal of Applied Linguistics* 13 (2), 159–178.
Canagarajah, A.S. (1999) *Resisting Linguistic Imperialism in English Teaching*. Oxford: Oxford University Press.
Condry, I. (2000) The social production of difference: Imitation and authenticity in Japanese Rap music. In H. Fehrenbach and U. Polger (eds) *Transactions, Transgressions, and Transformations* (pp. 166–184). New York: Berghan Books.
Coupland, N. (2003) Introduction: Sociolinguistics and globalization. *Journal of Sociolinguistics* 7 (4), 465–472.
Cowie, C. (2007) The accents of outsourcing: The meanings of 'neutral' in the Indian call centre industry. *World Englishes* 26 (3), 316–330.
Crawford, J. (2000) *At War with Diversity: US Language Policy in an Age of Anxiety*. Clevedon: Multilingual Matters.
Extra, G. and Kutlay, Y. (2004) *Urban Multilingualism in Europe: Immigrant Minority Languages at Home and School*. Clevedon: Multilingual Matters.
Foucault, M. (1980) *Power/Knowledge: Selected Interviews and Other Writings 1972–1977*. (Ed. C. Gordon; Trans. by C. Gordon, L. Marshall, J. Mepham and K. Soper). New York: Pantheon Books.
Gal, S. (1998) Multiplicity and contention among language ideologies: A commentary. In B. Schieffelin, K. Woolard and P. Kroskrity (eds) *Language Ideologies: Practice and Theory* (pp. 317–331). Oxford: Oxford University Press.
Gal, S. and Irvine, J. (1995) The boundaries of languages and disciplines: How ideologies construct difference. *Social Research* 62, 967–1001.
Giddens, A. (1990) *The Consequences of Modernity*. Stanford, CA: Stanford University Press.
Giddens, A. (1991) *Modernity and Self-Identity: Self and Society in the Late Modern Age*. Cambridge: Polity Press.

Grant, C. (1812) Observations on the state of society among the Asiatic subjects of Great Britain, particularly with respect to morals, and on the means of improving it. London: General Appendix to Parliamentary Papers 1812–1813, Vol. 10. No. 282.

Hoffman, C. (2000) The spread of English and the growth of multilingualism with English in Europe. In J. Cenoz and U. Jessner (eds) *English in Europe: The Acquisition of a Third Language* (pp. 1–21). Clevedon: Multilingual Matters.

Irvine, J. and Gal, S. (2000) Language ideology and linguistic differentiation. In P. Kroskrity (ed.) *Regimes of Language: Ideologies, Polities, and Identities* (pp. 35–83). Santa Fe: School of American Research Press.

Jenkins, J. (2006) Current perspectives of teaching world Englishes and English as a Lingua Franca. *TESOL Quarterly* 40, 157–181.

Jones, S. and Peter, B. (2007) *As You Like It: Catching Up in an Age of Global English.* Online document: http://www.demos.co.uk/publications/asyoulikeitpamphlet. Accessed 12 October 2008.

Kachru, B.B. (1976) Models of English for the third world: White man's linguistic burden or language pragmatics? *TESOL Quarterly* 10, 221–239.

Kachru, B.B. (1977) New Englishes and old models. *English Language Forum* 15 (3), 29–35.

Kachru, B.B. (1985) Standards, codification and sociolinguistic realism: The English language in the outer circle. In R. Quirk and H. Widdowson (eds) *English in the World, Teaching and Learning the Language and Literatures* (pp. 11–30). Cambridge: Cambridge University Press.

Kachru, B.B. (1994) The new Englishes. In K. Brown (ed.) *The Encyclopedia of Language and Linguistics* (pp. 2787–2791). Oxford: Pergamon & Aberdeen University Press.

Kachru, B.B. (1998) Raja Rao: Madhyama and mantra. In R. Hardgrave (ed.) *Word as Mantra: The Art of Raja Rao* (pp. 60–87). New Delhi: Katha.

Kachru, B.B. (2001) *On Nativizing Mantra: Identity Construction in Anglophone Englishes.* University of Illinois (mimeo).

Kandiah, T. (1998) Why new Englishes? In J. Foley *et al.* (eds) *English in New Cultural Contexts* (pp. 1–40). Singapore: Oxford University Press.

King, R.D. (2006) The beginnings. In B.B. Kachru, Y. Kachru and C. Nelson (eds) *The Handbook of World Englishes* (pp. 19–29). Malden, MA: Blackwell.

Lee, J.S. (2006) Crossing and crossers in East Asian pop music: Korea and Japan. *World Englishes* 25 (2), 235–250.

Lee, J.S. and Kachru, Y. (eds) (2006) *World Englishes Special Issue: Symposium on World Englishes in Pop Culture* 25 (2), 191–313.

Macaulay, T.B. (1957[1835]) Minute of 2 February 1835 on Indian education. In G. M. Young (ed.) *Macaulay, Prose and Poetry* (pp. 721–724, 729). Cambridge, MA: Harvard University Press.

Mcentee-Atalianis, L. (2004) The impact of English in postcolonial, postmodern Cyprus. *International Journal of the Sociology of Language* 168, 77–90.

Mesthrie, R. and Bhatt, R.M. (2008) *World Englishes: The Study of New Linguistic Varieties.* Cambridge: Cambridge University Press.

Mufwene, S. (1994) New Englishes and the criteria for naming them. *World Englishes* 13, 21–31.

Mufwene, S. (1998) Native speaker, proficient speaker, and norm. In R. Singh (ed.) *Native Speaker: Multilingual Perspectives*. New Delhi: Sage.

Omoniyi, T. (2006) Hip hop through the world Englishes lens: A response to globalization. *World Englishes* 25 (2), 195–208.

Parakrama, A. (1995) *De-hegemonizing Language Standards*. Basingstoke: Macmillan.

Pennycook, A. (2003) Global Englishes, Rip Slyme, and performativity. *Journal of Sociolinguistics* 7 (4), 513–533.

Perullo, A. and Fenn, J. (2003) Language ideologies, choices, and practices in Eastern African hip hop. In H. Bernger and M. Carroll (eds) *Global Pop, Local Language* (pp. 19–33). Jackson, MS: University Press of Mississippi.

Phillipson, R. (1992) *Linguistic Imperialism*. Oxford: Oxford University Press.

Platt, J., Heidi, W. and Mian Lian Ho. (1984) *The New Englishes*. London: Routledge.

Potter, R. (1995) *Spectacular Vernaculars*. New York: SUNY Press.

Prator, C. (1968) The British heresy in TESOL. In Joshua Fishman, Charles Ferguson and Jyotindra Das Gupta (eds) *Language Problems of Developing Nations* (pp. 459–476). New York: Wiley.

Pride, J. (1982) *New Englishes*. Rowley, MA: Newbury House Publishers.

Proshina, Z. (2005) Russian Englishes. *World Englishes* 24 (4), 437–438.

Quirk, R. (1985) The English language in a global context. In R. Quirk and H. Widdowson (eds) *English in the World: Teaching and Learning the Language and Literatures* (pp. 1–6). Cambridge: Cambridge University Press.

Quirk, R. (1990) Language varieties and standard language. *English Today* 21, 3–10.

Ramanathan, V. (1999) 'English is here to stay': A critical look at institutional and educational practices in India. *TESOL Quarterly* 33, 211–231.

Romaine, S. (1997) The British heresy in ESL revisited. In S. Eliasson and E. Jahr (eds) *Language and Its Ecology* (pp. 417–432). Berlin: Mouton de Gruyter.

Seidlhofer, B. (2001) Closing a conceptual gap: The case for a description of English as a lingua franca. *International Journal of Applied Linguistics* 11, 133–158.

Singh, R. (2007) The nature, structure, and status of Indian English. In R. Singh (ed.) *The Annual Review of South Asian Languages and Linguistics* (pp. 33–46). Berlin: Mouton de Gruyter.

Skutnabb-Kangas, T. (2000) *Linguistic Genocide in Education, or Worldwide Diversity and Human Rights*. Mahwah, NJ: Lawrence Erlbaum.

Sridhar, S.N. (1992) The ecology of bilingual competence: Language interaction in indigenized varieties of English. *World Englishes* 11, 141–150.

## Chapter 6

# EFL: From 'You Sound Like Dickens' to International English

MARIA GEORGIEVA

## Introduction

For the last 50 years, we have been witnessing the continual spread of English around the globe, impressed by the speed at which it has been diffusing into all spheres of life but also bewildered as to where this unprecedented expansion is taking us. Now Global English is a fact of life, a key feature of the new socio-political and economic world order, both a medium and a maker of new forms of interdependence, a product and a driver of globalization. Explorations into the causes of English globalization have uncovered a multiplicity of factors, not so much linguistic as geo-historical, socio-political, economic and technological. Thus, the emergence of the multitude of new Englishes currently in use is largely attributed to the expansion of British colonial power in earlier days and subsequent global demographic shifts. More recent diffusion processes are, in turn, associated with the fast development of communication technologies and the world expansion of US economy that have spurred large-scale English teaching in all states striving to partake in diverse transnational integration activities commonly subsumed under the term *globalization* (Brutt-Griffler, 2002; Crystal, 1997; Graddol, 1997; McArthur, 1998; Spolsky, 2004). Indeed, there are no sound linguistic arguments against the selection of any other language as a means of wider communication and many languages have been, and still are, used for that purpose. Yet, it is English, as Crystal (1997: 120) has put it, that 'happened to be in the right place at the right time' to take advantage of the running economic, technological and socio-cultural world developments. Small wonder that when Bulgaria, the subject of interest in this chapter, embarked on a course of democratization along with the other newly established democracies from Central and Eastern Europe, the expansion and modernization of English language teaching was high on the agenda for educational reform. There was an excessive demand for

English. People from all walks of life, not just the educated elite as in former years, hastened to catch up with Europe and perceived English as the instrument that would allow them to break away from local backwardness and appropriate European models of life. The ever growing demand for English has invigorated the ELT profession to such an extent that little attention was paid to the impact this might have on local traditions of foreign language teaching and learning.

On a global scale, though, the growth of English into an International Language (hereafter EIL) is far from uncontested. It has created a host of tensions that have deeply and irrevocably affected the ecology of the world language system and have sparked off heated debates among experts from all walks of life. One source of tension is the spread of English itself. Some scholars discard overly simple accounts of the causes of spread as a chain of happy coincidences and argue instead that the diffusion of English across the world results from artfully orchestrated expansion campaigns by identifiable human agents, that is, it is an outcome of language management (Roland, 2000; Skutnabb-Kangas, 2001). This purposefully pursued policy of English growth is closely bound up with intentional destruction of smaller languages (defined as 'linguicism' by Phillipson (1992)) and homogenization of world culture by entrenching in all communities of English users the beliefs, dispositions, values and practices of the 'sacred imagined community' of native speakers (Bhatt, 2002: 76).

Another source of tension is the inordinate heterogeneity of the formations claiming an English variety status. According to the type of English speaker in the world, these varieties are traditionally classified as *English as a native language* (ENL), *English as a second language* (ESL) and *English as a foreign language* (EFL), or, after Kachru (1985), as the Inner, Outer and Expanding Circle, respectively. Although they differ widely in more than one way, namely, speakers' proficiency level, degrees and types of input and contexts of learning and use, the relation of each circle of speakers to English standards and codification seems to be the pivotal demarcation line. ENL speakers, naturally, feel entitled to the role of custodians over what is acceptable usage of the language they have acquired by birth and are reluctant to sanction a place in the English mix of all those emerging varieties that threaten the monolithic nature of 'good English', one of the 'key achievements of Anglo-Saxon civilization' (McArthur, 1998: 214). Conversely, ESL speakers, particularly defendants of post-colonial 'New Englishes', argue in favour of pluralistic centres of reference for norms and standards. They discard as old-fashioned the concept of monolithic English as the exponent of cultures and norms of communication in all English-using countries. Instead, they strive to promote new norms of use that incorporate features of the local languages and cultural values, and that manifest bilingual writers' creativity, stylistic experimentation and 'intermeshing' of codes (Kachru, 1985; Kachru & Nelson, 1996; Kirkpatrick, 2001; Sridhar, 1996).

A third source of tension stems from the paradoxical situation in which Global English finds itself. It is a mother tongue, a stronghold of nationhood, characterized by standards and norms of use set and followed by its native speakers. At the same time, it is a world language that spearheads transnational communication, a role that divests it of cultural identity as it is shaped at least as much by its non-native as by its native speakers. This controversy has caused considerable confusion among EFL/ESL researchers and educationalists as it bears directly on the all-pervasive communicative approaches proclaiming native speaker behaviour as the only acceptable target language norm. Some scholars have questioned the relevance of the concept of speech community, as traditionally defined, to the new Global English language situation. Others have attempted to resolve the paradox by drawing a distinction between 'English as a foreign language' and 'English as a lingua franca' (House, 2003; Jenkins, 2006), insisting that hybridity and non-standard use should be accepted as natural manifestations of speakers' creativity and stylistic self-expression in lingua franca contexts of communication. Consequently, they argue in favour of codifying the variety used as lingua franca with the ultimate objective of 'making it feasible, acceptable and respected alternative to ENL in appropriate contexts of use' (Seidlhofer, 2001: 150).

All above debates deserve credit for bringing into relief problematic issues, for questioning the validity of concepts commonly accepted as axiomatic and for suggesting new ways of thinking about norms and standards of different Englishes. Nonetheless, the general opinion is that the different standpoints expressed by scholars would gain in credibility if substantiated by more concrete and more diverse evidence. One issue, for instance, that appears to be often neglected in current sociolinguistic research on EFL/EIL is EFL users' subjective perception of the current developments of the language (Kuo, 2006: 218). What role does English play in local societies? How does it co-exist with the other languages in individuals' repertoires? Do EFL speakers feel threatened or benefited from the new role of English? Starting from the assumption that knowledge and understanding of local conditions provide a valuable insight into the overall system, in this chapter, I focus attention on the Bulgarian language situation, especially on how EIL positions itself in it. In particular, the questions of my research interest are:

(1)   How is English positioned among all other languages in Bulgarian speakers' individual language repertoires? What are their preferred language choices, if any?

(2)   What role does English play in speakers' lives? Do they need it to satisfy some deeply private needs, for instance, for self-fulfilment; or, do they simply use it as a 'vehicular language – a tool of their trade' (Graddol, 1997: 56)?

(3)   Has the wider use of English brought about a change in Bulgarian people's attitudes towards the language?

(4)   Has the new role of English as a means of international communication affected Bulgarians' traditionally held views about standards and norms of its use?

My discussion is based on the results from a small-scale survey conducted electronically among Bulgarian speakers of English. Given the small size of the corpus, this should be taken as a pilot study that makes no claim to provide a thorough understanding of the complexities of the situation and no generalizations will be made in this respect. The small sample notwithstanding, the survey does shed light on how some of the most heatedly debated questions concerning Global English apply in a particular language situation. By showing what speakers themselves think of the English they use for transnational communication, therefore, the survey may be expected to provide a useful addition to the body of evidence needed for a fairer assessment of the credibility of some scholarly views on this topical issue.

## EIL in the Context of Plurilingual Europe: A Snapshot of Problematic Issues

The globalization of English has brought to bear on the very make-up of Europe's plurilingual and multicultural societies. Its overwhelming presence in major socio-economic spheres and its dominance as a lingua franca in influential international organizations have had a visible impact on all European languages in the way of massive influx of anglicisms, shrinkage of domains of use, erosion of functionality and marginalization of their role on the scene of international communication (Phillipson, 2001). This has caused national governments as well as institutions involved in the building up of unified Europe to place the language issue on their agendas and seek solution to the complex language situation. To demonstrate their firm commitment to safeguarding Europe's language and cultural diversity, the Council of Europe and the European Union have defined the promotion of large-scale plurilingualism and multiculturalism as a key goal of unified Europe. On a national level, some governments have passed laws to protect their national languages against the encroachment of English. Accordingly, the questions whether EIL is a threat to multilingualism and how to maintain Europe's rich cultural and linguistic heritage have assumed special significance for researchers and language policy makers alike.

Attractive as the idea of promoting multilingualism in Europe may seem, sociolinguists seem doubtful about its success. Some point out that its realization depends on how well European societies are prepared to accept multilingualism as the norm of communication (Graddol, 2001). Others, for instance, House (2003: 561), openly discard it as an 'illusion', an idea that is not only impractical but also 'costly and cumbersome'. As a counterproposal to Europe's 'ostensible multilingualism', House (2003: 562) suggests that a 'manageable number of working languages' be selected and the role of English as lingua franca (ELF) be recognized. Since ELF is simply a 'language for communication', it is argued, it does not threaten to displace local or national languages, which maintain their function of 'language for identification'. The functionally oriented distinction between 'language for communication' and 'language for identification' therefore can account for the 'division of labour' between English and local languages that is currently taking place and that will, eventually, lead to the establishment of a diglossic situation.

Indeed, the functional specialization of EIL and local native languages sounds clear and simple from a theoretical perspective, but any bilingual speaker would agree that it is not that easy to keep the two functions apart in practice. As Pennycook (2003: 517) has also pointed out, there are cases when non-native speakers of English may deliberately choose to use English 'to signify identification with some cultural affiliations'. In that event, the selection of a palatable minimum of working languages may prove rather problematic, as this would mean to officially endorse language inequality. Upon analyzing current communication practices in international organizations, Els (2005) propounds the solution to select different languages for different social practices and thus evade the inequality issue. This might appear a politically expedient proposal but, given the problems it might create for those in pursuit of jobs in international organizations and multinational companies, it virtually brings into sharper relief the seriousness of the issue.

Graddol (2006) provides a different interpretation of the situation. He argues that EFL is currently experiencing a 'paradigm shift' whereupon English is gradually taking the position of a basic skill, such as computer literacy, that all students have to master for an unproblematic functioning in society. Inasmuch as this presumption is realistic, then further research is needed in order to find how the role of English as a basic skill will affect speakers' overall language repertoire. Will knowledge of English be sufficient for them to get along in the world, in which case the establishment of a diglossic situation seems more likely? Or, will the changed status of English force people, those from the upwardly mobile circles at least, to extend their range of foreign language competencies in order to maintain their high social position which will step up the spread of plurilingualism?

Another group of problems stem from the changes that EFL practices of learning and use have undergone under the influence of English globalization. These changes do not concern so much the community of EFL users, which has always been very heterogeneous, comprising people of different language and culture background, with different communicative needs and levels of proficiency. What globalization of English has brought about is significant broadening of the range of functions and cross-cultural contexts of use of EFL among partners who are, more often than not, all non-native speakers. As a result EFL has shifted in status and has assumed a new socio-political role as a tool of wider communication that can be used cross-culturally, both intra- and internationally, and an instrument for providing access to the world's wealth of information. Some scholars have seen in these changes sufficient grounds for reassessment of the perception of EFL[1] varieties and speakers. From sheer 'performance varieties' (Jenkins, 2003: 15), without any official status and therefore dependent on the standard set by native speakers in the Inner Circle they are now considered to be entitled to some partial autonomy that permits a certain degree of systematic distinction from ENL. Given the utilitarian purposes for which the language is being used, EFL speakers are believed to owe 'no allegiance to any descendants of its ancestry in the present' (Widdowson, 1994) and have a legitimate right of 'appropriation of the language' for their own purposes (Seidlhofer, 2002). The corollary for EFL speakers of the new role attributed to the variety they speak is that they are now viewed as transformative agents willing to express their own social and cultural identity (Jenkins, 2006; Pavlenko & Lantolf, 2000; Seidlhofer, 2001), as users in their own right (Cook, 1993). Moreover, as expert communicators capable of adapting their speech performance to the requirements of the particular interactional context (Pennycook, 2003), EFL speakers are entitled to shape and be shaped by the language they are using.

The changed attitude towards EFL users has inevitably led to calls for reassessment of EFL methodology, especially, the validity of one of the basic tenets of the dominant communicative approaches – the native speaker as the ideal model of communicative behaviour. Scholars have questioned the concept of 'native speaker community' defining it as a 'linguistic myth' (Alptekin, 2002), an essentialist category that is poorly supported by sociolinguistic evidence (House, 2003). They have also challenged the adequacy of the communicative model, which fails to account for the particular needs of EFL users for participation in cross-cultural interaction being in complete disregard of the specificity of interchanges between non-natives and the transient nature of interacting groups in bilingual/multilingual settings (Jenkins, 2006; McKay, 2003). By focusing on cultural models of Britain and the USA, as some linguists have argued, communicative approaches tend to foster a specific kind of cultural hegemony, that is not just 'illogical' in cross-cultural communication (Modiano, 2001: 161) but even threatening for it may conflict with local religious, educational and political traditions (Kramsch, 1997). Inasmuch as the instruments of measuring EFL users' proficiency are based on the codified form of language represented by educated native speakers, their performance is often unjustly stigmatized (Byram, 1997). EFL users are doomed to a lifelong status of 'learners', forced to mimic a 'chimerical native speaker ideal' (Norrish, 1997) to avoid being marginalized as failed communicators.

The debates over all those problematic issues have provided a backdrop for the EIL (or, World Englishes) project. More and more linguists and language teaching educationalists stand by the conviction that the time is ripe for a paradigm shift in EFL research and teaching. This requires that a systematic description of the variety of English used for international communication be carried out to establish standards of use relevant to the specific context in which it is used (House, 2003; Seidlhofer, 2001). Furthermore, it is also necessary to design an adequate model of teaching, flexible and comprehensive, recognizing the various ways in which English is used by bilinguals and providing opportunities for students to benefit from interactions in bilingual settings (Llurda, 2004; McKay, 2002).

In sum, we may say that all explorers of EIL deserve credit for providing a comprehensive picture of the changes in EFL practices of use under the influence of globalization, for contesting long-established models and views and identifying problematic areas in need of special attention and for changing our thinking about bilingual speakers and the specificity of norms and standards in bilingual usage. At the same time, their work is also open to criticism. As pointed out by some linguists as well, EIL studies tend to operate with rather rigid 'conceptualization of globalization, national standards, culture and identity' (Pennycook, 2003: 217) and make sweeping generalizations without taking into account such important factors as tradition and cultural specificity of the separate groups of speakers (Bruthiaux, 2003: 168). Thus, such simple questions as 'Why people choose English', 'How people use English' or 'How people assess their own performance' remain inadequately answered. This study is an attempt to provide answers to exactly these questions with reference to a particular language situation.

## EFL in Bulgaria: Changing Perspectives

Globalization has reached the countries of central and eastern Europe (hereafter CEE countries), and Bulgaria as one of them, relatively late. Nonetheless, owing to the limited distribution of the languages spoken in the nation-states of the region, foreign languages have always been widely used as a means of international communication and foreign language competence has customarily been valued high as a 'passport to a successful career' (Enyedi & Medgyes, 1998: 2). Accordingly, English, along with the other major European languages, has had a distinctive place in school curricula even before the socio-political changes of the 1990s.

In spite of the positive attitude towards foreign language learning, however, the overall standard of instruction was low and inefficient, having educational rather than communicative goals. Students' accomplishments were far from satisfactory even at the elitist foreign language schools established to educate language professionals for all spheres of social life. EFL was regarded more like a school subject that had to equip students with knowledge about the language and culture of its native speakers, quite unlike ESL, for instance, which has always followed a native speaker model of communicative behaviour conducive to an eventual socialization into the respective target language community (Kramsch, 2002). The model for emulation was derived from the standardized grammar and spelling of the target language's formal register of academic prose, not from native speaker behaviour, as there were very few native speakers, or authentic materials around. Teaching was very traditional consisting of little more than grammar and vocabulary exercises, plenty of rote learning and huge texts that students had to grapple with unassisted. The ultimate objective of teaching was not to help students learn how to communicate in English, but to develop in them some basic academic skills, to teach them how to analyze and interpret English texts from the standard literary canon and instill in them some moral and civic virtues. Whatever innovative strategies there were, such as the teaching of some of the core subjects through the medium of English at the English language schools, they, too, were oriented towards developing skills that could manifest high educational standards, such as analytical and critical thinking, for instance, rather than good command of the instrumentalities of everyday talk. Students' motivation was customarily tied up with academic achievement. Their aspirations for the future were focused not so much on integration into communities of foreign practice but on such intellectual and social accomplishments that could ensure them a proper place among the well-educated citizenry of their own country. As one who has first-hand experience of the EFL teaching methods of those days, I can say that at the end of our schooling we felt much better prepared to come to grips with difficult literary or scientific texts than to ask about the way if we got lost. A good illustration of the kind of English we were speaking is the comment made by my first native speaker interlocutor, a British elderly woman. 'Your English is so quaint,' she said. 'You sound like Dickens to me.' Enyedi and Medgyes (1998: 3) argue that this statement could safely be generalized for the whole region. Indeed, our locally produced textbooks swarmed with writings of the classics while books other than textbooks were scarce. Owing to restrictions on travel and access to the mass media beyond national borders, opportunities to use the language in real communicative situations out of school were practically non-existent.

Things have changed radically nowadays. Having picked up fresh steam from the socio-political changes taking place in the region, the governments in all newly established democratic states have spearheaded large-scale reforms to assure their peoples a rightful place in the 'common European home'. Since internal changes were running in parallel with globalization processes world over, shortly after the 1990s watershed, people have become aware of the fast-spreading English and the dis/advantages associated with it. Those lacking adequate command of English have begun to feel linguistically impoverished and hastened to remedy the deficiency by taking language courses themselves, or by investing in foreign language education for their children from a very early age. This has forced governments to make a prompt about-face on their foreign language policy that has given fresh impetus to the profession. As a result, within a relatively short period of time EFL curricula have been modernized and brought in line with European standards. New teaching materials have been produced locally with a clear focus on communication and a fresh, 'polyvalent approach' to the teaching of culture (Grozdanova, 2002). The market has been flooded with resource materials, both imported and locally produced, aimed not only to prepare students to meet the challenges of intercultural contexts of communication, but also to instill into them the values of modernity entrenched in the well-established democracies of Europe. Cohorts of EFL teachers have taken training or re-training courses to brush up their English and gain command of the intricacies of teaching the language communicatively in an intercultural context. Notwithstanding the fact that native speaker norms still do not figure explicitly in any of the official educational documents,[2] on a grassroots level, learners, particularly the young ones, want to *talk*, *act* and *think* like native speakers.[3] Thus, English has quickly grown into a key feature of the region's present-day ecological setting, remarkably prominent not only among the educated circles who benefit directly from their proficiency in English but also among the masses who appreciate that the language provides them with a window on the world.

The question that concerns us in this study, therefore, is whether, and in what way, the radical socio-political and economic changes have affected the practices of EFL learning and use, given that people's milieu is among the factors exerting the strongest influence on their behaviour (Rose *et al.*, 1998: 17). How relevant to the Bulgarian situation is the conviction voiced by some linguists that the promotion of English as a major tool for 'catching up with Europe' would not have had the same success in the CEE countries had it not been for the 'finesse' of donor countries in marketing the language as a symbol of modernity and technological advance (Enyedi & Medgyes, 1998)?

## The Survey

The questionnaire for the current survey, written in English and distributed electronically, has been completed by 120 Bulgarians, the ratio of male to female being 23:77.[4] There are respondents from all over the country, although those from the capital form by far the largest group (75). There are also seven responses from Bulgarians living abroad, the USA, Canada, Great Britain, Malta and Luxemburg. About two-thirds of the respondents (87) have a university degree. The remaining 13% are divided between people with secondary education (8) and university students (5). Classified according to their university major, respondents fall into Humanities (73), Science (14), Economics (5), Law (3) and Information technologies (5). Although the group is highly varied in terms of respondents' occupation,[5] jobs requiring high language proficiency tend to predominate. One reason for this could be that the questionnaire was written in English, which may have prevented those with poor command of the language to participate. Since many of the respondents have chosen not to answer the question about their age, the age band is estimated approximately to be 20–50.

## Discussion of Survey Results

### Speakers' individual language repertoire

The results from the first question, aiming to define the position of English in speakers' individual language repertoires, show that the total number of languages spoken in this relatively small sample is 27. The largest is the group of speakers of two foreign languages (75) followed by those speaking three (19) and more (5) additional languages. The respondents with just one foreign language are less than 1%. These results are consonant with the findings from a previous study I have carried out among secondary students (Georgieva, 2005) and lend support to the expressed view on Bulgarians' prevailing positive attitude towards foreign language learning. Estimates of respondents' preferred language choices have yielded the following ranking of the corpus languages: English (100), Russian (60), German (45), French (23), Spanish (14), Italian (13), Greek (4), Turkish (4),[6] Serbian (4) and Other (21) (cf. Figure 6.1). This means that in addition to English, used by all respondents, over half of them speak also Russian; 45% speak also German and so on. As noted the list of languages registered in the corpus is 27,[7] but those not included in the table have been pointed by just one or two respondents each (cf. Figure 6.1 below).

To an extent, the current ranking replicates the results from the previous study with the only exception of Russian, which did not have such a distinctive position as a second choice in the teenagers' corpus. Presumably, the established difference is due to the age factor, as most of the respondents from the current sample must have been still at school when Russian was an obligatory first foreign language. The data from the two corpora are also at variance with regard to the level of competence[8] respondents have declared for each foreign language they speak. Students' registered competence in their first foreign language, usually one of the mainstream languages taught at school, tends to differ widely from that of subsequent languages, where partial or survival competence prevails. Conversely, some 73% of the respondents from the current corpus declare equal or almost equal proficiency (level A/B) in at least two languages. This may be taken as an indication of differences in the factors motivating individuals' selection in either case. My observations lead me to conclude that teenagers tend to be influenced to a much greater extent than adults by

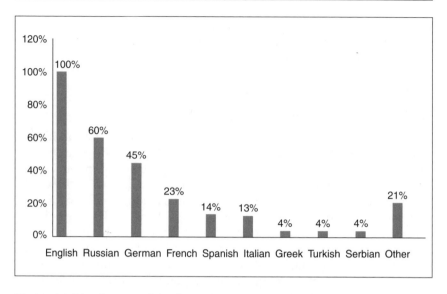

**Figure 6.1** Distribution of the foreign languages registered in the sample

attitudinal and emotive factors in their choice of foreign languages, conducive to what Spolsky calls 'folk plurilingualism' (2004) which is not likely to be very stable. In contrast, with adults pragmatic motives tend to prevail. To a large extent, young people's plurilingualism is a spin-off of their predisposition towards participation in multiplex social networks and development of solidarity ties with network members by picking up bits and pieces of their languages even if they are not so useful career wise. Because of the time and effort required to maintain a language however, they are likely to sustain in adulthood only those foreign languages in which they see some practical benefit. Consequently, it could be surmised that the languages spoken by the adult group will be entrenched in numerous and diverse social practices to ensure their maintenance. This leads us to the next question concerning respondents' preferred patterns and domains of use of the foreign languages they speak.

## Domains of EIL use

For the second question, namely, *Which of the languages you speak do you commonly use in the following situations?*, respondents had to specify their preferred choice of language, Bulgarian included, in 21 domains grouped into three categories. These categories were: HOME, concerned with dominant interaction patterns in a person's private life (family, friends, etc.);

WORK, bearing on patterns of communicative behaviour associated with one's professional life (communication with staff at workplace, professional contacts, business meetings, academic forums, seeking information on the internet, etc.); and ENTERTAINMENT, focused on the most preferred languages for entertainment – music, cinema and television. Taking as a starting point the habitual associations between languages and domains of use made by traditional sociolinguistics, I presumed that speakers would register Bulgarian as the language for the HOME domains and English for the WORK, and possibly, ENTERTAINMENT domains. Hence, considering the fact that HOME domains form the core of one's personal world associated with intimacy and self-actualization, while WORK domains are the customary place for establishing links with the outer world, language configurations of the expected type would lend support to the view that English and Bulgarian perform two separate, though complementary, sets of functions, that of communication and identification, respectively.

The survey results, however, have revealed a more sophisticated pattern of use. In the first place, English has leaked into all three categories and the HOME domains are no longer the preserve of Bulgarian.[9] In the WORK domains, in turn, English and Bulgarian happily co-exist, but the other foreign languages in the speakers' repertoire also take a significant place. Moreover, the internet domain does not appear to be a reserved territory for English alone, but is shared by all languages available. Similar is the situation in the ENTERTAINMENT category where the domains are shared by all languages available to the speaker. A respondent's comment (viz., *I watch what is interesting to me, the language doesn't matter*) aptly summarizes the situation.

In sum, the results manifest important changes in individuals' social networks that have taken place under the impact of globalization. New forms of social networks have been created with new patterns of social affiliation and new discourses. Existing social networks have been expanded and diversified including various forms of interpersonal relations across national and cultural boundaries. An important corollary of this process is that traditional associations between languages and domains of use have lost credibility, whereupon speakers' intent and the particular socio-cultural context begin to play a much greater role in the choice of a language. In light of the observed new situation we need to recognize that despite the undoubted dominance of English, especially in the WORK domains, the other languages in speakers' individual repertoire also have a distinctive and valued role to play in their practices of social life. It appears that the more English spreads as lingua franca, the weaker its position is becoming as a tool of professional advancement (Graddol, 2006). If this trend continues, it may plausibly serve as a natural stimulus for people in pursuit of more prestigious jobs to expand their foreign language repertoires. Consequently, the predictions about a diglossic or plurilingual future of Europe may prove complementary rather than opposing.

Language distribution across domains also seems to cast doubt on the propounded opposition between Acquisition and Participation Metaphors to account for EFL and ELF, respectively (Jenkins, 2006). Given the salient dominance of English in the WORK domains, it seems much more likely for speakers to have learnt the language driven by utilitarian motives rather than aspirations to personal excellence. Moreover, I am inclined to agree with Kuo (2006: 219) that a language of wider communication does not necessarily imply simplified, reduced variety. As mentioned earlier, speakers of smaller languages such as Bulgarian are learning English not just to communicate with fellow workers but also to compete, both intra- and internationally, for better job positions, for efficient fulfilment of their professional duties, for higher gains or recognition of their achievements. Considering the fast speed at which globalization is obliterating state borders and weakening their protective role, there are good grounds to suppose that good competence in English will continue to be highly prized as a prerequisite to a successful career. The analysis of speakers' attitude to English lends further support to this surmise.

### Attitude towards EIL

The item on speakers' attitudes included seven definitions[10] (cf. Table 6.1) of the role of global English, generalized versions of different views expressed in the literature, which respondents had to rank on a scale of 1 to 7. Three of the definitions (b, e and f) had a positive orientation, another three (a, c and d) were more towards the negative end of the continuum and the seventh (g) explored the impact of human agency. The answers are summarized in Table 6.1.

The results from the analysis clearly show speakers' preference for positive attributes, particularly those associated with prestige and professional advancement (f), which confirms what was said above of their pragmatic motivation for the use of EIL. Although not surprising, respondents' non-acceptance of the negative attributes is more interesting as it illuminates some important characteristics of the Bulgarian society in the transition period. According to some Bulgarian sociologists, a key feature of the period is peoples' overwhelming conviction that the rich

**Table 6.1** Speakers' attitude towards global English

| Criteria | most agree (1) | (2) | (3) | can't decide (4) | (5) | (6) | least agree (7) |
|---|---|---|---|---|---|---|---|
| (a) English kills motivation to learn other languages (%) | 6 | 5 | 5 | 15 | 26 | 24 | 19 |
| (b) English facilitates and strengthens intercultural relations (%) | 9 | 28 | 19 | 17 | 17 | 4 | 6 |
| (c) English causes erosion of national identities and shrinkage of language functions (%) | 2 | 7 | 10 | 12 | 23 | 35 | 11 |
| (d) English fosters Anglo-American cultural hegemony (%) | 6 | 2 | 8 | 10 | 11 | 17 | 46 |
| (e) English is a status marker – a talisman of democratization and modernity (%) | 6 | 14 | 26 | 27 | 12 | 7 | 8 |
| (f) English is a symbol of power, prestige and professional advancement (%) | 35 | 28 | 22 | 7 | 3 | 3 | 2 |
| (g) English is what speakers make of it (%) | 35 | 28 | 11 | 10 | 3 | 7 | 6 |

West holds the solution to all our problems, 'that it only gives away and does not want anything in return' (Dichev, 2001: 45) whereupon imitative repetition of western democracies is considered a supreme value (Mineva, 2001: 64). Inspired by the ideals propagated by the electronic mass media, the music and film industries, young people especially long to get access to all that counts as valuable in the 'normal' (i.e. rich) countries of Europe, and English provides the most efficient instrument to this effect. The consequences that blind imitation might have for their own self-image and cultural identity do not count, as it is exactly the backwardness of that image they want to break away from and build a new European identity. To a large extent, these attitudes towards Europe seem to hold good to this day, which explains why all negatively oriented roles of English have been discarded as unacceptable.

Nonetheless, the situation does not appear to be totally unchanged. Upon comparison of the current data with that from an analysis of an earlier period where the symbolic role of English as the language of freedom and high democratic ideals clearly stands out as one of the main drivers for its spread (Georgieva, 2002: 150), we see a slightly different picture. Notwithstanding its position at the positive end of the scale (cf. e), the symbolic role of English is now significantly outstripped by its pragmatic role as an instrument of prestige and social advancement. Because of the small scale of the study, it would be unwise to make any definitive conclusions about a turnabout in attitudes, for the registered difference may well be due to social characteristics of the examined group. Yet, the estimates for the two categories are substantial enough to deserve attention, especially, if we take into account the high value assigned to the role of agency (g) as well. The registered pragmatic orientation towards English may also be a corollary of speakers' growing awareness of globalization, which has caused commodification of the language 'as a means to control access to valuable resources' (Heller, 2003: 474). As it seems, more and more people are becoming alive to the complex plurilingual environment in which we are living and want to take advantage of the benefits that English can bring them by managing their knowledge and skills in a way that suits best their own purposes. Individuals' responses to the last question concerned with self-assessment of their English speech behaviour provide evidence in a similar vein.

### Standards and norms of use

Theoretical constructs of communicative competence may be useful as criterion reference device in the formulation of target objectives for foreign language teaching, but they tell us little about how these pre-formulated criteria of in/competence correlate with speakers' individual hierarchy of competences and skills. In their debates over what should count as EIL appropriate use, scholars and educationalists, too, rarely adduce evidence bearing on speakers' subjective opinion on the subject. Unlike what appears to be common practice in this study, I have addressed the issue from a speaker's perspective. In particular, the questions of interest were what variety Bulgarian speakers accept as standard target language norm and how they assess their speech performance with reference to that standard.

The estimates of respondents' preference for a standard variety are as follows: British English (39), American English (16), British/American English (38), EIL (16) and Bulgarian English (2). These results reflect in the main the traditions of EFL teaching in the country. The new moment is the relatively high level of indeterminacy. Alongside those who have marked both British and American English, more than half of the subjects who have opted for EIL, and all who have chosen Bulgarian English, have underlined a standard variety as well. One reason for respondents' hesitancy as to which answer to choose could be the fact that they are conscious of the hybrid nature of the variety they are using. But there seems to be yet another reason, implied in a comment added by a respondent as motivation for her choice, namely, *Deep in my heart I am all for British English, although I am perfectly aware that what I speak is International English.* By way of explanation of the registered ambivalence, I want to argue, with Kramsch (2002: 13), that the selection of a particular target language variety or norm of use is not determined solely by external – educational, social, economical, and so forth – factors. Affiliation to a particular language variety is also dependent on one's 'habitus', in Bourdieu's terms, one's psychological and socio-cultural capital that provides the referential framework against which the correctness of one's own or other people's behaviour is judged (Bourdieu as quoted by Grenfell, 1998: 14). Accordingly, the observed wavering between varieties may be accounted for by some speakers' intuitive desire to draw a distinction between a 'model for emulation' and a 'model for use'. EIL is the model for everyday use. The model for emulation, in turn, is not for use. It has the higher function of serving as a 'frame of reference' against which individuals' creativity, ingenuity, originality or beauty of expression are measured. Hence, affective factors and an individual's discursive history have a stronger role in its selection. On the other hand, selecting a native speaker variety as a model for emulation may not cause the displacement of the mother tongue or any other language from one's individual repertoire if they serve different functions.

The observed duality persists in speakers' self-assessment reports as well.[11] In the first place, claims for high proficiency (about 25% have underlined *I may pass for a native speaker in casual conversation.*) parallel open admissions for usage problems bearing, in the main, on pragmatic appropriateness (22), genre and style variation (33) and idiomaticity and fluency in casual conversation (21). It is possible that, for some respondents at least, 'pass for a native speaker' associates with fluency and communicative effectivity rather than accent. It is also likely that the registered problems are not regarded a serious impediment to mutual understanding in communication. Whatever the reason, it seems clear that respondents lay greater emphasis on meaning than on form. A second contradiction emerges in relation to norms of use and models of correctness. All but 10% of the respondents have signaled a preference to abide by the rules as defined in grammar books and dictionaries, that is, ENL norms. At the same time, the native speaker concept has proved a debatable point. Some openly reject it; others heatedly defend it, as illustrated in examples (1) and (2), respectively. In addition, over a third of the group admits that they like to use strategies of self-expression, that is, they attach importance to human agency.

> I do not think that I have to respect the native speakers because it is their language, but I have to respect the language rules. After all, I am not the one who has the right to choose.
>
> I do not approve of bending the language to suit one's own personality; the preference for speaking some kind of an 'adjusted' and 'individualistic' English rather than the native speaker's version, in my opinion, indicates acute self-consciousness and in almost all cases is a sign of insecurity and low self-esteem or fear from losing one's identity (which in its turn again points towards insecurity. (....) Aiming to reach a native speaker level of proficiency does not threaten in any way one's identity; this is merely a matter of perfectionism.

This seeming contradiction may again be accounted for by respondents' understanding of the notion 'norms of use'. The definitions that appear to prevail are closer to those used in EFL teaching, that is, a standard variety as codified in dictionaries and grammar books, which do not refer to the native speaker explicitly. Hence, following the rules is not deemed contradictory to the statement bearing on the role of agency, namely, *I prefer to be myself when I speak English*. Speakers' attitude towards communication strategies is presented in much the same vein. Twenty-three percent of the respondents admit that they often employ language crossing, in the sense of Rampton (1999), for social purposes, and over half of the group (54) emphasize the importance of context for their communicative performance. See, for example, 3.

> 3. For me, when I speak English it is very much like when I speak Bulgarian. It depends very much on who I speak to. I mean the person I speak to, no matter native or non-native, influences my performance so much that in every instance I may sound an entirely different person altogether.

The last example is indicative of how bilinguals assess their performance in more than one way. It shows that speakers are aware that rules of grammar only partially overlap with rules of communication. They are aware that in real life communication, many other factors relevant to the particular communicative context may influence one's performance; hence it may appear more or less fluent or native-like. That is why the focus is on getting their meaning across, whereas the form varies according to context and interlocutor. The statement also provides a clue as to why most respondents have not regarded affiliation to ENL norms as threatening their identity. By their communicative experience as bilinguals they have realized that identities do not exist as something static within people but are constructed in interaction, in performance, as Pennycook also argues (2003: 528). Communication is a cooperative endeavour in which all communicative partners in a particular encounter jointly contribute to the establishment of common ground, to the mutual understanding, to the unproblematic unfolding of the interaction process and to the construction of each other's identities. In an intercultural communicative situation, this may prove a real tall order, so communicators will have to use all kinds of strategies – compensatory, accommodation and social – to make up for flaws in their knowledge, to neutralize differences in ritual behaviour or to signal solidarity and respect for the other. And the way one manages to cope with the demands of the particular situation will also contribute to his/her identity as communicator. The registered high level of allegiance to rules of grammar clearly shows that blatant deviations from established norms would not be accepted as 'good' English even in a lingua franca communicative context. At the same time pragmatic inappropriateness, stylistic inconsistencies or clumsiness of expression will not only be 'let pass', but may even be regarded as adding colour and charm to one's speech performance. ⚡

## Conclusion

In conclusion, we may say that English has firmly positioned itself as the first foreign language in Bulgarian language situation. Nonetheless, interest in other foreign languages, not only the major European languages at that, is very much alive and well, too. Moreover, the more English is growing as a means of wider communication, the more it seems to be loosening its hold as a marker of prestige and an instrument of professional advancement. As a result, new opportunities arise for other languages to find a proper place in people's language repertoire. For now, there is not enough evidence to judge whether this tendency is not restricted to upwardly mobile circles of society, but considering the fast rate of development of such industries as tourism, for instance, it may be presumed that it might pertain to some groups of service workers as well.

People's growing awareness of globalization, on the other hand, has brought about a shift of attitude towards English. In the early years of transition, the symbolic role of English was a vehicle to the 'treasures' of the rich West that made people particularly vulnerable to assimilationist ideologies canonizing (or beautifying) Anglo-American socio-cultural values. Now, it is being gradually superseded by a more sober, pragmatic attitude towards the language. People are getting increasingly aware of the benefits that knowledge of English can bring them and feel entitled to consciously select a variety and manage their competences in ways that suit best their own needs and aspirations as professionals. This explains why the majority of the examined group, and this may be generalized to all Bulgarian speakers of English as well, are not conscious of being EIL users, or are not willing to be taken as such. Rather, they perceive themselves as speakers of EFL who abide by rules based on a standard variety of the language as codified in dictionaries and grammar books. That being the case, it seems unlikely that Bulgarian EFL users would wholeheartedly accept a new world standard established solely for the purposes of international communication and teaching, quite distinct from currently existing standard varieties. The construct EIL seems tenable as a supranational variety only if it is viewed as a complex composite of varieties, held together by sharing a core of features pertaining to what are traditionally known as ENL standard varieties, yet different in some respects due to the diverse language and cultural background of EIL speakers. The various forms of overlapping of languages and cultures in EIL find realization in specific nuances of use that bring colour, freshness and singularity of expression. At the same time, because of the excessive variability of EIL its users will have to resort to a much broader and much more diverse range of communication strategies – accommodation, compensatory and social – to assure mutual intelligibility of conversational partners' speech and smooth away social barriers to successful communication.

## Notes

1. It is important to note that the scholars arguing in favour of a partial autonomy of the variety of English spoken by foreign users tend to draw a distinction between EFL (the kind of English taught at schools which is exonormative, i.e. it obeys the widely recognized ENL standards) and English as a lingua franca (ELF) (the variety employed by nonnative users to

communicate with other nonnative users which is endonormative, i.e. develops rules of its own) (Jenkins, 2006). Taking into account the ever growing use of English for communication among non-native speakers, the proponents of the ELF model (e.g. House, Jenkins or Seidlhofer) suggest that ELF should be treated as a specific variety in its own right. It deserves according to them a thorough unprejudiced description conducive, eventually, to its codification and acceptance as a respected alternative to ENL. Attractive though it may seem, the proposal raises a number of problems. Firstly, it would be difficult to describe a variety that has neither a relatively stable community of speakers nor a distinctive set of social practices or contexts of use. Choosing 'non-nativeness' as the most salient feature of the variety, on the other hand, would practically lead to the exclusion of native speakers from participation in joint transnational activities which is neither realistic nor fair. Finally, as becomes evident from survey results, EFL speakers themselves are not particularly enthusiastic to be treated as 'people from another planet'. These are all very serious questions that deserve more profound investigation.

2. Thus in the rationale of 'A World of English', one of the most widely used locally produced textbooks, the promoted socio-cultural model is to raise students' awareness of the world language and cultural diversity and allow a balanced and realistic projection of one's social and cultural identity upon the wider context of the multicultural world (Grozdanova, 1996).

3. Cf. Impact Study on the Teaching of English to Young Learners Project. British Council, Bulgaria 1999–2001, unpublished manuscript.

4. All estimates hereafter are %.

5. The breakdown, according to respondents' occupation, is as follows: university lecturers (10), teachers (25), students (21), interpreters/translators (8), Civil servants (14), media workers (7), Public affairs specialists (2), IT specialists (3), sales assistants (1) and other (9).

6. It is noteworthy that Turkish is not widely spread outside the Turkish community in Bulgaria and its use for intergroup communication is almost nil. One reason for this could be that the Ottoman Empire of which Bulgaria used to be a part had a multiethnic principle of state organization which made possible the preservation of the religious and linguistic identity of local peoples. So Bulgarians did not feel pressed to learn Turkish. Another important reason seems to be that from the very first awakening of the national spirit in the early 16th century, Bulgarians have always shown stronger affinity for European models of literature, arts, music and lifestyle (Stefanova, 2006; Angelov & Marshall, 2006).

7. The other languages occurring in the corpus are Arabic, Armenian, Bosnian, Croatian, Czech, Dutch, Hebrew, Hindi, Japanese, Macedonian, Maltese, Norwegian, Polish, Portuguese, Romanian, Slovak and Swedish.

8. Competence is as declared by respondents on a scale of five levels described verbally, namely, A – I can understand, speak, read and write fluently in different genres and styles; B – I can understand standard speech, produced at normal speed, but I have problems with speaking/writing, especially in less familiar genres; C – I can understand the gist of written or spoken texts in the standard variety but I speak with a lot of mistakes and I cannot write; D – With some help, I can generally understand what a text is about but I can speak very little and I cannot write; E – I know just a few phrases that can help me survive when I'm abroad.

9. The diffusion of English in the HOME domains is possibly a side effect of the country's policy of greater openness to the world in present-day times providing more favourable conditions for international mobility, mixed marriages, cohabitation with foreigners, establishing friendly relationships with English-speaking foreign settlers or workers in the country, and so forth. The situation, however, needs a more thorough investigation.

10. All definitions were given as extended statements. See, for example, (d) The spread of English unavoidably fosters a form of Anglo-American neo-colonialism that conflicts with local, religious, educational and political traditions and weakens the status of national languages, and (f) The fast spread of English worldwide could be accounted for by its newly acquired symbolic value as the language of power, prestige and progress. Knowledge of English can guarantee upward mobility and affluence to those who speak it.

11. For this task, respondents were asked to either select from a list of ten descriptors provided in the questionnaire or submit their own description. They could also underline only those sections from a descriptor which they considered relevant to their situation. The descriptor that seems to have aroused most mixed feelings was the one bearing on native speaker standards and read as follows: _When I speak English, I prefer to follow the rules as they are given in the dictionaries and grammar books. After all, we have to show respect for the standards of those whose language we are using._

## References

Angelov, A.G. and Marshall, D.F. (2006) Introduction: Ethnolinguistic minority language policies in Bulgaria and their Balkan context. _International Journal of the Sociology of Language_ 179, 1–28.

Alptekin, C. (2002) Towards intercultural communicative competence in ELT. _ELT Journal_ 56 (1), 57–64.

Bhatt, R.M. (2002) Experts, dialects, and discourse. _International Journal of Applied Linguistics_ 12 (1), 74–109.

Bruthiaux, P. (2003) Squaring the circles: Issues in modeling English worldwide. _International Journal of Applied Linguistics_ 13 (2), 159–178.

Brutt-Griffler, J. (2002) _World Englishes: A Study of Its Development._ Clevedon: Multilingual Matters.

Byram, M. (1997) Intercultural communicative competence – The challenge for language teacher training. In R. Cherrington and L. Davcheva (eds) _Teaching Towards Intercultural Competence_ (pp. 92–103). Sofia: The British Council.

Cook, V. (1993) _Linguistics and Second Language Acquisition._ Basingstoke: Palgrave Macmillan.

Crystal, D. ([1997]2003) _English as a Global Language_ (2nd edn). Cambridge: Cambridge University Press.

Dichev, I. (2001) Europe as a legitimization. _Sociologicheski problemi Journal_ 1–2, 2000. Translation in Blagovest Zlatanov (ed.) _New Publicity: Bulgarian Debates in 2000_ (pp. 42–60). Sofia: Otvoreno Obshtestvo.

Els, T. van (2005) Multilingualism in the European Union. _International Journal of Applied Linguistics_ 15 (3), 263–281.

Enyedi, Á. and Medgyes, P. (1998) ELT in Central and Eastern Europe. *Language Teaching: The International Abstracting Journal for Language Teachers, Educators and Researchers* 1, 1–12.

Georgieva, M. (2002) On developing intercultural communicative competence in EFL learners. In D. Thomas and M. Georgieva (eds) *Smaller Languages in the Big World* (pp. 146–159). Sofia: British Council/Lettera Publishers.

Georgieva, M. (2005) English as a converging and diverging force in sociocultural relations. In M. Georgieva (ed.) *Spaces, Gaps, Borders: Proceedings of the 8th International Conference of the Bulgarian Society for British Studies, 2003* (pp. 63–74). Sofia: St Kliment Ohridski University Press.

Graddol, D. (1997) *The Future of English?* London: The British Council.

Graddol, D. (2001) The future of English as a European language. *The European English Messenger* X (2), 47–55.

Graddol, D. (2006) *English Next*. The British Council.

Grenfell, M. (1998) *Bourdieu & Education: Acts of Practical Theory*. Florence, KY: Taylor and Francis.

Grozdanova, L. (1996) A World of English: Rationale of the English coursebook for the preparatory class of English Medium Secondary Schools (in Bulgarian). *Foreign Language Teaching* 5, 9–20.

Grozdanova, L. (2002) Cultural diversity in a unifying world – A new challenge for English textbook writers. In D. Thomas and M. Georgieva (eds) *Smaller Languages in the Big World* (pp. 126–145). Sofia: The British Council/Lettera Publishers.

Heller, M. (2003) Globalization, the new economy and the commodification of language and identity. *Journal of Sociolinguistics* 7 (4), 473–492.

House, J. (2003) English as a Lingua Franca: A threat to multilingualism? *Journal of Sociolinguistics* 7 (4), 556–578.

Jenkins, J. (2003) *World Englishes*. London: Routledge.

Jenkins, J. (2006) Points of view and blind spots: ELF and SLA. *International Journal of Applied Linguistics* 16 (2), 137–162.

Kachru, B.B. (1985) Standards, codification and sociolinguistic realism: The English language in the outer circle. In R. Quirk and H. Widdowson (eds) *English in the World: Teaching and Learning the Language and Literatures* (pp. 11–30). Cambridge: Cambridge University Press.

Kachru, B.B. and Nelson, C.L. (1996) *World Englishes*. In S.L. McKay and N.H. Hornberger (eds) *Sociolinguistics and Language Teaching* (pp. 71–102). Cambridge: Cambridge University Press.

Kachru, Y. (1985) Discourse analysis, non-native Englishes and second language acquisition research. *World Englishes* 14 (2), 223–232.

Kirkpatrick, A. (2001) *English as an Asian Language*. http//www.guardian-unlimited.co.uk [downloaded August 2001].

Kramsch, C. (1997) Culture and self in language learning. In R. Cherrington and L. Davcheva (eds) *Teaching Towards Intercultural Competence* (pp. 14–29). Sofia: The British Council.

Kramsch, C. (2002) Beyond the second vs. foreign language dichotomy: The subjective dimensions of language learning. In K. Sp. Miller and P. Thompson (eds) *Unity and Diversity in Language Use* (pp. 1–19). BAAB/Continuum.

Kuo, I-Chun (Vicky) (2006) Addressing the issue of teaching English as a Lingua Franca. *ELT Journal* 60 (3), 213–221.

Llurda, E. (2004) Non-native-speaker teachers and English as an international language. *International Journal of Applied Linguistics* 14 (3), 314–323.

McArthur, T. (1998) *The English Languages.* Cambridge: Cambridge University Press.

McKay, S.L. (2002) *Teaching English as an International Language.* Oxford: Oxford University Press.

McKay, S.L. (2003) Toward an appropriate EIL pedagogy: Reexamining common ELT assumptions. *International Journal of Applied Linguistics* 13 (1), 1–22.

Mineva, M. (2001) Points of view and boundaries of the analysis. *Sociologicheski problemi Journal* 1–2, 2000. Translation in Blagovest Zlatanov (ed.) *New Publicity: Bulgarian debates in 2000* (pp. 61–69). Sofia: Otvoreno obshtestvo.

Modiano, M. (2001) Ideology and the ELT practitioner. *International Journal of Applied Linguistics* 11 (2), 159–173.

Norrish, J. (1997) english or English? Attitudes, Local Varieties and English Language teaching. *TESL-EJ* 3 (1), 37–51.

Pavlenko, A. and Lantolf, J.P. (2000) Second language learning as participation and the (re)construction of selves. In J.P. Lantolf (ed.) *Sociocultural Theory and Second Language Learning* (pp. 155–177). Oxford: Oxford University Press.

Pennycook, A. (2003) Global Englishes, Rip Slyme, and performativity. *Journal of Sociolinguistics* 7 (4), 513–533.

Phillipson, R. (1992) *Linguistic Imperialism.* Oxford: Oxford University Press.

Phillipson, R. (2001) English yes, but equal language rights first. *The Guardian Weekly.* http://www.guardian.do.uk/GWeekly/Story/0,3939,475284,00.htm [downloaded 2002].

Rampton, B. (1999) Language crossing and the redefinition of reality. In P. Auer (ed.) *Code-Switching in Conversation* (pp. 290–317). Florence, KY: Routledge.

Roland, J-L.Breton (2000) Can English be dethroned? http://www.unesco.org/courier/2000_04/uk/doss11.htm [downloaded 2004].

Rose, R., Mishler, W. and Haerpfer, C. (1998) *Democracy and Its Alternatives: Understanding Post-Communist Societies.* Baltimore, MD: John Hopkins University Press.

Seidlhofer, B. (2001) Closing a conceptual gap: The case for a description of English as a Lingua Franca. *International Journal of Applied Linguistics* 11 (2), 133–158.

Seidlhofer, B. (2002) *Habeas corpus* and *divide et impera*: 'Global English' and applied linguistics. In K. Sp. Miller and P. Thompson (eds) *Unity and Diversity of Language Use* (pp. 198–215). BAAB/Continuum.

Skutnabb-Kangas, T. (2001) Murder that is a threat to survival. The Global English Debate. *The Guardian Weekly.* http://www.guardian.co.uk/GWeekly/Story/0.3939.464614,00.html [downloaded 2001].

Spolsky, B. (2004) *Language Policy: Key Topics in Sociolinguistics.* Cambridge: Cambridge University Press.

Sridhar, K.K. (1996) Societal multilingualism. In S.L. McKay and N.H. Hornberger (eds) *Sociolinguistics and Language Teaching* (pp. 47–70). Cambridge: Cambridge University Press.

Stefanova, J. (2006) The four transitions in Bulgarian education. *International Journal of the Sociology of Language* 179, 155–167.

Widdowson, H.H. (1994) The ownership of English. *TESOL Quarterly* 28 (2), 377–389.

## Chapter 7

# Glocalization of English in World Englishes: An Emerging Variety among Persian Speakers of English

FARZAD SHARIFIAN

## Introduction

In the invitation letter sent to authors of the chapters of this volume, the editors noted that

> Globalisation is perhaps one of the most troubled concepts in the social sciences. Under the umbrella of investigating the phenomenon, numerous and sometimes variant or in fact conflicting perspectives on what it is have emerged in economic, cultural, religious, political and other disciplinary analyses. From those researching the global spread, forms and functions of English, there has been a modest response to this phenomenon's pattern of interfacing with structural issues around diversity and multiple centres to which the World Englishes paradigm is anchored.

While the response on the part of World Englishes scholars researching World Englishes may have been modest, speakers of World Englishes themselves have provided a strong response to the globalization of English by glocalizing it to varying degrees and in various ways. This is exactly what researchers within the paradigm of World Englishes have been trying to show, though without calling it 'glocalization of English'. Within studies of globalization, 'glocalization' is a term used to refer to the modification of a global product to meet local needs and norms, and make it more marketable in various parts of the globe (Robertson, 1995). In the world of business, this may be done by non-local businesses. In the case of World Englishes, however, the process of localization is carried out by local speakers. The localization of English in the form of World Englishes is driven by local as well as global forces, specifically by the perceived needs of speech communities and individuals, either consciously or sub-consciously.

English has spread around the world for various reasons and through various routes, either through the front door, the back door or even the window, and different relationships with it have been developed by different speech communities as well as by individual speakers. The role English plays in particular contexts determines the degree to which different speech communities and individuals localize this globalized language. Needless to say, speakers across different societies are not automatons who can be homogenously programmed with a set language programme: they use language to express, among other things, their dynamic *cultural conceptualizations* (Sharifian, 2003, 2008b). Studies in applied linguistics have firmly established that factors such as one's identity (or identities), ideology, culture, emotions, and so forth have a significant influence on how one learns a second language (e.g. Dewaele, 2005; Norton Peirce, 1995; Pavlenko & Dewaele, 2004; Sharifian, 2007b). These factors also determine the degree to which a speech community and the individual go 'local' or 'global' in their use of English. One important – and obvious – factor in this choice is whether English is used for intracultural or intercultural purposes. These are, however, not mutually exclusive: some people, for example, Aboriginal Australians, may need English for both purposes. Indeed, many speakers of English are glocalizing English in a more comprehensive sense: they are simultaneously developing global norms and local norms as they come to use English for both intercultural and intracultural purposes.

What appears to be modest in the World Englishes paradigm is the description of how the process of rapid glocalization of English, together with the multiple roles this language plays in people's lives, is leading to the explosive development of new Englishes. Such studies are likely to have significant implications for language policies within each country in terms of whether governments view English, for example, as a local product, or, alternatively, as an imperialistic imposition. In this chapter I will make an attempt to reflect on how Persian speakers[1] are responding to the increasing global dominance of English as an international language.

## The Case of Iran

The history of the relationship between English and the society of Iran has been complicated by the political events of the last few decades. While eschewing an exhaustive account of the history of the English language in Iran, I will, in this chapter, try to capture an account of some of the diverse responses to the forces and events that have brought Persian speakers into contact with English.

English has become significant as an international and an intra-national language in Iran over the last 50 years. At the beginning of the 20th century, French was the dominant European foreign language in Iran. It had an elite status since France was the country of choice for those seeking higher education abroad. English came to replace French in response to the presence of British companies, the British Army and the Americans who developed close relationships with the former king of the country, Mohammad Reza Pahlavi (also known as the Shah). The United States established a strong military and economic presence in Iran during the Shah's reign, which became the impetus for the development of English as the most significant foreign language (see also Tollefson, 1991). The Shah had a very strong vision for turning Iran into a 'modern' country, which, for him, meant Westernization. English thus came to be viewed as the language of 'modernity', or *tamadon-e bozorg* ('great civilization'), which was the Shah's goal for Iran. Learning and speaking English became a prestigious exercise which would open many 'horizons' for the Iranian people. During the 1960s and 1970s, hundreds of thousands of government-funded and self-funded Iranians went to the United States, mainly for higher education. Many American companies opened branches in Iran, bringing expatriates into Iran and also employing local Iranian people. This created a need for the use of English in the workplace for those who worked with foreigners.

One of the most important institutions that promoted English was the Iranian Army, which hosted a significant number of American personnel. During this period, many Americans came to Iran to teach English and many language schools that recruited native speakers of English were opened. Two other main centres for the promotion of the English language in Iran at the time were the Iran-America Society (IAS) and the British Council. Under such circumstances, then, English was thought to be 'owned' by the Americans and the British, and these two varieties were considered the only correct forms of English.

The Islamic Revolution of 1979, however, complicated the relationship the Iranian people had with English. The post-revolutionary government at first viewed English as the language of the 'Great Satan' (i.e. the US government) and several attempts were made to ban any form of English in Iran. However, the government soon realized that its aim of 'exporting the Islamic Revolution to the rest of the world' would require an international language that could reach the non-Muslim world, and thus learning English appeared again on the state agenda.

During the years after the Iranian revolution, several developments shaped the fate of the English language in Iran. On the one hand, the government made an attempt to 'cleanse' English of its Western 'baggage' by commissioning local experts to develop local materials in English for school and university curricula. Thus, the English books students now study at school contain localized content written in English. The following examples are from the prescribed high school text books used in Iran.

- <u>Takhti</u> was a great athlete. In fact, he is the father of wrestling.
- <u>The 5th of Sha'ban</u> is a great religious celebration. (Birjandi *et al.*, 2006: 53)
- How is he going to travel to Tabriz? (Birjandi *et al.*, 2006: 14)

It can be seen that the local content includes local words such as people (Takhti, a most famous wrestler in Iranian history), places (Tabriz, a city in the north of Iran) or events (5th of Sha'ban, birth date of a Shi'a Imam) that would generally be known to Iranians. These books also include lessons that make use of religious content, such as the following:

God has sent many prophets for the guidance of mankind. They all taught us to be good and to do good. Our Holy Prophet Muhammad (peace be upon him) was the last of the prophets. He was born in 571 A.D. in Mecca. The people of Mecca liked him. They highly admired his truthfulness, honesty and sense of duty. They gave him the title of 'Al-Amin' which means 'the trustworthy'. He received God's message at the age of 40, and began to preach Islam. He told the people of Mecca not to worship idols but the One God who is the creator of the entire universe. The people of Mecca, who worshiped idols, turned against him. They became his enemies. They did not want him to preach Islam. The Holy Prophet left Mecca with his followers and went to Medina. The people of Medina received him with open arms. They were very happy to see the prophet of God. (Birjandi *et al.*, 2000: 104)

At the tertiary level, as part of the government's attempt to localize textbooks, the Centre for Studying and Compiling Books in Humanities commissioned experts to develop English for Specific Purposes (ESP) textbooks.

The general public has responded with mixed feelings to such developments. Many of those who support globalization (in the sense of Americanization) view such attempts as futile, but those who support the government's anti-West movement endorse attempts to localize English. Many Iranians still associate English with social prestige, as a tool which can not only open educational, social and professional opportunities but also help in the construction of an educated, elite social identity. For many, then, English provides a 'modern-citizen' identity that distances them from less cosmopolitan identities. As during the last three decades, Iran has gained a new political identity in international contexts, which is often closely associated with religious fundamentalism, for some Iranians speaking English, particularly with a Western accent, may be an attempt to reject this alleged 'national political identity'.

This is, however, just the beginning of the story. The last two decades have witnessed remarkably widespread use of the internet and of satellite communications in Iran. Many Iranians therefore have new motives for learning English: these range from expressing their political opinions, to accessing entertainment and to conducting business both within the country and outside.

Such developments have coincided with a number of other international engagements. Since the end of the Iran–Iraq war, the government of Iran has promoted international trade to boost the country's economy. The government has also tried to re-open the country to tourists, for both cultural and economic reasons. One important motivation in this area is for tourists to experience Iranian society as it is, and not as it is portrayed in the international media. Iranian universities are recruiting foreign students. Concurrently, an increasing number of Iranian citizens are travelling to neighbouring countries and to East Asian countries such as Singapore and Malaysia, mainly for trade, higher education and holidays. All these developments have led to an expanded role for English in Iranian society, and, now, almost everyone wants to learn English. Individual motives may be quite different: one citizen may want to migrate to a Western country and so need to take an English test, while another may want to be a 'modern' and literate citizen who can use the internet and watch foreign movies. This interest has resulted in an unprecedented growth in the number of language schools opening in Iran.

The significant point, here, is that these often sharply contrasting motives for learning English – and perhaps dozens of different motives could be found – have led to just as many different perceptions about what type of English should be taught. It is obvious that someone enamoured of the West would want to learn a Western variety of English, yet I doubt that a government official who is learning English to send anti-Western communiqués would wish to sound American or British.

These factors seem to be leading to the development of a distinct variety of English that could be referred to as 'Persian English'. One of the significant matrixes for this variety is the use of English by the relatively large population of Persian speakers who live in European and Western countries. One aspect of globalization is the huge increase in diasporas. Large numbers of people now move to form communities in English-speaking countries and as a result ethnolects develop from their interactions in English, both among themselves and with others (Clyne, 2000; Clyne *et al.*, 2001). Thus the development of new world Englishes is not tied so much to national boundaries and may take a transnational nature.

A large number of Persian speakers are actively present on the internet, developing blogs, Yahoo groups, and so forth, which are mostly written in English. The use of English in email correspondence between speakers of Persian has also become commonplace. The rationales behind this phenomenon range from convenience (such as the use of an English keyboard) to the desire to construct certain English-based identities.

In terms of its sound system, this emerging variety of English may be described as ranging from a basilect to an acrolect (Platt & Weber, 1980). The acrolect version of English among Persian speakers sounds like either British Received Pronunciation (RP) or American English in terms of phonology and grammar, depending on which variety a particular individual has mostly been exposed to and tried to imitate. The basilect version includes phonetic features that are close to the sound system of the Persian language. For example, /d/ is likely to be pronounced as dental rather than alveolar. This dental /d/ may also be used to pronounce /ð/ sounds in English. Samples of speech in English by Persian speakers can be found on IDEA website (http://web.ku.edu/idea/middleeast/iran/iran1.mp3).

At least one factor determining whether a person develops a basilect or an acrolect seems to be their attitude towards English. As mentioned above, it is doubtful that the government official who has strong anti-Western sentiments would wish to cultivate the accent of either standard American or British English. On the other hand, while having an integrative pro-Western motivation does not guarantee a native-like American or British accent, it would certainly facilitate one. Thus, the development of a native-like accent in Persian English may be driven by an integrative motivation.

However, I maintain that it is not so much the sound system that qualifies the English language used by speakers of Persian as a distinctive emerging variety of English; rather, it is the use of Persian *cultural conceptualizations* (Sharifian, 2003, 2008b) which provides a basis for semantic as well as pragmatic meaning which give a distinctive character to this emerging variety. In the following section I will elaborate on the notion of *cultural conceptualizations* in general before proceeding to a discussion of specifically Persian cultural conceptualizations.

## Cultural Conceptualizations

Our experience of the world is not a universally homogeneous phenomenon; rather, people across different cultural groups *conceptualize* at least some experiences differently. This extends to their internal as well as external experiences. Anthropologists have provided ample evidence of this from various cultural groups. Human languages play a significant role in these culturally constructed conceptualizations, or *cultural conceptualizations* (Sharifian, 2003, 2008b), in that language embodies, preserves and communicates these conceptualizations. Cognitive scientists refer to the components of cultural conceptual systems as 'schema', 'category' or 'conceptual metaphor' (e.g. Lakoff & Johnson, 1980; Rice, 1980; Rosch, 1978; Rumelhart, 1980). 'Schemas' and 'categories' are conceptual structures that are derived from human experiences and are used to make sense of, and organize, new experiences. The main difference between the two is their principle of organization; 'schemas' capture conceptual elements that are related thematically but 'categories' include 'instances' that are conceptually perceived as belonging to one class. As an example, the category of 'food' for a group of people may include instances such as 'rice', 'curry' or 'pizza', but the schema of 'dining out' for a speaker may include conceptual components such as 'going to a restaurant', 'ordering food' and 'paying the bill'. Schemas and categories are not mutually exclusive: a schema includes various categories and categories are usually associated with certain schemas.

Conceptual metaphors draw on more than one domain of experience. For example, in many industrial cultures 'time' is conceptualized as a 'commodity', reflected in expressions such as 'saving time', 'spending time' or 'budgeting time'. While many cognitive scientists view such conceptual structures as components of an individual's cognition, I view them equally as properties of a cultural group's *cultural cognition* (Sharifian, 2008b). A group's cultural cognition is more than the sum of the cognitive systems of its members. Cultural cognition is an emergent property of the interaction between members of a cultural group. Speakers across cultural groups develop their own cultural conceptualizations through their communicative interactions, and constantly negotiate and renegotiate them across time and space. These conceptualizations are by no means equally imprinted in the minds of the members of a cultural group but are rather *heterogeneously distributed* across the group, and as such 'cultural cognition' is a form of 'distributed cognition' (Hutchins, 1995).

The relevance of cultural conceptualizations to the global spread of English and the case of World Englishes is that many speakers use English to express and encode the conceptualizations of their culture of origin. This results in the localization of English, or, in other words, the development of new Englishes.

## Cultural Conceptualizations in World Englishes

An important aspect of the glocalization of English by speakers of World Englishes, and in particular new Englishes, has been how the speakers of these varieties use English to instantiate their cultural schemas, categories and metaphors. For example, speakers of Aboriginal English have encoded their cultural schemas, categories and metaphors that constitute their world view in English. Even everyday words such as 'family', 'home' or 'sit' in Aboriginal English are associated with schemas and categories which derive from Aboriginal cultural experiences (e.g. Malcolm & Sharifian, 2005, 2007; Sharifian, 2005a, 2006, 2007a). 'Home', for an Aboriginal English speaker, for instance, may refer to wherever a member of their extended family lives. Thus, 'home' in Aboriginal English captures an Aboriginal category. Similarly, the term 'family' for an Aboriginal English speaker involves cultural schemas that are largely culture-specific (e.g. Birdsall, 1988). This association of English words with cultural conceptualizations also abounds in other varieties of English. For example, in Ghanaian English the word 'linguist' refers to an 'interpreter, spokesperson, especially attached to chiefs in southern tradition. Visitors must speak through the linguist even when the chief is familiar with their language' (Blench, 2006, online source).[2] This is not simply a new meaning for the word 'linguist', but a new cultural category and its associated cultural schemas. An understanding of why the chief would not speak to the visitors, or what the role of a chief is or what 'southern tradition' refers to would require the knowledge of cultural schemas and categories that move beyond the scope of a dictionary definition. I now turn to the case of cultural conceptualizations among Persian speakers of English.

## Cultural Conceptualizations among Persian Speakers of English

As noted above, Persian speakers have increasingly come to learn and use English for various reasons, providing a meeting place for the English language and Persian cultural conceptualizations. Persian has, compared to Western varieties of English, a highly sophisticated sociocultural basis (e.g. Beeman, 1976, 1986, 1988, 2001; Eslami Rasekh, 2004, 2005;

Keshavarz, 2001; Modarressi-Tehrani, 2001; O'Shea, 2000; Sharifian, 2005b, 2008a). Persian has a rich repertoire of politeness and courtesy, which enters the exchange between the speakers in all forms and contexts of communication. Foreigners who learn Persian often find the sociocultural basis of the language its most difficult aspect. Through their socialization into the language, speakers of Persian learn how to address every single member of society according to their socially perceived standing. One single verb often has several forms that mark different levels of intimacy between the speakers. Additionally, the plural morpheme is used with verbs as a marker of politeness. Many Persian speakers of English often attempt to express these nuances of courtesy and politeness in English. Consider the following from a conversation between an American lecturer and a Persian speaker:

**American lecturer:**  Here's the recommendation letter that you asked for.
**Iranian student:**  Thanks very much. I am ashamed.
**American lecturer:**  What have you done?!

(Personal data)

Here the Iranian student has literally translated the Persian expression *sharmandam* ('I am ashamed') into English to express her gratitude to the lecturer. I would assert that this is not simply a mistake, but a reflection of a cultural schema. The Persian cultural schema of *tashakor* ('gratitude') encourages the expression of gratitude in ways that may seem more intense than is normally found in Western varieties of English. A simple act of thanking a person often translates into several turns in which the speaker expresses sincere appreciation. The concept of 'shame' here highlights the fact that the speaker is (painfully) aware of the time and energy that the addressee has invested in order to fulfil her request and that she feels uncomfortable about it. Thus, even if one tends to ascribe a lack of fluency to a speaker who would use such an expression, even those Persian speakers who are quite at home in English will tend to express their appreciation and gratitude more intensely than is the norm in Western varieties of English. I have observed several emails in which a writer has code-switched to Persian in order to express gratitude. For example:

I really don't know how to thank you, 'sharmandeh' (Personal data)

This clearly reflects a feeling on the part of the writer that English does not have a word that can replace the Persian concept of *sharmandeh*. The case of switching to Persian, or giving the Persian word and explaining it, is frequent among Persian speakers of English, again owing to the speaker's awareness that what she/he wants to say may not be covered completely by any English word. The following examples from Persian speakers were found on the internet:

Seriously, I'll take you to an awesome Persian restaurant then we'll hit the city. That is no taarof either. You must come to Sydney![3]

I haven't given up the habit of ta'arof, but now I say it up front that it is a cultural habit .... [4]

Since then, I have returned a few times to the place I know as my 'second homeland'

(and this is not a ta'arof): in 1982, in order to take part in two official forums in Tehran and Esfahan; ... [5]

I can say, without any taarof and trying to be polite, that Pouria was one of the few people that I consider myself very fortunate to have been acquainted with in Toronto.[6]

I suppose that if I were bettered versed in the 'game' of ta'arof (something of an ingrained politeness) I had felt it coming, but as it was, we left Hossein with not even enough cash to buy a packet of cigarettes.[7]

Now, i am going to buy some other fishes lol! by the way, please let me know if you have any farsi questions (taarof nakon). thanks again for everything:)[8]

Dear bbkhiav:
My compliments to you were truly sincere (no taarof here).[9]

It can be seen here that the Persian speakers have used the Persian word *târof* (also spelt as 'taarof', 'tarrof', 'ta'arof' and 'tarof') in their English writing. A Google search delivers thousands of pages either trying to explain what has been labelled 'untranslatable *taarof*' (also spelt as *ta'arof*) in Persian culture or asking about an explanation for it. *Târof* captures a significant Persian cultural schema that influences most speech events in Persian (see also Sharifian, 2007b). It is mainly driven by considerations of 'face' and politeness but to an extent that many foreigners find it an exclusively Iranian phenomenon (Beeman, 1986; de Bellaigue, 2004). Acts and gestures of *târof* include hesitation about making requests and complaints, hesitation about accepting offers and invitations, as well as offering 'ostensible' invitations (see more in Eslami Rasekh, 2005). All these acts, in themselves, may sound unexceptional, with variations existing in all cultures and languages. But it is the extent to which they take place in Persian conversations that has attracted a great deal of attention. The following is a description of *târof* from an internet posting by an Iranian:

> Iran has the sometimes charming, and sometimes superfluous, 'tarof', or pleasantries. Its domain spans from repeatedly offering someone food, even when they have refused it numerous times; to allowing other people to go through a door before you do, to insisting that someone come to your house, even though the moment you hang up, you complain about not having wanted guests (the reverse side of course is that the invitee has to reject the invitation until the host has offered at least five times). This etiquette comes naturally to many Iranians (although not to all; some people, like my dad, are playfully reprimanded amongst family members if they don't know how to 'tarof').[10] (Sadr, 2006, accessed 8 February 2007)

The above posting appears to be from an Iranian who lives in the United States but who also travels to and lives periodically in Iran. It clearly shows that its writer feels that the concept of *târof* is a characteristic of Iranian culture. The speaker refers to this cultural schema as 'etiquette', thus suggesting that in Persian English gestures of *târof* may be captured by the words 'pleasantries' and 'etiquette'. Wikipedia now has a webpage dedicated to the explanation of *târof* (http://en.wikipedia.org/wiki/Taarof). It notes that *târof* is very prevalent among Persian speakers and that it governs a wide range of social behaviour and communication. The Wikipedia page notes, for example, that

> The prevalence of t'aarof often gives rise to different styles of negotiation than one would see in a European or North American culture. For example, a worker negotiating a salary might begin with a eulogy of the employer, followed by a lengthy bargaining session consisting entirely of indirect, **polite** language – both parties are expected to understand the *implied* topic of discussion.[11]

The distinctiveness of *târof* to Persian culture is usually soon noticed by members of the Persian-speaking diaspora in other countries. For example, the *Washington Post* reports a camp held by Iranian American Youths where one of the main activities is playing and workshopping *târof*. The following excerpts are from the *Washington Post* report:

> The campers had played dodge ball, sung along with the guitar, horsed around. Now it was time for a hot-blooded battle of ta'arof, the Persian art of hyper politeness.

Ta'arof, which involves both parties insisting they are not worthy of the other, is in constant play in Iranian society – people refuse to walk through a door first, cabdrivers refuse to accept payment as passengers beg them to, hosts must offer pastries even if guests don't want them, and guests must say they don't want them even if they do. But at Camp Ayandeh, a leadership camp for Iranian American teenagers, ta'arof is one of several games and workshops that address growing up between two often-conflicting cultures. … Ta'arof can be hard to translate, and campers said they are careful not to do it around their American friends.[12]

Many Persian-speaking members of the Iranian diaspora have also posted explanations of *târof* on the web, which again suggests their awareness of culture-specificity of this cultural schema. The following excerpts are from a web posting by a retired dentist and freelance writer living in San Diego:

One of the most complicated aspects of Persian culture – and language – is the untranslatable ta'arof. Depending on the circumstance, it can mean any number of things: To offer, to compliment and/or exchange pleasantries. But that's only the tip of the iceberg. I doubt if any study can lead to a full understanding of Ta'arof. A born and raised Persian, even I find myself losing my grasp on it from time to time. … Those of us who have lived in the West for decades may feel westernized, but when it comes to Ta'arof, we remain Persians. I knew this when the other day at the local hamburger joint my teenage son grabbed the bill in the air before it reached me.[13]

As it can be seen from the above posting, the Persian-speaking writer who has lived in the United States for decades maintains that *târof* is still very much part of the culture of the Persian-speaking diaspora. The same writer notes how the exercise of *târof* in a Western context often leads to miscommunication. She notes:

Although ta'arof plays a basic role in politeness and indeed is one of our best traditions, there are embarrassing times when we make an absolute scene. I remember once after performing a small dental procedure on a friend, I refused to charge her. As she pushed a large bill into my hand, I tried to push it back and when she held my arm and tried to put it in my pocket I must have raised my voice in protest. The commotion brought my American secretary into the room. Seeing our struggle, she thought I was being attacked and asked if she should call security. Do I need to mention the scenes we make at restaurants over who pays the bill? We have all seen the frightened look on the waitress's face when we play tug-of-war with the check until it's torn in the middle.

The distinctiveness of this Persian cultural schema is often also noted by non-Persian-speaking people who interact with the community of Persian speakers. The following is an example:

> You are very correct. I've been fortunate enough to 'meet' many Iranians via the Internet, due to a medical condition that has brought us together. A year ago, I didn't even know what language was spoken there. Now, I plan to visit once I have time and money – hopefully soon. I've promised several people that I'll stay at least a day with them when I go. (Their offers were not just taarof, either.) Finding a hotel isn't a problem; getting a long enough visa to visit everyone will be the trouble. (posted by Eddie)[14]

It can be seen here that the non-Iranian English speaker here uses the word 'taarof' to suggest that the offers of invitations that he has received from Iranians have been genuine and not ostensible. Foreign visitors to Iran often soon become conscious of this cultural schema as a result of their daily interactions with Iranians. The following is an example from a foreign visitor to Tehran:

> Moving across town in a taxi, the driver offers me his own cup of tea as ta'arof, or a polite custom. His generosity is as intense as the tinted light — in a city of more than twelve million. (Caroline Morrell)[15]

The significance of the cultural schema of *târof* goes beyond the level of everyday communicative interactions. For example, it may affect international political discourse between the Persian-speaking government officials of Iran and those of the United States. During an interview between David Ignatius, Associate Editor and columnist at the *Washington Post*, and Iranian Foreign Minister, the Minister used the word *taarof*, which is reported in Just World News as follows:

> Ignatius said that during a recent interview with Iranian Foreign Minister Muttaqi, in New York, he had discussed the idea of 'a Kissinger style of "grand regional bargain." between the two nations ... But Muttaqi was skeptical and said it would only be a form of *taarof* (making nice); and that we should start the negotiation with small things, instead.'[16]

It can be seen here that the use of the word *taarof* by the Iranian Foreign Minister is reported in its Persian version with 'making nice' as its translation. Within the context of the discussions presented so far in this chapter, it should be noted that such translations do not fully capture the Persian concept and may thus lead to miscommunication, with either rewarding or damaging consequences depending on the nature of interpretation. It should be noted that Persian cultural conceptualizations are not always expressed by code-switching among Persian speakers of English: English words may be used instead. For example, the Persian cultural schema of *ehterâm* is usually referred to as 'respect' by Persian speakers of English. Many communicative acts and gestures that are categorized as *ehterâm* in Persian are unlikely to be labelled as 'respect' in Western varieties of English.

Sadr (2006) observes that 'the list of Iranian *de facto* gestures of respect are endless: In a closed setting, never having your back to anyone, especially an elder, even if the arrangement of a room makes it very difficult to sit otherwise' (accessed 8 February 2007). Several scholars have observed that *ehterâm* is closely associated with *târof* and politeness in Persian in the sense that a failure to observe an act of *târof* may be construed as 'disrespect' (Eslami Rasekh, 2005; Koutlaki, 2002; Sahragard, 2003). For example, a failure to offer an invitation, either genuine or ostensible, or to inquire about the health of the interlocutor's family in daily conversations may be considered 'disrespectful'. Sahragard (2003: 408) maintains that for Iranians, '[*ehterâm*] is essentially concerned with all kinds of social interactions' and observes that it is 'the most pivotal aspect in human relations among Iranians' (2003: 507). *Ehterâm* among Persian speakers is closely tied to the perceived social status of individuals (see also Behzadi, 1994) which is in turn tied to the perceived social standing of their family, either nuclear or extended. Koutlaki (2002: 1742) observes that

> Ehteram (near equivalents 'honour', 'respect', 'esteem', 'dignity') establishes the positions and statuses of the interactants with respect to one another and is shown through the adherence to the established norms of behaviour according to the addressee's position, age, status and interlocutors' relationship.

An important indicator of the degree of *ehterâm* that a speaker shows for her/his interlocutors is the address terms that are used. An interlocutor may be addressed in dozens of ways depending on the relationship between the individuals and also the perceived social status of speakers. A common term of *ehterâm* which also indicates certain degree of intimacy between friends in Persian is *jân* (also spelt as *jaan* or *jan*), which is usually used after a person's first name but can also be used with someone's surname. Many speakers of Persian express this as 'dear' when speaking in English even though 'dear' does not capture the degree of intimacy and respect involved in the use of *jân*. Some Persian speakers use this address term untranslated in their English. The following excerpts come from the beginning of a web correspondence between two Persian speakers:

> Dear Afshin, We have been using Unicode since RH7.3 ... Mohsen. Mohsen jan, Thanks for your reply, unfortunately i didn't check your respond [*sic*] until today, since there was no email notification... Afshin[17]

It is clear that the second speaker felt that the word 'dear' was not an adequate substitute for *jân* and has therefore addressed his interlocutor using the Persian word. The followings are other examples of the use of this address term among Persian speakers:

> Babak jaan,

> nice post, he is popular in iran. In Europe 99.9% percent of 20–30 year old generation haven't even heard his name. Older people like more his songs and know him better. Probably calm gentle music suits better the taste of the majority of Iranians.[18]

> Motori jaan; While you may be correct about the state of the Iranian Air Force, this account of the process of qualification of pilots may not be entirely true and although there are general guidelines, IATA member states exercise the training and qualification of their pilots with sovereignty.[19]

> majid jan, I think suggesting switching the two games against N korea would be even better. as ala suggested in the other thread.[20]

> Hi Navita jaan,

> Yes, in fact Iran had a very active movie industry and even now, after the revolution, when almost everyone left, they had to redevelope and have produced some very moving works.[21]

> Borzou jaan, your agenda is clear as a whistle. Of course you are going to get a negative response when you form a question like that.[22]

> Reza Jan, I am not sure when they will show the games. There are few games that will be played at the same time (last game in group stage).[23]

> alam Reza jan, Seems you set things right! may I have a look at the site?[24]

> Noushin jan salam

Thanks for your kind words and your support. My website does not accept Farsi scripts for some reason, we are working on that. However, i send this beautiful poetry to our Rooyesh webblog.[25]

Again the language-culture specificity of such feature of communication among Persian speakers is becoming increasingly taken up by non-Iranians. As an example, the following exchange has taken place on the internet by a British English speaker and a Persian speaker.

| | |
|---|---|
| **British English (BE) speaker:** | Salaam!! What category of people do you address attaching -jan to their name? And is it only ever attached to the first name? |
| **Persian Speaker 1 (PS1):** | It is used among friends and relatives. No, it can also attach to one's last name e.g. I can call a colleague as 'Ahmadi jân'. |
| **BE speaker:** | So, no way you can use it to a colleague or somebody who is not a good acquaintance of yours? |
| **PS speaker 1:** | Not normally, especially for one of the opposite sex. |

.
.
.

| | |
|---|---|
| **PS 2:** | Well the ending 'jaan' exactly means 'soul'/ 'ability to live' (∼also the word 'jaanevar' in meaning of 'animal'/'creature' < Old Iranian 'viana-bhere'). It might be attached to any kind of name! I could ever translate it 'dear'/'sweetie'/'darling'. e.g. 'ali jaan' ∼ 'dear ali'. |
| | The word exactly is derived from Old Iranian 'viyana-*'∼'soul/spirit' > Parthian 'giyan'∼'soul/spirit' > Kurdish 'giyan' and Persian 'jaan'. Also in Kurdish we use the same: 'dayke giyan' ∼ 'dear mom', 'role giyan' ∼ 'dear son', 'Ako giyan' ∼ 'dear Ako', etc. ....[26] |

A thorough description of Persian cultural conceptualizations that are increasingly being realized in the use of the English language by Persian speakers is beyond the scope of this chapter; but the examples given above

should indicate how the emergence of what I have termed Persian Eng͟
is tied to its cultural-conceptual basis. In the following section, I will dr̲ ̲ᵥ
on these observations in order to address a number of issues that have
been raised in the context of the globalization of English.

## Globalization and Standardization

One issue that has often been discussed in relation to the globalization
of English is an aspiration for standardization accompanied by a working
towards, or recommendation of, a core model or variety as a *Lingua Franca*.
In the light of the fact that speakers are largely localizing English on the
basis of their cultural conceptualizations, I am not certain how one could
offer a core variety that would fulfil the needs of such different speech
communities and cultural groups. Discussions of a 'standard variety' or
a core variety largely focus on grammar and often also on the sound system. But is this all there is to language? Drawing on my background in
cultural linguistics (Palmer, 1996; Sharifian & Palmer, 2007), I maintain
that all levels of language, particularly semantic and pragmatic meanings,
emerge from our conceptualization of experience. Even everyday words
such as 'family', 'home' and 'friend' may be conceptualized differently
across different cultures (Sharifian, 2005a). Studies of Aboriginal English
reveal that this dialect of English is significantly different from Standard
Australian English in its cultural-conceptual basis, even when Aboriginal
English speakers sound similar to Australian English speakers. The question would then be whether forcing the speakers to develop a grammatical
and sound system that is close to the Standard variety would help intercultural communication with non-Aboriginal English speakers. In fact this
is more likely to lead to miscommunication, since the Standard Australian
English speaker would then assume that because the Aboriginal speaker
sounds as if she/he is speaking the Standard variety, the underlying
meanings and conceptualizations would be shared. One solution might be
to explore the communicative strategies that speakers of different varieties
of English can employ as they work towards explicating their cultural
conceptualizations in English.

I now turn to the criticism of the World Englishes paradigm. It seems
that evaluations of the paradigm as a whole are often simply equated with
the work of Braj Kachru. I find it difficult to accept such a limited view.
This myopia reflects the conceptual metaphor of A RESEARCH PARADIGM IS
A PERSON.

Pennycook (2003: 517) argues that 'it [World Englishes] has tended to
operate with a limited and limiting conceptualisation of globalization,

national standards, culture, and identity.' One could agree with Pennycook that most publications that have focused on any of the World Englishes have addressed issues of culture and identity in a limited way. I believe this is partly because the World Englishes paradigm has previously been mainly a sociolinguistic enterprise, whereas identity has traditionally been viewed mainly a psychological concept, and culture is generally an anthropological one. There has, however, recently been an expansion in the scope of and approaches to World Englishes. For example, the recently published *Handbook of World Englishes* (Kachru *et al.*, 2006) includes sections that are devoted to 'Ideology, Identity, and Constructs' as well as 'World Englishes and Globalization'. Also, a cognitive and cultural linguistic perspective (e.g. Polzenhagen & Wolf, 2007; Sharifian, 2006) has been developed, which also underpins the description of Persian cultural conceptualizations offered in this chapter. It is noteworthy that in my own dealings with the situation of English among Persian speakers, I could not avoid addressing issues of identity and the political context.

It should, however, be mentioned that some scholars would argue that the more issues of political context and identity are included, the less the researcher deals with the key *linguistic* points of the nature of language and language variety. At some earlier stage the job of linguistics was to present a descriptive account of a language or a dialect. Today, however, it is clear that language cannot be studied in a socio-political or cultural vacuum. Moving beyond studying language in isolation naturally entails expanding the linguist's comfort zone by borrowing the analytical tools of other disciplines.

Finally, another objection Pennycook (2003: 519) raises against the paradigm of World Englishes is that it 'constructs speaker identity along national lines within these circles'. I agree with Pennycook on this point, and an appropriate example is that of Australia. Within Kachru's (1985) three circles, Australia is considered to be an inner-circle country, since Anglo-Australians speak Australian English as their native language. This conceptualization, though, overlooks the fact that many Aboriginal Australians speak Aboriginal English, which is an indigenized variety of English. There are also many other varieties of English spoken by migrants and refugees in Australia which do not lend themselves to the conception of an 'inner-circle' version.

In this chapter I discussed how the development of Persian English has partly been generated by those Persian speakers who are currently living outside Iran. This again means explorations of World Englishes should not be limited by national boundaries. I have also shown how speakers of Persian English may bring their own 'norms', such as politeness rituals, into the speaking of English, and thus these speakers may be best described as 'norm-developing'. Within Kachru's three circles, speakers of Persian English would be classified as 'norm-dependent', as Iran is categorized as an 'expanding circle' country. These observations obviously call for a revised taxonomy of World Englishes.

## Concluding Remarks

In this chapter, I have made an attempt to show how responses to the globalization of English may best be viewed as glocalization of this international language. I have shown how English has 'met' with Persian cultural conceptualizations through the increasing use of English by Persian speakers. The case of Persian speakers of English provides a good example of how different individuals have developed different relationships with English in terms of the different roles that it plays in their lives and also in terms of how it is employed in constructing their individual, social and/or political identities. The complexities that arise from the interactions between language, politics, culture and identity in the case of English force us to expand the scope of World Englishes and to borrow analytical tools from other disciplines such as cultural linguistics. I hope this chapter can serve as a small step in this direction.

## Notes

1. In this chapter, I use 'Persian speakers' rather than Iranian speakers because the data presented comes from speakers of Persian living both inside and outside Iran.
2. http://www.rogerblench.info/Language%20data/Africa/Ghana/Ghana%20English%20dictionary.pdf (accessed January 2007).
3. http://www.irankicks.com/ikboard/archive/index.php/t-27214.html (accessed January 2007).
4. http://parents.berkeley.edu/madar-pedar/blunders.html (accessed March 2009).
5. http://www.tavoosonline.com/Articles/ArticleDetailEn.aspx?src=69&Page=1 (accessed March 2009).
6. http://babakfakhamzadeh.com/site/index.php?p=0&k=0&c=12&i=856 (accessed March 2009).
7. http://www.italki.com/T000959005.htm (accessed March 2009).
8. http://boards.ipersians.com/archive/index.php/t-3820.html.
9. http://legofish.com/weblog/2004_06.php (accessed March 2009).
10. http://www.boston.com/yourlife/blogs/mideast/2006/10/15-week/index (accessed January 2007).
11. http://en.wikipedia.org/wiki/Taarof (accessed March 2009).

12. http://www.washingtonpost.com/wp-dyn/content/article/2007/07/06/ AR2007070601974.html (accessed March 2009).
13. http://www.iranian.com/Ghahremani/2005/March/Taarof/index.html (accessed March 2009).
14. http://blogs.sciencemag.org/scienceinsider/2008/12/us-science-acad.html (accessed March 2009).
15. http://www.wooster.edu/magazine/winter2006/morrell.php    (accessed March 2009).
16. http://justworldnews.org/archives/003015.html (accessed March 2009).
17. http://www.linuxiran.org/modules/newbb/viewtopic.php?post_id=2505& topic_id=782&forum=12 (accessed January 2007).
18. http://freethoughts.org/archives/000581.php (accessed March 2009).
19. http://forums.iransportspress.com/showthread.php?p=631045    (accessed March 2009).
20. http://www.persianfootball.com/forums/archive/index.php/t-60731.html (accessed March 2009).
21. http://www.asianoutlook.com/aoforum/archive/index.php?t-2220.html (accessed March 2009).
22. http://latimesblogs.latimes.com/babylonbeyond/2008/04/iran-you-vote. html (accessed March 2009).
23. http://www.irankicks.com/ikboard/archive/index.php/t-46225.html (accessed March 2009).
24. http://drupal.org/node/167444 (accessed March 2009).
25. http://middlepeace.com/(accessed March 2009).
26. http://forum.wordreference.com/showthread.php?t=1068034    (accessed March 2009).

## References

Beeman, W.O. (1976) Status, style and strategy in Iranian interaction. *Anthropological Linguistics* 18, 305–322.
Beeman, W.O. (1986) *Language, Status, and Power in Iran*. Bloomington: Indiana University Press.
Beeman, W.O. (1988) Affectivity in Persian language use. *Culture, Medicine and Psychiatry* 12, 9–30.
Beeman, W.O. (2001) Emotion and sincerity in Persian discourse: Accomplishing the representation of inner states. *International Journal of the Sociology of Language* 148, 31–57.
Behzadi, K.G. (1994) Interpersonal conflict and emotions in an Iranian cultural practice: *qahr* and *ashti*. *Culture, Medicine, and Psychiatry* 18, 321–359.
Birdsall, C. (1988) All one family. In I. Keen (ed.) *Being Black: Aboriginal Cultures in 'Settled' Australia* (pp. 137–158). Canberra: Aboriginal Studies Press.
Birjandi, P., Soheili, A., Noruzi, M. and Mahmoodu, G. (2000) *English Book 1*. Tehran, Sherkat chap va nashr ketabhaye darsi iran.
Birjandi, P., Noruzi, M. and Mahmoodu, G. (2006) *English Book 3*. Tehran, Sherkat chap va nashr ketabhaye darsi iran.

Blench, R. (2006) *A Dictionary of Ghanaian English*. Available online at http://www.rogerblench.info/Language%20data/Africa/Ghana/Ghana%20English%20dictionary.pdf (accessed March 2009).

Clyne, M. (2000) Lingua Franca and ethnolects in Europe and beyond. *Sociolinguistica*, 14, 83–89.

Clyne, M., Eisikovits, E. and Tollfree, L. (2001) Ethnic Varieties of Australian English. In D. Blair and P. Collins (eds) *English in Australia* (pp. 223–238). Amsterdam: John Benjamins.

de Bellaigue, C. (2004) *In the Rose Garden of the Martyrs: A Memoir of Iran*. London: HarperCollins.

Dewaele, J. (2005) Investigating the psychological and emotional dimensions in instructed language learning: Obstacles and possibilities. *The Modern Language Journal* 89, 367–380.

Eslami Rasekh, Z. (2004) Face-keeping strategies in reaction to complaints: English and Persian. *Journal of Asian Pacific Communication* 14 (1), 179–195.

Eslami Rasekh, Z. (2005) Invitations in Persian and English: Ostensible or genuine? *Intercultural Pragmatics* 2 (4), 453–480.

Hutchins, E. (1995) *Cognition in the Wild*. Cambridge, MA: MIT Press.

Kachru, B.B. (1985) Standards, codification and sociolinguistic realism: The English language in the outer circle. In R. Quirk and H.G. Widdowson (eds) *English in the World: Teaching and Learning the Language and Literatures* (pp. 11–30). Cambridge: Cambridge University Press, for The British Council.

Kachru B.B., Kachru, Y. and Nelson, C.L. (eds) (2006) *The Handbook of World Englishes*. Oxford: Blackwell.

Keshavarz, M.H. (2001) The role of social context, intimacy, and distance in the choice of forms of address. *International Journal of the Sociology of Language* 148, 5–18.

Koutlaki, S.A. (2002) Offers and expressions of thanks as face enhancing acts: Tae'arof in Persian. *Journal of Pragmatics* 34 (12), 1733–1756.

Lakoff, G. and Johnson, M. (1980) *Metaphors We Live By*. Chicago: University of Chicago Press.

Malcolm, I.G. and Sharifian, F. (2005) Something old, something new, something borrowed, something blue: Aboriginal students' schematic repertoire. *Journal of Multilingual and Multicultural Development* 26 (6), 512–532.

Malcolm, I.G. and Sharifian, F. (2007) Multiwords in Aboriginal English. In P. Skandera (ed.) *Phraseology and Culture in English* (pp. 375–398). Berlin/New York: Mouton De Gruyter.

Modarressi-Tehrani, Y. (2001) Aspects of sociolinguistics in Iran. *International Journal of the Sociology of Language* 148, 1–3.

Norton Peirce, B. (1995) Social identity, investment, and language learning. *TESOL Quarterly* 29 (1), 9–31.

O'Shea, M. (2000) *Cultural Shock: Iran*. Portland, OR: Graphic Arts Publishing Company.

Palmer, G.B. (1996) *Toward a Theory of Cultural Linguistics*. Austin: University of Texas Press.

Pavlenko, A. and Dewaele, J. (eds) (2004) Multilingualism and emotions. Special issue. *Journal of Multilingual and Multicultural Development* 25 (1).

Pennycook, A. (2003) Global Englishes, Rip Slyme, and performativity. *Journal of Sociolinguistics* 7, 513–533.

Platt, J. and Weber, H. (1980) *English in Singapore and Malaysia: Status, Features, Functions.* Singapore: Oxford University Press.

Polzenhagen, F. and Wolf, H. (2007) Linguistic expressions of corruption in African English: A cultural-linguistic approach. In F. Sharifian and G.B. Palmer (eds) *Applied Cultural Linguistics: Implications for Second Language Learning and Intercultural Communication* (pp. 125–168). Amsterdam/Philadelphia: John Benjamins.

Rice, G.E. (1980) On Cultural Schemata. *American Ethnologist* 7, 152–171.

Robertson, R. (1995) Glocalization: Time-space and homogeneity-heterogeneity. In M. Featherstone, S. Lash and R. Robertson (eds) *Global Modernities* (pp. 25–44). London: Sage Publications.

Rosch, E. (1978) Principles of categorization. In E. Rosch and B.B. Lloyd (eds) *Cognition and Categorization* (pp. 27–48). Hillsdale, NJ: Erlbaum.

Rumelhart, D.E. (1980) Schemata: The building blocks of cognition. In R.J. Spiro, B.C. Bruce and W.F. Brewer (eds) *Theoretical Issues in Reading and Comprehension* (pp. 33–58). Hillsdale, NJ: Erlbaum.

Sadr, A. (2006) *Etiquette* – Online document: http://www.boston.com/yourlife/blogs/mideast/2006/10/15-week/index

Sahragard, R. (2003) A cultural script analysis of a politeness feature in Persian. *Proceedings of the 8th Conference of Pan-Pacific Association of Applied Linguistics* – Online document: http://www.paaljapan.org/resources/ proceedings/PAAL8/pdf/pdf034.pdf

Sharifian, F. (2003) On cultural conceptualisations. *Journal of Cognition and Culture* 3 (3), 187–207.

Sharifian, F. (2005a) Cultural conceptualisations in English words: A study of Aboriginal children in Perth. *Language and Education* 19 (1), 74–88.

Sharifian, F. (2005b) The Persian cultural schema of *shekasteh-nafsi*: A study of compliment responses in Persian and Anglo-Australian speakers. *Pragmatics & Cognition* 13 (2), 337–361.

Sharifian, F. (2006) A cultural-conceptual approach to the study of World Englishes: The case of Aboriginal English. *World Englishes* 25 (1), 11–22.

Sharifian, F. (2007a) Aboriginal language habitat and cultural continuity. In G. Leitner and I.G. Malcolm (eds) *The Habitat of Australia's Aboriginal Languages* (pp. 181–196). Berlin/New York: Mouton De Gruyter.

Sharifian, F. (2007b) L1 cultural conceptualisations in L2 learning. In F. Sharifian and G.B. Palmer (eds) *Applied Cultural Linguistics: Implications for Second Language Learning and Intercultural Communication* (pp. 33–51). Amsterdam/Philadelphia: John Benjamins.

Sharifian, F. (2008a) Cultural schemas in L1 and L2 compliment responses: A study of Persian-speaking learners of English. *Journal of Politeness Research* 4 (1), 55–80.

Sharifian, F. (2008b) Distributed, emergent cognition, conceptualisation, and language. In R.M. Frank, R. Dirven, T. Ziemke and E. Bernárdez (eds) *Body, Language, and Mind (Vol. 2): Sociocultural Situatedness* (pp. 241–268). Berlin/New York: Mouton de Gruyter.

Sharifian, F. and Palmer, G.B. (eds) (2007) *Applied Cultural Linguistics: Implications for Second Language Learning and Intercultural Communication.* Amsterdam/Philadelphia: John Benjamins.

Tollefson, J. (1991) *Planning Language, Planning Inequality.* New York: Longman.

## Chapter 8
# Local Networks in the Formation and Development of West African English

AUGUSTIN SIMO BOBDA

## Introduction

The two main concerns relating to globalization and the spread of English in the world, which Bamgbose (2001), representative of most views, identifies, are the dominance of English over the other languages and calls in some quarters for uniformization of the language. This chapter focuses on the latter concern. It is generally agreed today that it is neither possible nor desirable to uniformize English; it seems, therefore, anachronistic to dwell on this issue. Of greater interest, it appears, are the various forms that English has taken across the world, and the circumstances leading to this phenomenon. This is what this chapter attempts to study. It shows the patterns of transplantation of English in West Africa, from the 15th century to the present, and the modes of its diffusion throughout its history in the region. Of particular interest are the networks which, in these local patterns of globalization, have developed from historical, geographic and other bonds between some countries in the region, a phenomenon which by no means precludes the existence of clear national and sub-national identities. Clear links are found between the period of transplantation, the modes of diffusion and the networks, on the one hand, and the sociolinguistics of English and the structural features of the emerging varieties in the various settings, on the other hand. The chapter covers essentially the following countries of the former British Empire and American sphere of influence from the west to the east: The Gambia, Sierra Leone, Liberia, Ghana, Nigeria and Cameroon (see Figure 8.1). In general geographic and economic terms (e.g. its membership to the Central African Monetary and Economic Community), Cameroon is in Central Africa, but its common history with the Anglophone countries to the west argues for its inclusion in West Africa in works of this nature.

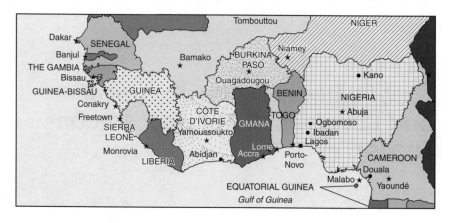

**Figure 8.1** Map of West Africa

## Patterns of Transplantation of English in West Africa, and Sociolinguistic and Linguistic Correlates

Some form of English must have been used on the West African coast as far back as the late 15th century. The first notable group of Europeans to visit the coast were the Portuguese. Their communication need with the indigenous population is generally believed to have bred an early form of Portuguese-based pidgin. But there were probably some English people among their staff; for example, Mbassi-Manga (1973) reports the presence of English privateers in Portuguese boats.

There is more tangible evidence of English presence on the West African coast in the 1560s, when William Hawkins stopped there en route to Brazil (Holm, 1989: 410); his son John Hawkins is later reported to have made three expeditions to take slaves from Sierra Leone to the Spanish Caribbean (1989: 410). Holm (1989: 410) reports further references in the literature to the use of English on the West African coast by the end of the 16th century. There are also reports of West Africans being taken to England as early as 1554 to learn English in order to serve as interpreters in trading expeditions, constituting what Spencer (1971: 10) calls 'a scattered band of Africans capable of interpreting between English and a number of the vernaculars'.

Having lived in the River Gambia area by the end of the 16th century, the English, using force when necessary, gradually took control of the coast hitherto in the hands mostly of the Dutch, and gained a number of forts in the 17th century in what is today Ghana. The latter part of the 17th century and the 18th century witnessed a firmer presence of the English. The use of some restructured form of English also increased significantly, notably through African middlemen in the slave trade, the women who had closer contacts with the whites and the mulattoes that these contacts produced (for details, see Holm 1989: 406–433; Huber 1999: 45–70).

A much larger influx of English-speaking immigrants to West Africa arrived in the late 18th century through Sierra Leone, which received successive groups of Black native speakers, namely, 411 settlers who were brought back to Africa from Britain in 1787 and founded Freetown; some 1131 former slaves who had fought for Britain in the American War of Independence, and had for some years been settled in Nova Scotia and arrived in Sierra Leone in 1792; 550 Jamaican Maroons, who were deported to Sierra Leone in 1800; other former slaves after the formal abolition of the slave trade by Britain in 1807 who were taken from illegal slave ships and who could not easily be returned to their original homelands (Görlach, 1991: 126).

Until the partition of Africa in the last two decades of the 19th century, the British were not keen to establish permanent settlements in Africa. Görlach (1991: 126) rightly notes that '[A]ll the British needed were stepping stones to the Caribbean and to India and Australia, and this objective could be achieved by the possession of islands (such as St Helena and Mauritius) or ports and forts,' and that 'larger colonies would have been considered rather a burden' (1991: 126). One of the dissuading factors was diseases, mostly malaria, on the mosquito-infested African continent. Hancock and Angogo (1982: 306) quote in this connection the saying that 'West Africa owes a debt to the mosquito for having been spared extensive European settlement.'

It was the presence of the Krios which was mostly felt before British colonization proper. Krios were the initial occupants of Freetown, as indicated above. They spoke an English-based creole called *Krio*, which came to also designate the speakers. Todd (1982: 284) reports that the Krios were found in large numbers from The Gambia to Fernando Po (present-day Malabo, Equatorial Guinea). Having served for a long time as preachers, teachers and traders, they became the main agents of administration under British rule. It is during the 20th century that West African colonies saw the arrival of a sizable number of British and Irish, and also other European (namely, German, Dutch, Swiss and French) settlers (see, e.g. Simo Bobda (2006: 219–223), and especially, in the case of South Africa, Mesthrie (1998) for the type of English the missionaries spread).

The above picture shows the specific environment in which English was transplanted in West Africa, an environment which was to determine its ecology as different from that of other world Englishes. The major points to note include the fact that, although its spread to a sizable portion of the population is fairly recent, mostly dating to the beginning of the 20th century, West African English is arguably one of the oldest Englishes in the world, if we take the possible presence of some form of English in the 15th century, and its more documented presence in the 16th century, to be its beginning.

Jenkins (2003: 5) associates the emergence of Englishes outside Great Britain to what she calls the two *dispersals* or *diasporas*. The first resulted in new mother-tongue varieties in America, Australia and New Zealand. The second resulted from colonization and yielded the Englishes of Africa and Asia. But this is only a simplified picture. For example, in Africa, English was brought to southern and eastern Africa much later than in West Africa. As Jenkins herself notes, 'the British did not arrive [in South Africa] until 1795 when they annexed the Cape, and did not begin to settle in large numbers until 1820,' although this part of the continent was colonized by the Dutch from the 1620s. English came to East Africa even much later, from the 1850s through British settlers after the expeditions of explorers like David Livingstone.

Also worth noting is the fact that English in West Africa, unlike in southern and eastern Africa, first developed through trade, mostly slave trade.

The above features of the transplantation of English in West Africa, namely, the period of transplantation, the agents of diffusion and the activities in which these agents were engaged, add to the fact that English in various parts of West Africa was superimposed over basically the same family of Niger-Congo languages, and evolves in a large set of conditions common to the region which, predictably, have sociolinguistic and linguistic correlates.

One of the major sociolinguistic correlates is the existence of pidgins and creoles in all the countries of the region: Aku in The Gambia, Krio in Sierra Leone, varieties of West African Pidgin English in Ghana, Nigeria and Cameroon and a range of pidgins and creoles in Liberia, which include Liberian Pidgin English, Kru Pidgin, Merico and Kepama (Görlach, 1991: 128). English-based pidgins and creoles do not exist in any other part of Africa. These idioms are generally found in countries with a history of slave trade like those of West Africa and the Caribbean, or of indentured plantation labour, like countries of the Pacific (e.g. Papua New Guinea, with its well-known Tok Pisin).

The many structural English features found across West Africa are also due to shared circumstances which helped to shape the ecology of the language in the region. For example, most West Africans realize the STRUT vowel as /ɔ/, which contrasts with East and southern African /a/; Harris (1996) convincingly attributes this difference to the fact that, at the time English was transplanted to (the Caribbean and to) West Africa, STRUT still had a rounded realization, and the gradual change to /ʌ/ and /a/ in many varieties occurred much later, explaining the occurrence of /a/ in East and southern Africa where the language was transplanted much later, mostly in the 20th century. (Asian Englishes also have /a/ for the STRUT vowel, resulting from the same phenomenon.) In West Africa, most divergences from /ɔ/ are due to some national parameters. For example, Ghana, where the vowel has changed only over a generation from /ɔ/ to /a/ and /ɛ/ in some words as seen later, owes this change to some psychological reconditioning to be discussed later. The case of northern Nigeria, where /a/ equally occurs in many STRUT words, is explained by the fact that, having for a long time resisted British penetration, this part of the country was permeable to English much later than the south, in fact around the same time as southern and eastern Africa.

Other common and exclusive West African phonological features include the occurrence of [-ɪn] for the <ing> form as in *goin'*, *comin'*, *eatin'*, contrasting with southern and eastern African [-ɪŋg]. West African [-in] is clearly the heritage of the Krios, as shown by Montgomerry (1999) in the case of Sierra Leonean English. A further example of a West African feature in English pronunciation is the occurrence of /ɔ/ for the *lettER* vowel in words with orthographic <-or, -our, -ure> as in [sɛktɔ, kɔlɔ, piktʃɔ] *sector, colour, picture* (except again in Ghana and northern Nigeria, which may have /a/). This feature contrasts with southern and eastern African /a/.

In lexis, borrowings from West African pidgins and creoles clearly distinguish West African Englishes from the others; for example, *okrika* 'used clothes' (for sale), *chakara (man)* 'trouble maker'. West African Englishes also have in common, and sometimes exclusively, a number of lexical peculiarities. Some features associated by some authors (e.g. Igboanusi, 2002; Kujore, 1985; Sey, 1973) with particular varieties are in fact characteristic features of more or less the whole of West Africa. *Go slow*, *senior/junior brother, to be on seat, invitee* (traffic jam, elder/younger brother, to be in the office, guest) are examples of such features. And even more convincing examples, tested in the field as part of Peter and Wolf's (2008: 228) preliminary findings, are *chief* 'traditional ruler'; *brown bag* 'bribe'; *a child's play* 'an event or situation that does not require much energy'; *conscientize, -se* 'raise awareness of something'; *dash* 'bribe, small gift'; *petty trader* 'person involved in small scale trading, usually by the roadside'.

## Sub-Regional Networks

The patterns of transplantation of English and the environments in which it was transplanted in various West African countries have been similar, but by no means identical. Particular countries have been involved in networking of one kind or another, creating some group identity which has shaped the ecology of English in these particular sets of countries. Examples of such networks are what I have earlier (Simo Bobda, 2003) called the 'Krio Connection', the Sierra Leone–Gambia network, the Ghana–Nigeria–Cameroon network and the Nigeria–Cameroon network.

Countries of the Krio Connection are those which experienced the greatest Krio impact. They are Sierra Leone, The Gambia and Nigeria. The base of the Krio community was Freetown in Sierra Leone, as shown above. But another group of Krios settled in Bathurst, present-day Banjul, in The Gambia. It happens that a large number of Krios were of Nigerian, especially Yoruba, origin. Holm (1989: 415) thus reports that '[o]f the 11,000 liberated Africans in Sierra Leone noted in the 1848 census, no less than 7,114 were identified as Yoruba.' That is why, in their dispersion to various parts of Africa, their preferred land of resettlement was Nigeria, as indeed some freed slaves managed to return to their native lands (Holm, 1989: 412). One linguistic correlate of this connection is that countries forming it have a number of shared phonological features which include large-scale realization of the NURSE vowel with <er, ear, ir, yr> as /a/ as in [tam, lan, tati] *term, learn, thirty*, where the other West African accents have mostly /ɛ/ ([tɛm, lɛn, tɛti]); the prevalence of /u/ in final /Cl/ clusters as in [tebul, devul, aŋgul] *table, devil, angle*, where the other countries will more often have [-əl]; a recurrence of [-in] for the <-ing> form, for a more common [-iŋ] elsewhere.

The Nigerian variety of West African Pidgin also shares more lexical and grammatical features with Krio than the other varieties. Common lexical or functional items are the many words which are of Yoruba origin like *oyibo* 'white man', and others like *sissy* 'sister, girl', *boku* 'many, plenty of', *bato* 'ship'. Shared grammatical features include *him* and its variants used as subjects for 'he, she', *them* and its variants equally used as subjects, for 'they'.

The Sierra Leone–Gambia network is a subset of the Krio Connection. The two countries involved have in common the use of Krio, called Aku in The Gambia, as one of the main languages. The overall sociolinguistic landscape, however, is different from one country to the other, as will be shown later.

The Ghana–Nigeria–Cameroon network comprises the three eastern-most countries in the region under investigation, which also happen to be the biggest, in terms of the population as well as the surface area: Nigeria has a population of about 132 million on an area of 923,768 sq km, Ghana 22 million on 238,537 sq km and Cameroon 16 million on 475, 000 sq km. Nigeria and Cameroon are contiguous, while Ghana is sepa-rated from Nigeria only by a thin strip of about 200 km formed by Benin and Togo. Not having, like Sierra Leone and Gambia, experienced a mas-sive Krio settlement at the beginning, Nigeria, Ghana and Cameroon have not inherited Krio, but another form of restructured English, West African Pidgin English, very close to Krio with which it has a high degree of intel-ligibility. Attitudes to this idiom and to standard English, however, vary tremendously from one country to another, as will be seen later.

Elements of the Nigeria–Cameroon network include a long common border of 1239 km which, predictably, dozens of transborder languages straddle, for example, Efik, Korop and Ejagham. This border is also very porous, letting in and out millions of people from both sides involved in trade and other activities. There are about 4 million Nigerians in Cameroon, for a total Cameroonian population of about 16 million, as stated above; conversely, about 500,000 Cameroonians live in Nigeria.

Historical facts make the network even tighter. The British part of Cameroon was administered as part of the federation of Nigeria during the time of British trusteeship. In 1961, after the independence of French Cameroon from France on 1 January 1960, British Cameroon was to decide in a plebiscite whether to have their independence as part of Nigeria or as part of Cameroon. The southern part opted to join Francophone Cameroon, while the northern part, in an election alleged by Francophone Cameroon to be rigged, voted to be attached to Nigeria. This formerly Cameroonian territory is now in north-eastern Nigeria.

During the colonial days, Cameroon underwent the influence mostly of southern Nigerians, in several ways. The influence of Yorubaland came from the fact many of the Krios who dispersed to the various corners of West Africa, as indicated above, were of Yoruba origin. Yoruba influence was further strengthened by the fact that Lagos, the capital of the Feder-ation of Nigeria, was situated in Yorubaland. Also worth noting is that Lagos was an important seaport and university centre like Ibadan, also situated in Yorubaland; Ibadan had one of the first and most prestigious universities in West Africa, in which a good part of the elite of this region received their education. Nigerians of both Yoruba and Ibo ethnic groups held very important administrative and educational positions. There were also many Cameroonians working in Nigeria for British administration. Iboland in eastern Nigeria was the chief source of religious influence. The Catholic mission, which was well established in this part of Nigeria, was an important link to Cameroon, as Nigerians and Cameroonians crossed the border both ways for missionary work, and as staff and students of Catholic education (for more facts, see Awonusi, 1986; O'Neil, 1991; and Simo Bobda, 2006).

The linguistic correlate of these long-standing contacts between Nigeria and Cameroon is the fact that the varieties of English used in the two countries are closest to each other than they are to any other at all levels of analysis (see, e.g. the phonological similarities between the two varieties in Simo Bobda (1995), and Nigerian features described in works like Kujore (1985) which overwhelmingly reflect Cameroonian usage).

## National and Sub-National Identities

The regional and sub-regional similarities discussed above conceal peculiarities associated with each country and even regions within a given country. Although the patterns of transplantation and growth of English have roughly been the same everywhere, each country has its own story to tell about the environment in which English was transplanted and the way it developed, indeed the ecology of the language, as Mufwene (2001) would term it. I am going to survey in turn Liberia, The Gambia, Sierra Leone, Ghana, Cameroon and some regions of Nigeria for these differing stories, and find out what the sociolinguistics and/or the structural features of local Englishes owe them.

Liberia was founded by the Americans to perform a similar function to Sierra Leone, founded by the British. In 1847 the American Colonization Society granted independence to this territory, recognized by the United States in 1862. The initial settlers on the land bought by the Americans around present-day Monrovia were called Americo-Liberians or Mericos, who considered themselves superior to the indigenous population. According to Holm (1989: 424), '[t]the speech that most of the Settlers brought from America was the creolized (or decreolizing, [. . .]) ancestor of modern Black English Vernacular.' This information is very important, as it makes Liberian English the only African variety the colonial input to which clearly descended from American English.

This, added to the fact that Liberia, before the recent wars that have caused massive displacements of population, had not had many contacts with the other West Africans, has given rise to a cluster of Liberian

Englishes which are very distinct, especially with regard to their phonological features. These features include some American English, and other typically Liberian ones like the following: realization of the LOT vowel as /ɑ, a/ as in [pat, gad] *pot, God*; raising of the TRAP vowel to DRESS as in [hɛnd, mɛn] *hand, man*; realization of the *happY* vowel as /ɛ/ as in [bebɛ, hɛvɛ] *baby, heavy*; monophthongization of the PRICE vowel in some words to /ɛ/ as in [lɛk, tɛm] *like, time*, **and in others to /a/ as in [fan, nan]** *fine, nine*; monophthongization of the MOUTH vowel sometimes to /ɔ/ as in [tɔn, abɔt] *town, about*; **realization of the *lettER* and *commA* vowels as /ɔ/ as in [famɔ, tugɛdɔ]** *farmer, together*; [labiriɔ, afrikɔ] *Liberia, Africa*; occurrence of intervocalic flap /ɾ/ [waɾɔ, paɾɔ] *water, potter*; deletion of /t/ between /n/ and a following vowel as in [twɛnɛ, nani] *twenty, ninety*; deletion of post-vocalic consonants as in [fu, wa, tʃa] *foot/food, wash, child* (literature on Liberian English, where such data can be found, includes Singler (1981, 1997, 2005)).

Although The Gambia shares with Sierra Leone a common historical resettlement of the Krio community, its own story within the Krio Connection and the Gambia–Sierra Leone connection is different. The difference stems mainly from the fact that only a small Krio community settled there, and exerted less influence on the country than in Sierra Leone. According to recent findings (e.g. from field work by Lothar Peter and Hans-Georg Wolf reported in Wolf, 2001: 35; Peter *et al.*, 2003; Juffermans, 2006), which differ from earlier claims (e.g. Crystal, 1995: 102 reported by Wolf, 2001: 35), the lingua franca which competes with English in The Gambia is not Aku (the Gambian name for Krio), but Mandingo; in Juffermans' (2006: 34) study, Aku comes far down the list, after English and Arabic, and Mandingo, Wolof, Fula, Jola, Serahule, Mandjago and Serer.

Gambian English does not seem influenced as much by Aku as it is influenced by Mandingo. The main phonological features of this variety of English, many induced by Mandingo, include the confusion between /p, b, f, v, β/ (e.g. [pita, kasafa, sɛβən] *bitter, cassava, seven*) and, even more characteristically, the replacement of Received Pronunciation (RP) /Σ/ by /s/; for example, [sip, sɔp, sus] *ship, shop, shoes*.

About 10% of Sierra Leoneans are first language speakers of Krio and 90% are second language speakers. Because of the influence of the Krio settlers, the Krio language has become overwhelmingly the lingua franca of Sierra Leone and the Krio culture permeates every aspect of Sierra Leonean life. Examples of Krio features in Sierra Leonean English include phonological features like /h/ deletion, for example, *'ammer, 'andsome, 'orrible* (hammer, handsome, horrible) or corresponding hypercorrect /h/ insertion, as in *[h]eat, [h]also, [h]element*; and occurrence of uvular [R] for RP post-vocalic /r/; for example, *[R]iver, p[R]ide, t[R]avel.*

Many authors (e.g. Nelson & Todd, 1992: 440) report Ghana to have had the longest and most intimate (in both the literal and figurative meanings) contacts with English-speaking expatriates over the years. There were already many mulattoes on the present-day Ghanaian coast in the early years of the 16th centuries. There were also a sizable number of Ghanaians overseas in the 16th century. And many schools were built at that period for mulattoes and middle-class Ghanaians. For a more detailed documentation of the early history of English in Ghana, see, for example, Huber (1999), Simo Bobda (2000) and Adjaye (2005).

As a result of this early, long and intimate exposure to English, Ghanaians have traditionally shown a strong attachment, and a very positive attitude, to English; they are also very proud of their English, and boast that their English pronunciation is nearer to RP than that of any West African country (Gyasi, 1991: 26). Of the three West African Pidgin English-speaking countries, Ghana has the least favourable attitude to this idiom (see, e.g. Huber, 1999; Simo Bobda, 2000).

Against this background, it is understandable why, despite a shared colonial experience with the other West African countries and a similar sociolinguistic background, Ghana has developed an accent of English quite distinct in the region. The features of this accent include the realization of the KIT vowel as /ɪ/ as in [sɪt, bɪt, lɪp] *sit, bit, lip,* contrasting with mainstream West African English [i]; the realization of the STRUT vowel as /a, ɛ/ as indicated above, as in [bat, kap, dʒɛst, stɛdɪ] *but, cup, just, study;* the possible realization of the *lettER* vowel with <er> and <or, our> as /ɛ/ as in [lɛtɛs, nɛbɛ] *letters, neighbour* (contrast mainstream West African /a/ for *letters* and [ɔ] for *neighbour,* respectively); the pronunciation of <wh> words as [hw] as in [hwai, hwɛn] *why, when* (recent descriptions of Ghanaian English, which contain these findings, include Simo Bobda (2000), Adjaye (2005) and Huber (2005)).

The main sociolinguistic specificity of Cameroon is the use of French as a co-official language to English, and its overwhelming dominance. This situation results in Cameroon English showing a heavy influence of French, notably in the register of administration and education where terms such as *concours* 'competitive exam', *mandate* 'money order' *and vignette* 'vehicle tax' are common. The many authors who have studied this phenomenon include Simo Bobda (1994), Mbangwana (1999) and Kouega (2003a, 2003b). In fact, *Franglais,* as is found in other English-French bilingual communities, is fast developing, while a more typically Cameroonian school slang called *Camfranglais,* made up of the mixture of English and French, Pidgin English and/or other local languages, has emerged. An example of *Camfranglais* taken from Kouega (2003a: 25) is: *Tu ne know pas qu'on go dans le même quat?* ('Don't you know that we are going to the same neighbourhood?')

Nigeria is a typical example of a country where the differing patterns of transplantation of English and its local ecology have yielded clearly identifiable varieties, especially at the phonological level. The division is generally in terms of the north versus south, but the south lends itself to a further breaking into the western, mainly Yoruba, region and the eastern, mainly Igbo, part. In addition to the language substratum mostly made up of Hausa and other smaller northern Niger-Congo languages, as well as the domination of Islam, the north is characterized by its late colonization, and the early transplantation of English by the British, rather than by the Krios as in the south. The western part of the Yoruba-dominated south is marked, *inter alia*, by the influence of the Krio in the spread of English, while the Igbo-dominated east is marked by the historical influence of the Irish in religion and education.

The sociolinguistics of English correlates with this division. Pidgin English is not widespread in the north, where the lingua franca is Hausa instead. But it is a dominant inter-group language in the south.

Features of the three accents of English have been described by Jibril (1982), who labels them Hausa English, Yoruba English and Igbo English. Notable descriptions of Yoruba and Igbo English accents also include Igboanusi (2006). Characteristic features of Hausa English include the realization of the NURSE vowel with <ir, ur> as /a/ (e.g. [fast, mada] *first, murder*; the *lettER* vowel with orthographic <or, our, ure> and other cases of RP /ə/ with <u> as /a/ (e.g. [tela, kanda, piktʃa, vasas, sɔgam] *tailor, candour, picture, versus, sorghum*. Yoruba English is marked by features like the following: replacement of RP /tʃ/ by /ʃ/ as in [ʃɔʃ, kaʃ, tiʃa, lɔnʃ] *church, catch, teacher, lunch*; replacement of //v/ by /f/ as *fanguard, fanilla, efaluation* 'vanguard, vanilla, evaluation'; replacement of /z/ by /s/ as in *sip, sinc, soo* 'zip, zinc, zoo'; /h/ deletion as in *and, ungry, eat* 'hand, hungry, heat'; replacement of /ʒ/ by /j/ as in *mea[j]ure, plea[j]ure*; nasalization of pre-nasal vowels as [pɛ̃n, mãn, mɔdãn] 'pen, man, modern' (Igboanusi, 2006: 494). According to Igboanusi (2006: 494), one of the main diagnostic features of Igbo English is the confusion between /l/ and /r/ as in *ranguage, pray, crass* 'language, play, class' on the one hand, and *liver, lubber, yerrow* 'river, rubber, yellow' on the other.

It should be noted that recent or ongoing movements of population are breaking the homogeneity of the entities identified in the foregoing analyses. War has been the main cause of such movements. Tens of thousands of people have left their countries of origin and settled in other countries, for long and sometimes permanent settlement. Omoniyi (2006: 180) reports a United Nations High Commission for Refugees (UNHCR) source that gives the number of refugees in West Africa for 2000 as indicated in Table 8.1.

**Table 8.1** Refugees by donor and receiving nations in West and Central Africa (reported by Omoniyi, 2006: 180)

| *Refugees* | | *Asylum seekers* | *Returned refugees* | *IDPs*[a] | *Total population of concern* |
|---|---|---|---|---|---|
| Benin | 5,021 | 314 | – | – | 5,335 |
| Burkina F. | 457 | 377 | – | – | 834 |
| Cameroon | 58,288 | 5,308 | – | – | 63,596 |
| Chad | 33,455 | 1,034 | 51 | – | 34,540 |
| Gabon | 13,473 | 5,663 | – | – | 19,136 |
| Gambia | 12,120 | – | – | – | 12,120 |
| Ghana | 33,515 | 8,762 | – | – | 42,277 |
| Guinea | 182,163 | 367 | – | – | 182,530 |
| Ivory Coast | 44,749 | 1,142 | – | 100,000 | 145,891 |
| Liberia | 64,956 | – | 21,901 | 304,115 | 390,972 |
| Mauritania | 405 | 12 | – | 29,917[b] | 29,917 |
| Niger | 296 | 44 | – | – | 340 |
| Nigeria | 7,355 | 30 | 114 | – | 7,499 |
| Senegal | 20,711 | 1,928 | 15 | – | 22,654 |
| Sierra L. | 63,494 | 277 | 75,978 | – | 139,749 |
| Togo | 12,294 | 123 | – | – | 12,417 |

[a] Internally displaced people.
[b] 29,500 of these are Malians and Saharawis.

The refugees take along their languages and their language varieties, changing the sociolinguistic and linguistic picture of the recipient communities. They are also affected by the languages and language varieties of their new communities. As Omoniyi (2006: 180) rightly notes, of particular interest are the movements across the traditional Francophone/Anglophone divides such as Liberia/Ivory Coast, Liberia/Guinea, Sierra Leone/Guinea and Nigeria/Cameroon. The huge numbers of refugees across these divides from UNHCR statistics are shown in Table 8.2.

**Table 8.2** Refugees in West Africa across Anglophone/Francophone divides (reported by Omoniyi, 2006: 180)

| Donor | Refugee numbers and receiving nations | | | | | | | |
|---|---|---|---|---|---|---|---|---|
| Nation | Ivory Coast | Ghana | Guinea | Liberia | Mali | Nigeria | Sierra Leone | Gambia |
| Ivory Coast | – | – | 2,188 | **19,158*** | – | – | – | – |
| Liberia | **122,846** | 8,865 | **82,792** | – | – | 1,505 | 10,771 | |
| Sierra Leone | – | 1,998 | **95,527** | 54,717 | **1,415** | 2,041 | – | 7,734 |

*Intercolonial figures are in bold type.

One can easily imagine the impact of the encounters of these different languages across the border in a generation or less.

Examples of movements not caused by wars include the settlement of Nigerians in Bakassi, an oil-rich peninsula disputed in the late 1990s by Nigeria and Cameroon, and finally recognized by the International Court of Justice of The Hague to be Cameroonian. A sizable portion of the Nigerian population, mostly fishermen, has lived there, some for decades, carrying into the Cameroonian territory features of Nigerian English. Another example of a movement of population, still in Cameroon, but much older, is the case of the Mbororo-Fulanis from the north of Nigeria who settled in the north-west only in the 20th century. According to the figures reported by Isa Jaeh (2007), they were 6636 in 1946, a number which rose to 120,000 by the end of the century. The presence of this new English-speaking population has yielded pronunciation features traditionally associated with northern Nigerian English, like /β/ or /b/

for /v/, as in [sɛβɛn, ɛlɛβɛn, baksin] *seven, eleven, vaccine* (Isa Jaeh, 2007). Phenomena like these make it impossible to assign somebody a nationality on the basis of the language or variety of language they speak, although it arguably remains possible to determine somebody's place of socialization on the basis of the person's accent or other linguistic features.

## Conclusion

Common patterns of transplantation and diffusion of English in countries of West Africa have yielded the specific sociolinguistic and linguistic characteristics that West African English has, and which are different from the other world Englishes. Sub-regional networks have in turn yielded group identities shared by some countries, which maintain in most cases specific national and sub-national specific sociolinguistic and linguistic features, the linguistic features being noticeable mostly at the phonological level. As shown in a previous study (Simo Bobda, 2003) focusing on African accents of English, the linguistic substratum is only part of the explanation for the emergence of African English varieties. This chapter has highlighted the diversity of factors leading to the specific emergence of West African Englishes, and the dynamic nature of these factors.

The chapter has thus shown, with reference to West Africa, how and why, in the process of its global spread, English acquires local identities at regional and lower levels. These local identities manifest themselves in the exclusive sociolinguistic, but mostly linguistic, features they display at each level, which make it possible to identify an English speaker from West Africa, or from sub-regional networks. Interestingly, the study has demonstrated how networks can be formed beyond immediate geographic vicinity, as indeed a wide variety of historical and other factors contribute to the ecology of each variety of English.

As a matter of fact, in this era of globalization, it can be predicted that greater population mobility will increasingly favour convergence and indistinguishability at the structural level within the West African region, at least.

## References

Adjaye, S.A. (2005) *Ghanaian English Pronunciation.* Lewston, NY: The Edwin Mellen Press.
Awonusi, V.O. (1986) Regional accents and internal variability in Nigerian English: A historical analysis. *English Studies 67,* 550–560.

Bamgbose, A. (2001) World Englishes and globalization. *World Englishes* 20 (3), 357–363.

Crystal, D. (1995) *The Cambridge Encyclopedia of the English Language.* Cambridge: Cambridge University Press.

Echu, G. and Grundstrom, A.W. (eds) (1999) *Official Bilingualism and Linguistic Communication in Cameroon.* New York: Peter Lang.

Görlach, M. (1991) English in Africa – African English? In M. Görlach (ed.) *Englishes: Studies in Varieties of English 1884–1988* (pp. 122–43). Amsterdam/ Philadelphia: John Benjamins.

Gyasi, I.K. (1991) Aspects of English in Ghana. *English Today* 26, 26–31.

Hancock, I.F. and Angogo, R. (1982) English in East Africa. In R.W. Bailey and M. Görlach (eds) *English as a World Language* (pp. 306–323). Ann Arbor: University of Michigan Press.

Harris, J. (1996) On the trace of short 'u'. *English World-Wide* 17 (1), 1–40.

Holm, J. (1989) *Pidgins and Creoles.* Vol. II: *Reference Survey.* Cambridge: Cambridge University Press.

Huber, M. (1999) *Ghanaian English in its West African Context.* Amsterdam/ Philadelphia: John Benjamins.

Huber, M. (2005) Ghanaian English: Phonology. In E.W. Schneider *et al.* (eds) *A Handbook of Varieties of English* (Vol. I) (pp. 842–865). Berlin/New York: Mouton de Gruyter.

Igboanusi, H. (2002) *A Dictionary of Nigerian Usage.* Ibadan: Enicrownfit Publishers.

Igboanusi, H. (2006) A comparative study of the pronunciation features of Igbo English and Yoruba English speakers of Nigeria. *English Studies* 87 (4), 490–497.

Isa Jaeh, A. (2007) Interference difficulties faced by the Anglophone Fulanis of the North West Province of Cameroon learning English as a second language. Unpublished postgraduate dissertation for DIPES II, Ecole Normale Supérieure, University of Yaounde I.

Jenkins, J. (2003) *World Englishes: A Resource Book for Students.* London: Routledge.

Jibril, M. (1982) Variation in Nigerian English. Unpublished PhD thesis, University of Leeds.

Juffermans, K. (2006) English and literacy practices in The Gambia: Sociolinguistic investigations in education, media and public life. Unpublished MA dissertation, Ghent University.

Kouega, J. (2003a) Camfranglais: A novel slang in Cameroon schools. *English Today* 74, 23–29.

Kouega, J. (2003b) Word formation processes in Camfranglais. *World Englishes* 22 (4), 511–538.

Kouega, J. (2006) *Aspects of Cameroon Lexical Usage.* München: Lincom Europa.

Kouega, J. (2007) *Dictionary of Cameroon English Usage.* Frankfurt: Peter Lang.

Kujore, O. (1985) *English Usage: Some Notable Nigerian Variations.* Ibadan: Evans.

Mbangwana, P. (1999) Linguistic deculturation of English usage in Cameroon. In G. Echu and A.W. Grundstrom (eds) *Official Bilingualism and Linguistic Communication in Cameroon* (pp. 87–102). New York: Peter Lang.

Mbassi-Manga, F. (1973) English in Cameroon: A study of historical contexts, patterns of usage and current trends. Unpublished PhD thesis, University of Leeds.

McArthur, T. (ed.) (1992) *The Oxford Companion to the English Language.* Oxford: Oxford University Press.

Mesthrie, R. (1998) Imagint excusations: Missionary English in the nineteenth century Cape Colony, South Africa. *World Englishes* 15 (2), 139–158.

Montgomerry, M. (1999) Eighteenth century Sierra Leone English: Another exported variety of African American English. *English World-Wide* 20, 1–34.

Mufwene, S. (2001) *The Ecology of Language Evolution*. Cambridge: Cambridge University Press.

Nelson, C.L. and Todd, L. (1992) East African English. In T. McArthur (ed.) *The Oxford Companion to the English Language* (pp. 333–334). Oxford: Oxford University Press.

Omoniyi, T. (2006) West African Englishes. In B. Kachru, Y. Kachru and C. Nelson (eds) *The Handbook of World Englishes* (pp. 172–185). Oxford: Blackwell.

O'Neil, R.J. (1991) *Missions to the British Cameroons*. London: Mission Book Service.

Peter, L., Wolf, H-G. and Simo Bobda, A. (2003) An account of distinctive phonetic and lexical features of Gambian English. *English World-Wide* 24 (1), 43–61.

Peter, L. and Wolf, H-G. (2008) Compiling an exclusive dictionary of West African English. In A. Simo Bobda (ed.) *Explorations into Language Use in Africa* (pp. 221–234). Frankfurt: Peter Lang.

Peter, L., Wolf, H-G. and Simo Bobda, A. (2003) An account of distinctive phonetic and lexical features of Gambian English. *English World-Wide* 24 (1), 43–62.

Sey, K.A. (1973) *Ghanaian English: An Exploratory Survey*. London: Macmillan.

Simo Bobda, A. (1994) Lexical Innovation Processes in Cameroon English. *World Englishes* 13 (2), 245–260.

Simo Bobda, A. (1995) The phonologies of Nigerian English and Cameroon English. In A. Bamgbose, A. Banjo and A. Thomas (eds) (1995) *New Englishes: A West African Perspective* (pp. 248–268). Ibadan: Mosuro Publishers.

Simo Bobda, A. (2000) The uniqueness of Ghanaian English pronunciation in West Africa. *Studies in the Linguistic Sciences* 30 (2), 185–198.

Simo Bobda, A. (2003) The formation of regional and national features of African English pronunciation. *English World-Wide* 24 (1), 17–42.

Simo Bobda, A. (2006) Irish presence in colonial Cameroon and its linguistic legacy. In H.C.L. Tristram (ed.) *The Celtic Englishes IV: The Interface between English and the Celtic Languages* (pp. 217–231). Potsdam: Potsdam University Press.

Singler, J.V. (1981) *An Introduction to Liberian English*. Michigan: Peace Corps/Michigan State University African Studies Center.

Singler, J.V. (1997) The configuration of Liberia's Englishes. *World Englishes* 16 (2), 205–231.

Singler, J.V. (2005) Liberian Settler English. In Schneider *et al.* (eds) *A Handbook of Varieties of English* (Vol. I) (pp. 874–884). Berlin/New York: Mouton de Gruyter.

Spencer, J. (1971) The English language in West Africa. In J. Spencer (ed.) *The English Language in West Africa* (pp. 1–34). London: Longman.

Todd, L. (1982) English in West Africa. In R.W. Bailey and M. Görlach (eds) *English as a World Language* (pp. 281–305). Ann Arbor: University of Michigan Press.

Wolf, H-G. (2001) *English in Cameroon*. Berlin: Mouton de Gruyter.

Chapter 9

# The English Language, Globalization and Latin America: Possible Lessons from the 'Outer Circle'

KANAVILLIL RAJAGOPALAN

## Introduction

In this chapter,[1] I shall be concerned with the effects of globalization and the spread of English language as the lingua franca of the globalized world. My focus will be on Latin America in general and Brazil in particular. As of now, English is, by all established criteria, still a *foreign* language in most of the countries of Latin America, but it is spreading like wildfire. This is so even in countries like Cuba which has had a difficult time in its relations with its mighty neighbor, the United States of America (Rajagopalan, 2005a, 2006). Graddol (2006) prophesies that, in 10–15 years, there will be as many as 2 billion people across the world learning English. He also predicts that, with the language spreading at this breathtaking speed, English will soon cease to be a foreign language in many of these countries. Now, what does it mean to say that English will cease to be a foreign language? It means that the language will slowly take roots in these new environments, begin to develop its own endonormative standards and start to live, in each of these environments, a life of its own. Needles to say, it will develop its own local characteristics. It will, in other words, become progressively 'nativized'. If one might hazard a guess, this process should take, in Brazil's case, anywhere between 50 and 100 years to come to fruition. Now, by no means is the process going to be uniform or homogeneous across the board.[2] This means that we need to be prepared for important changes in the way we look at problems of English language teaching worldwide. I shall conclude this chapter by arguing that the world at large may have an important

175

lesson or two to learn from the so-called Outer Circle countries in this regard.

## The Geopolitical Backdrop

'If you've just turned 60 and still consider yourself a Leftist, then you have a serious problem.' This was how Luiz Inácio 'Lula' da Silva (aged 61 at that time), Brazil's maverick President, popularly known as 'Lula', defended himself against the barrage of criticism, coming from many of his own disenchanted former supporters, that he had moved to the center of the political spectrum – or to the right-of-center. Or, as some of his most vociferous critics insist, to the very Right that he had spurned all through his meteoric rise from a low-paid metal worker to a charismatic head of state and a cynosure of all eyes on the international stage. Lula had just been returned to office for a second term after a landslide win over his principal adversary who, incidentally, had also claimed to be right-of-center.

In Brazil, as in many other countries in Latin America, the electorate nowadays are by and large wary of the extremes and the politicians, with an eye constantly on the polls, are careful not to scare away their prospective voters. At the 2007 World Social Forum at Nairobi, Kenya, Lula, an assiduous frequenter in the years past, was conspicuous by his absence. That more and more heads of state in Latin America are opting for a middle-of-the-road foreign policy might strike some as swimming against the tide, given the widely publicized fact that many countries of the Andean region have recently elected heads of state with manifestly leftist agendas. But, as recent polls on the continent showed, Lula is by far the most popular leader right across the continent, far ahead of such populist figures and firebrands as Hugo Chavez of Venezuela and Evo Morales of Bolivia, despite the spasmodic bursts of enthusiasm that these local leaders have occasioned, leading to the widespread feeling, fanned by the international media, that the continent is sliding to the Left.

An important element of Lula's political profile – one that especially endeared him to the public at large, avid for a major change in the way the country had been run until then by a select coterie of politicians widely suspected of representing the interests of only the rich – was the fact that *he spoke no English*, in fact no language other than his own native Portuguese and that too in ways that often scandalized nitpicky grammarians. In fact, he has long made a fine art of cashing in on his working-class Portuguese, claiming thereby to represent the person-in-the-street. This puts him in stark opposition to his immediate predecessor Fernando Henrique Cardoso, sociologist and professor emeritus of a leading Brazilian university, who spoke fluent English, French and Spanish besides Portuguese.

Cardoso was perceived as a world citizen, more interested in rubbing shoulders with his peers around the world and an apologist for the new world order ushered in by globalization. In Lula's case, his unscripted public pronouncements are a source of constant embarrassment for the diplomats who accompany him on trips overseas. However, unlike, say, the much-talked-of 'Bushisms' that made their eponym a laughing stock, Lula's verbal gaffes and rhetorical blunders only helped him be perceived as 'one of us' by the Brazilian electorate at large who readily approved of his 'rustic' and uncouth style, not in the least bothered about 'bourgeois' mannerisms and rules of etiquette.

The truth of the matter is that in Latin America – as indeed in many other parts of the world – being a Leftist is today often equated with being anti-US. Recalling the famous remark by historian H.C. Allen to the effect that men change their ideas to suit the circumstances, Brazilian political commentator and columnist Demétrio Magnoli (2004) wrote in his weekly column:

> The new set of circumstances brought about by the fall of the Berlin wall and the USSR instantly echoed in the diverse currents within the Left. Their 'Marxism' (the scare-quotes are absolutely necessary here) quickly adapted itself to the setback and recycled itself as vulgar anti-[north-] Americanism: the U.S.A. (the Empire) now assumed the place formerly occupied by Capitalism.

And sure enough, the public at large, including celebrities not particularly renowned for their political acumen, were quick to grab the headlines by wholeheartedly embracing the new trend. The Argentine football player and national celebrity Diego Maradona is reported to have told a journalist, avid for a scoop: 'Lula! Lula! I'm Chavez, Fidel Castro and Lula. We, who are Chavez, are anti-American. Anti-American.'

On closer inspection, it turns out that it is the ongoing trend of globalization that is the favorite target of the fury of the intelligentsia who rightly or wrongly see it as old capitalism in new bottle. Understandably (which is not saying the same thing as justifiably), more and more of these intellectuals have taken up blatantly nationalist – often aggressively chauvinist – agendas (Rajagopalan, 2003a). As Ollanta Humala, leader of the Peruvian Nationalist Party (PNP) and runner-up in the race for Peru's presidency in 2006 (ironically enough, both Chaves and

Morales explicitly – and in a brazenly meddlesome manner – declared their preference for him), put it:

> My nationalism is a march against globalization, which snuffs out national interests and both the Right, and the Left have a place in it. We are not separated by ideology [on this issue]. (cited in Magnoli, 2006)

## Globalization and the Role of English

'Globalization' has been a buzzword for quite some time now but it remains the case that there is very little agreement among laypeople – or, for that matter, scholars trying to get to grips with this phenomenon – as to what it is really all about. Many people see it as a writing on the wall saying that, from now on, it is going to be a new ball game altogether. It is going to be the old dream of laissez-faire come true at last! International trade is going to be practiced on a level playing field. And, furthermore, that playing field is shrinking fast, so that what is happening in one corner of the world will soon impact life on another, in fact on every other part. But, the skeptics insist, on *whose* turf are we being asked to play the new ball-game?

If there is agreement on one thing in relation to the much-talked-about but as-yet-little-understood phenomenon of globalization, principally among the intelligentsia in Latin America, it is that, having been spawned in the northern hemisphere, it just can't be a good thing for the rest of the world. What is sauce for the goose may well be sauce for the gander, but not so for the lowlier ducks and drakes.

In fact, conspiracy theories of all sorts find a fertile breeding ground in many of these countries – theories that conjure up a very carefully laid-out Machiavellian scheme designed to lure the unsuspecting poor nations of the world into the snare of worldwide corporate capitalism. Hardt and Neri's bestseller *Empire* (Hardt & Neri, 2000) had a telling effect on millions of readers in Latin America. Its instant success could be attributed to its seeming to confirm what the people at large felt they 'already knew'. Terms like 'MacDonaldization' and 'Coca-colonization' that have been floated around are self-explanatory in some sense and drive home the point that the developing world will soon be easy prey for corporate (North) America and their cohorts in Western Europe. The following news report that appeared in December 2006 under the heading 'Argentina's tango with globalization' on Salon.com makes no secret of the desire on the part of some of the emerging economies to outwit the economically powerful to survive in this globalized world:

'The continuation of strong economic growth in Argentina,' says economist Dean Baker, 'is one of the five most important economic news stories of 2006.' The reason: Argentina defaulted on billions of dollars of international debt in 2001, and then despite harsh entreaties from the International Monetary Fund, agreed to pay only 30 cents on the dollar to its creditors in 2003. But since then, despite numerous warnings from A-list economists predicting that Argentina's self-imposed 'exile' from the global economy would lead to imminent doom, Argentina has done quite nicely, thank you very much. Right now, along with Venezuela, it is one of the fastest growing economies in Latin America. (Downloaded on 14 December 2006 at http://www.salon.com/tech/htww/2006/12/13/argentina/index.html)

The untold moral of the story, namely, 'It pays to be smart and play tough with your creditors,' is played down later on with the warning that the country's creditworthiness may be negatively affected in the long run.

It is not all that difficult to see how the English language figures in all this. After all, it is no secret that English is caught up in the geopolitics currently playing out around the world (Rajagopalan, 2003a, 2003b, 2005d). Commenting on Thomas Friedman's best-seller *The World Is Flat: A Brief History of the Twenty First Century* (Friedman, 2005), Brazilian journalist Élio Gaspari wrote in his weekly column:

The world of Friedman is flat, but in it a working knowledge of English is a mountain-range of obstacles. Since English is hardly likely to be replaced by Portuguese, there is precious little one can do about it. (Gaspari, 2005)

Gaspari's remark is very much to the point: there is a general feeling right across the country that knowledge of English is going to be absolutely vital (along with access to information technology) in the rat race for a competitive edge that has resulted from the progressive dismantling of trade barriers. Gaspari's advice to his readers is: since you and I cannot do anything about the advance of English into our daily lives, the best thing to do is to grin and bear it. But, in what may appear to many to be a blatantly ambivalent attitude (Rajagopalan, 2002, 2003b, 2005a, 2005b, 2006; Rajagopalan & Rajagopalan, 2005), there are also those who are alarmed by the advance of English and the threat they think this poses to the local language (Portuguese) and culture. As for globalization, recent publications such as *Flat World, Big Gaps* (Sundaram & Baudot, 2007) have only stoked up lingering suspicions.

It is interesting to note that some of the most passionate and vociferous calls for resistance to English include an outright ban on the use of the language in all but a handful of very specific domains. In 1999, a congressman in Brazil by name Aldo Rebelo attempted just that when he presented a bill prohibiting the use of English (Rajagopalan, 2002, 2005c). The underlying logic would seem to be: if Argentina can get away with debt default, and force the richer nations to concede exceptional loan repayment conditions, why can't one use a similar strategy in dealing with the advance of English? In other words, have no trucks with the language of the Empire and see what happens. Maybe, despite Gaspari's apprehensions and despair, the powerful may succumb and speak to us in 'our language'. Wouldn't that be great, them speaking *our* language for a change! In the next section, I shall point out a number of reasons why I think such an attitude is ineffective (not to say, quixotic) and, in the final analysis, suicidal.

## Dealing with English: Why Simply Shutting the Doors Is Not an Option

### The thesis of linguistic imperialism

In the wake of Phillipson's trail-blazing work titled *Linguistic Imperialism* (Phillipson, 1992), there was a much-needed and long overdue awakening worldwide of the English as a foreign language (EFL) enterprise, which had over the years become unmindful of its own soft ideological underbelly and impervious to charges of aiding and abetting the hegemonic pretensions of the Empire. Pennycook's *The Cultural Politics of English as an International Language* (Pennycook, 1994) and *English and the Discourses of Colonialism* (Pennycook, 1998) further brought the stark reality of the world of EFL to public gaze and scrutiny.

But it is probably true to say that the whole idea of linguistic imperialism also caused a tremendous amount of scare-mongering in countries across the world, especially the ones on the periphery, where, as already noted, conspiracy theories tend to find fertile breeding ground. The idea of 'linguistic genocide' (Skuttnab-Kangas, 2000) raised that alarm to feverish pitches. But many concerned intellectuals also went on to register that most teachers of English were unaware of the ideological dimensions of the EFL enterprise, despite all the efforts by a handful of scholars to expose them to public scrutiny. In Brazil, Moita Lopes (1996) and Cox and de Assis-Peterson (2001) lamented that most teachers of EFL went about their business in complete unconcern with the ideological dimensions of their trade, thus proving beyond any doubt their own state of alienation and, in the ultimate analysis, complicity. The following words of de Assis-Peterson and Cox (1999: 433) speak volumes for the state of affairs:

> Considering that critical pedagogy has its roots in the work of Brazilian educator Paulo Freire, we investigated what 40 Brazilian English teachers know about/think of critical pedagogy in ELT. Our findings showed that they are unaware of it. Attached to the strong appeal of a dominant integrative discourse, English teachers see themselves as agents of good in that they prepared students to be successful in the world.

Now, it is incontestable that Phillipson, Pennycook and others did a valuable service by showing the world the dark side of the English language teaching enterprise. The ELT community was rudely awakened from the state of stupor resulting from conformity and acritical acquiescence in the order of things and forced to review its past practices.

## Objections to Phillipson's thesis

However, there were also voices of dissent. Speaking from a Marxist standpoint, Holborow (1999) took Phillipson to task for failing to perceive that his own solution to the problem that he had identified was ideologically suspect in that it bolstered the classic right-wing agenda of promoting nationalism as an antidote to foreign influences, now paraded as imperialism. In other words, Phillipson was on the right track when he denounced the imperialist agenda behind the spread of English. But his exaggerated Marxist fervor blinded him to the fact that his own solution was contrary to the very spirit of Marxism and in advocating it he unwittingly played into the hands of the very ideological forces he was seeking to counter.

In earlier work (Rajagopalan, 1999a, 1999b), I questioned the logic of linguistic imperialism on the grounds that the very thesis that Phillipson advances is caught up in an argumentative vein typical of the imperialistic attitude. In other words, despite all its initial attractiveness, the logic of imperialism presents a most depressing portrait of erstwhile colonial subjects (like the present writer), reduced to the status of the hapless flies as described by the Earl of Gloucester in Shakespeare's *King Lear* when he says,

As flies to wanton boys are we to th' gods.
They kill us for their sport.

The colonial subject is denied agency and the power to react, to resist. In his ground-breaking work *Resisting Linguistic Imperialism in English Teaching*, Canagarajah (1999) showed how wrong Phillipson was in this regard. John E. Joseph (2006: 52–53) nicely sums up this argument in the following words:

> But [many] scholars from the Periphery have lined up to reject Phillipson's model – which after all depicts them as suffering from a false consciousness at best, and at worst as traitors to their own cultures – or at least propose amending the model in ways that still cut the legs from under it. In the views of Bisong (1995), Makoni (1995) and Rajagopalan (1999a, b), the ongoing existence of linguistic imperialism is a myth, an invidious myth that embodies a kind of imperialism every bit as bad as the one it purports to critique. Phillipson's notion that people in the third-world countries are the objects of hegemonic choices that make it impossible for them to exercise any free choice, though intended 'for their good', is patronizing in the extreme.

But the fact remains that Phillipson's diatribes against the hegemonic role of the English language have inspired a number of people in Brazil and the rest of South America, where the English language is viewed by many as the unmistakable symptom of Uncle Sam's formidable influence on the countries to the south (Rajagopalan, 2001a, 2002, 2003a, 2003b, 2005a, 2005b, 2005c, 2006). And they continue to attract more and more sympathizers.

Perhaps the roots of such an attitude should be traced to the history of language policy and language planning in Latin America in general.

## The history of language policy (or lack thereof) in Latin America

In an article titled 'Portuguese and Brazilian efforts to spread Portuguese', Silva and Gunnewiek (1992) stated that

> In Brazil the thought seems to prevail that a language policy has to be first and foremost a policy directed toward the preservation and consolidation of the language as a medium of culture. This concern is clearly restricted to the national level, which in a certain sense will force the postponement of any more direct preoccupation with language policy abroad.

That situation has changed considerably since that paper was written. Teaching Portuguese as a foreign language has gained a lot of attention in recent years. In fact, the whole idea of spreading the language has become a matter of national pride, as evidenced by the reaction from the academic community in Brazil to a recent decision by the University of Cambridge, UK, to close down their Department of Portuguese as part of their budget-trimming drive. An irate commentator sent an impassioned plea to her colleagues on the internet to invest more and more in the propagation of our 'marvelous language' instead of trying to curb foreign influences.

What does not seem to have undergone any significant change over the years is the attitude toward foreign languages. Foreign language is by and large regarded with either distrust or unconcern and 'a policy directed toward the preservation and consolidation of the [Portuguese] language as a medium of culture' seems to underwrite most of the language planning, whether overt or covert. Maria Antonieta Alba Celani, one of Brazil's leading applied linguists and a pioneering figure in ELT, wrote as early as in 1984:

> The (recent) educational reform, after having identified the democratisation of education as its main objective, paradoxically created an extremely elitist state of affairs when it rendered the possibility of learning foreign languages, with reasonable chances of success, unavailable to all but a handful. (1984: 32)

In other words, if there is a single thread running through successive governments and policies relating to language, it is one of serving a nationalistic agenda. In her book *Colonização Lingüística* [Linguistic Colonization], Bethania Mariani argues that language policies were enacted, right from the beginning, in response to the exigencies of the wider project of nation-building:

> The case of the Portuguese language vis-à-vis the indigenous languages was that of the imposition of language of the conqueror, a language which, thanks to its ties to the Portuguese nation, was believed to act as an imaginary link that would pave the way for an 'understanding' between the Crown and the subjects [. . .] (Mariani, 2004: 96)

Or, in the words of Oliveira (2001: 127),

> The Portuguese State and, after independence, the Brazilian State, had as their policy, throughout history, the project of imposing Portuguese

as the only legitimate language, considering it 'the handmaid of the empire'.

*Rejection of English as a form of rejecting linguistic imperialism*

Theories of language policy and language planning are primarily about politics. They address language issues in order to serve political exigencies of specific historical moments. Brazil has a long history of looking to its neighboring countries to formulate its own language policies (Rajagopalan, 2008). Even essentially nationalistic agendas such as the promotion of Portuguese as the country's only language against the interests of the hundreds of indigenous languages (that were smothered in the process – a process that went on until the newly revised Constitution of 1988 guaranteed them their right to exist – Oliveira, 2001) were promoted by way of emulating practices in the neighboring countries. The idea of claiming a distinct linguistic status for the national language as distinct from the language of the metropolis was in the main inspired by examples from the outside – in this case, by Noah Webster and his successful call for the linguistic independence of the United States.[3]

With regard to the spread of English, too, *paradoxically* enough, the United States plays an important role in shaping the reaction of many people in Brazil and elsewhere on the continent. The desire to keep the country rigorously monolingual is very much in line with the thesis promoted by movements such as 'English only' in the United States. In other words, here we need to distinguish between the United States as a role model and the United States as an elder brother (at once protective and domineering). Latin Americans reject the latter even as they enthusiastically embrace the former.

This rather schizophrenic attitude toward the United States may help explain the ambivalence in the attitude of many Latin Americans toward the English language. Brazil is no exception to the rule. On the one hand, the people admire the way the United States has over the years striven to declare their linguistic independence and try to model their own attitude to Brazilian Portuguese. The following claim by Manuel Bandeira (1886–1968), a leading literary figure, attests to this: 'The language is Brazilian for the simple reason that it is the language of the country' (cited in Pinto, 1981: xiv). On the other hand, the same people also distrust the United States, looking askance at the pretensions of 'the Big Brother' vis-à-vis its neighbors to the south. This easily translates into a rejection of English, or in some cases, a rejection of English with an American accent. A series of reports called 'Landmark reviews' on the status of English in the different countries of South America, commissioned by the British Council, contained several snippets such as the following:

English is the preferred second language of Uruguayans. Within English, the British variety is preferred to the American.

The American English language schools with their resources and materials from the USA dominate the market [in Chile]. However, British English generally holds greater prestige amongst EFL students.

No doubt, these observations were made with a view to orienting the interests of marketing the British variety of English and there is no doubt that the British Council has been clever enough to exploit a general preference for European cultural products noticeable among the upper and middle classes in many Latin American countries. But there can be no doubt either that, with regard to the different varieties of English, the long-standing distrust of the United States ends up playing into the hands of institutions promoting British English.

The most convincing evidence for this is the number of private language institutes that offer courses in English and make a point of trumpeting in their advertisements that the variety of English they promote is British or English. Institutes like 'Cultura Inglesa' and 'Centro Britânico' tout their 'Englishness' or 'Britishness' as a special selling point. A television campaign run by the former recently emphasized that it is not just the language they teach but *culture* as well. All this might seem somewhat odd, given that in Britain itself they have been struggling hard to come to a proper understanding of just what constitutes 'Britishness'.

## English in Latin America: Possible Lessons from the 'Outer Circle'

### Language and the question of culture

As must be clear from the last paragraph above, the idea that languages are indissociably tied to specific cultures is very much part of popular imagination. It is one of the leftovers of the mindset typical of the 19th century. And many theories about language have also incorporated the idea. But the usefulness of this idea, especially in relation to languages like English that have long ceased to be the monopoly of their original 'native speakers', has increasingly been questioned by a number of researchers, including the present writer. In Rajagopalan (2004: 111), I argued that 'World English (WE)[4] belongs to everybody who speaks it, but it is nobody's mother tongue.' And, furthermore,

WE is a linguistic phenomenon that is altogether *sui generis*. It defies our time-honoured view of language which is structured around the unargued assumption that every natural language is typically spoken by a community of native speakers, and exceptionally, or marginally (that is to say, from a theoretical point of view, in a none-too-interesting sense) by a group of non-natives.

Now, many of our EFL/ESL practices are based on the wrong assumption that those who learn English in these contexts do so 'in order to be able to communicate with the so-called native speakers of English' – 'to be able to order a pint of beer in a London pub or hail a taxi on the southern end of Manhattan'. More recently, Jenkins (2006: 137) made the same point when she wrote that '[...] English is still taught as though the primary aim of learners is to be able to communicate with its native speakers and with the assumption that correct English is either Standard British or Standard American English.'

In fact, this was the unstated claim that led Ellis (1996) to doubt the appropriateness of the communicative language teaching (CLT) in contexts such as Asia and Africa. Ellis' thesis was that, if the English language is treated as a product of, say, the English culture, its introduction in alien settings will be tantamount to cultural domination or, at the very least, brazen interference, and, insofar as CLT relies heavily on the cultural context of given languages, it must face the charge of promoting culture under the pretext of teaching language (see also, Collins, 1999).

As a matter of fact, CLT has been critiqued from a number of angles. While Ellis and others disapprove of its overemphasis on English culture, Bax (2003) complains that it pays insufficient attention to the cultural contexts where teaching/learning often takes place. Others such as Swan (1985a, 1985b) have objected to it, among things, on formal grounds and for reasons of practicability.

What has escaped the attention of many of these critics is that there is no such thing as a single culture backing up what I prefer to call 'World English' (Rajagopalan, 2004). The simple reason for this is that World English has no native speakers. Or, as McArthur (2002) has forcefully argued, it has no center, no mooring. It is not, in other words, tethered to any specific culture. Not that it is culturally neutral or that it knows no culture. Rather, it is multicultural in its very essence. Once again, not an amalgam of cultures, where different and disparate cultures co-exist peacefully, but an arena where different cultures are engaged in a constant tug-of-war (Rajagopalan, 2001b, 2007).

In retrospect, it seems to be fairly easy and straightforward to conclude that CLT was a last-ditch effort on the part of certain sectors of the ELT enterprise worldwide to safeguard their vested interests. These interests were safe and secure so long as the myth of the native speaker persisted. Once the native-speaker-centered approach to ESL/EFL teaching was called into question, there was apprehension that the whole enterprise would spin out of control. The issues of authenticity and cultural-rootedness – essential ingredients of CLT – were raised in order to reinstate the native, only this time through the back door.

In Rajagopalan (2003a), I argued that the notion of communicative competence – the mainstay of CLT – was likewise hijacked to mean just good old linguistic competence (monopoly of the native), duly 'enriched' and refurbished in order to recover the centrality of the native – in spite of the fact that Hymes (1972) himself, in his original formulation of the concept, had meant it to be in opposition to the center-piece of the Chomskyan paradigm rather than a simple additive or afterthought. This clearly brings out the allure of what I have elsewhere called 'the apotheosis of the native speaker' (Rajagopalan, 1997: 229), especially if one bears in mind that this has enormous implications for the billion-dollar ELT industry worldwide.

Krishnaswamy and Burde (2004: 74–77) have persuasively argued that the concept of the native speaker is fundamentally a brainchild of European psyche and definitely alien to non-European cultures. As Wright (2004: 42) says,

> The history of the politics of nation state reveals how the conscious promotion of language convergence was part of the development of the nation state. The national language takes on a number of important roles in the nation building process.

Krishnaswamy and Burde contrast the European psyche that conjured up nation-states, national languages and native speakers with the reality of Africa and Asia, where multilingualism is the norm. 'Native-speakerhood' is often a matter of *choice*, since all-too-frequently several candidates to the status of 'mother-tongue' are readily available. The following case reported by Mallikarjun (2001) clearly illustrates the linguistic reality of many of the countries in Africa and Asia.

> On March 7, 2001, H.Y.Sharada Prasad [...] wrote in his column, 'All in All,' in *The Asian Age* about a census enumerator who visited his house. His wife 'told him that her mother tongue was Telugu and mine was Kannada but that our children had only a mother but no mother-tongue, having been born in Delhi and gone to school here without any opportunities to study either of the parents' language. His (the census enumerator's) response was that since they must be speaking

Hindi, that would be deemed to be their mother tongue'. This story is not new. Most Indians who earn their livelihood outside their own linguistic province face this problem every ten years.

The idea of 'multicompetence' (Cook, 1992, 1995) does recognize the phenomenon, but it is beset with problems of its own, some of which have been brought out by Hall *et al.* (2006). But I think there is a more fundamental flaw in many attempts to get to grips with the complexities of multilingual reality. It is that such theoretical constructs as 'multicompetence' are still concerned with the individual speaker and his/her knowledge of more than one language. As it happens, societal multilingualism plays by different rules. For one thing, it simply cannot be equated with a number of multilingual speakers cohabiting the same physical space. In a multilingual society, speakers do not necessarily have comparable competencies in the different languages that make up their multilingual repertoire. The following observation made by John Joseph (2006: 145) apropos of the so-called New English(es) may be extended to *all* the languages that partake of societal multilingualism:

> The linguist who rushes in to systematize a New English prematurely runs a serious risk of misrepresenting as fixed what is actually still quite fluid.

What distinguishes societal multilingualism is the fact that the different languages of which it is comprised form a complex mosaic where the choice of language is not haphazard, but mostly rule-governed. The communicative competence – if you want to insist on using the term – of a societal multilingual includes knowledge of which language to use and when, as well as knowledge of what social codes one is breaking when one practices code-switching in ways not sanctioned by the social mores.

## The Outer Circle Model

In many countries that belong to the so-called Outer Circle, English is used in linguistic environments that are societally multilingual in the sense thumbnailed above. This is true of India. It is true of South Africa (Kamwangamalu, 2006), Singapore (Lourdes *et al.*, 2006) and Nigeria (Bisong, 1995; Omoniyi, 2006) – to name just a handful of examples. Particularly interesting in this context is Modiano's (2006) notion on 'Euro-English'. With the formation of the European Union and the abolition of most traditional barriers among the nations that make up the Euro-zone, the entire continent has come to acquire the characteristics of a multilingual nation where, in Modiano's words (2006: 223), 'English is gaining ground at the expense of all other European languages, continues to lay claim to an increasing number of domains, and is considered by many to be a threat to minority languages and cultures.' In this sense, Euro-English can be seen as showcasing what has been a growing trend elsewhere in the world. In all these contexts, it is important to bear in mind that English is part of a multilingual mix. In the example cited by Mallikarjun (2001), the language that is not mentioned is English. But, as anyone with a nodding acquaintance with the linguistic reality of India, especially with that of a metropolitan city like New Delhi, knows, English is one language effectively used by the parents and their two children as part and parcel of their multilingual repertoire, with each one of them having a different command of and ease with the language. In such contexts, the question to ask is not how well they know each of these languages. It is much more worthwhile to wonder how the society as a whole (as well as different sub-groups thereof) stage-manages its collective stock of languages and to what end.

One consequence of English, originally a foreign language in India, finding its way into a societally multilingual reality is that it immediately loses its 'foreign' status. In due course, it develops (as it already has) a distinctive local flavor and coloring. The result is it becomes a local language like any other. This is how the outer circle varieties of English developed in the first place. According to Graddol (1997), this process of what one might call 'deforeignization' is already under way in Argentina, described by Friedrich (2003: 178) as 'probably the "most British" of Latin American countries'.

In the absence of studies specifically aimed at monitoring this process whereby countries from the expanding circle slide into the outer circle (with the exception of some interesting preliminary studies, mostly restricted to Singapore and a few other cases), one can only make some educated guesses at how the change may come about. It seems reasonable to speculate that the changes would begin at the phonological and lexical levels. That is to say, certain phonological characteristics and peculiarities of the 'foreign' language become consolidated as the defining features of the 'second language'. At the lexical level, 'foreign' words are incorporated intact or with slight phonological modifications to the vocabulary of the second language. An excellent example of this is the use of the English word *point* to refer to a meeting point or a rendezvous in Brazil. The word *outdoor* has been transformed into a substantive and is today used to mean a billboard ('hoarding' in the UK).

The key point about such gestures of nativization (the final stage of a process that began with deforeignization) is that people who use the neologisms regularly find it hard to believe that such uses are inexistent in the donor languages. The best example of this was given to me by an English friend of mine who visited India a few years ago. When he was in Mumbai, he was curious about an old friend of his, of whom he only had an old address on a tattered piece of paper. Having decided to take his chance, he took a taxi and found his way to the apartment building and asked the janitor about his friend. Dumbfounded by the reply 'Oh, he's out of station,'[5] my friend asked if the janitor could be more specific and tell him which station he had in mind. 'Don't you speak English?' was the answer he received from the incredulous janitor.

Needless to say, considerations such as the ones made in the foregoing paragraphs have important implications. As Canagarajah (1999) has convincingly argued, so-called native competence is of no use whatever to people going about their work-a-day lives in such settings. Rather, people in those circumstances need to mold the language to their specific needs and lived reality.

Khushwant Singh, a doyen of Indian journalism, expressed the underlying sentiment in the following words:

> I am entirely in favour of making English an Indian language on our terms. Maul it, misuse it, mangle it out of shape but make it our own *bhasha*. The English may not recognise it as their language; they can stew in their own juice. It is not their *baap ki jaidaad* — ancestral property. (Singh, 2001)

This, I think, is what is in store for people in the 'expanding circle' which is where Brazil currently belongs. It is just a matter of time before people decide to 'maul it, misuse it and mangle it out of shape but make it their own *idioma*'.[6] One thing is for sure: many of the countries that today belong to the expanding circle are going through a process that is comparable to the one that made the outer circle countries what they are. In fact, the difference between the two types of countries may have to do only or primarily with the number of years they have been in contact with the language. This was brought out by the editors of *The Handbook of World Englishes* (Kachru *et al.*, 2006) when they signaled the worldwide spread of English in terms of four successive diasporas: the first diaspora covering Wales, Ireland and Scotland, the second covering North America (i.e. the United States and parts of Canada) as well as Australia and New Zealand and finally the third and the fourth extending to South Asia, East Asia,

Southeast Asia, South America, South Africa, West Africa, East Africa, the Caribbean island and Europe (of course bearing in mind the differences between countries that were, until not very long ago, colonies of Great Britain and the ones that were not). This means that we may soon need to rethink the very terms 'inner', 'outer' and 'expanding' as adequately explaining the status of World English in countries across the world. In his review of the volume, Todd (2008) says that '[t]he metaphor of "diaspora" is both valid and helpful' but goes on to observe that

> The sections on the third and fourth diasporas have 'Englishes' rather than 'English' in the title of each of the chapters and, in this way, the range and diversity of coverage are clearly indicated. Of course, one might ask if there is any country, including Australia, New Zealand and the British Isles, where 'Englishes' would not be the more appropriate designation. (Todd, 2008: 251)

What Todd is alluding to is the utter impossibility of distinguishing between the different realities attested in each of these countries in any cut-and-dried terms. Rather, one must admit that the situation is fluid and volatile, and destined to remain so for many more years to come. If I am right about this, then it is from the outer-circle countries that the countries that belong to the expanding circle today may have a lesson or two to learn.

## Notes

1. I am grateful to the CNPQ, a funding agency under Brazil's Ministry of Science and Technology, for financing my research (Process no. 304557/2006-4).
2. To be sure, the situation varies enormously from one country to another. If one is to go by the attitude of the people towards English, this process of 'nativization' will be more rapid in Argentina (Friedrich, 2003) than, say, Columbia (Velez-Rendon, 2003) or Ecuador (Alm, 2003).
3. The movement for declaring Brazil's linguistic independence from Portugal reached its apex in 1922 when a conference called 'Primeiro Congresso da Língua Nacional Cantada' was held in the city of São Paulo. The participants discussed at length a possible new name for the language. The candidates included 'brasiliano', 'brasilina' and so forth.
4. Note that I am using the expression WE in the singular (World English), not plural (World Englishes). This is because I am interested in underscoring not what these different Englishes have about them that make them different, but what they have in common in order to serve as a common language, as a lingua franca.
5. An old-fashioned expression from Indian English, probably of colonial origin, meaning 'so-and-so is away, traveling'.
6. Portuguese word for 'language' or Khushwant Singh's 'bhasha'.

## References

Alm, C.O. (2003) English in the Ecuadorean commercial context. *World Englishes* 22 (2), 143–158.

Bax, S. (2003) The end of CLT: A context approach to language teaching. *ELT Journal* 57 (3), 278–287.

Bisong, J. (1995) Language choice and cultural imperialism: A Nigerian perspective. *ELT Journal* 49 (2), 122–132.

Canagarajah, S. (1999) *Resisting Linguistic Imperialism in English Teaching.* Oxford: Oxford University Press.

Celani, M.A.A. (1984) Uma abordagem centrada no aluno para os cursos de letra (A student-centered approach to language courses). In M.A.A. Celani (ed.) *Ensino de Línguas* (Language Teaching) (pp. 32–39). São Paulo: Educ.

Collins, S. (1999) Communicative methodology: A health warning? *Explorations in Teacher Education* 7 (1) (online).

Cook, V.J. (1992) Evidence for multicompetence. *Language Learning* 42 (4), 557–591.

Cook, V.J. (1995) Multi-competence and the learning of many languages. *Language, Culture and Curriculum* 8 (2), 93–98.

Cox, M.I.P. and de Assis-Peterson, A.A. (2001) O professor de inglês: entre alienação e a emancipação. *Linguagem e Ensino* [Language and Teaching] 4 (1), 11–36.

de Assis-Peterson, A.A. and Cox, M.I.P. (1999) Critical pedagogy in ELT: Images of Brazilian teachers of English. *TESOL Quarterly* 33 (3), 433–452.

Ellis, G. (1996) How culturally appropriate is the communicative approach? *ELT Journal* 50 (3), 213–218.

Friedman, T.L. (2005) *The World Is Flat: A Brief History of the Twenty First Century.* New York: Farrar, Straus and Giroux.

Friedrich, P. (2003) English in Argentina: Attitudes of MBA students. *World Englishes* 22 (2), 173–184.

Gaspari, E. (2005) Um livro muito bom: 'O Mundo é Plano' [A very good book: 'The World Is Flat']. *Folha de São Paulo*, 18 December.

Graddol, D. (1997) *The Future of English?* London: The British Council.

Graddol, D. (2006) *English Next: Why Global English may Mean the End of 'English as a Foreign Language'.* London: The British Council.

Hall, J.K., Cheng, A. and Carlson, M.T. (2006) Reconceptualizing multicompetence as a theory of language knowledge. *Applied Linguistics* 27 (2), 220–240.

Hardt, M. and Neri, A. (2000) *Empire.* Boston, MA: Harvard University Press.

Holborow, M. (1999) *The Politics of English: A Marxist View of Language.* London: Sage.

Hymes, D. (1972) On communicative competence. In J.B. Pride and J. Holmes (eds) *Sociolinguistics* (pp. 269–285). Harmondsworth: Penguin.

Jenkins, J. (2006) Points of view and blind spots: ELF and SLA. *International Journal of Applied Linguistics* 16 (2), 137–162.

Joseph, J.E. (2006) *Language and Politics.* Edinburgh: Edinburgh University Press.

Kachru, B., Kachru, Y. and Nelson, C. (eds) (2006) *The Handbook of World Englishes.* New York: Blackwell.

Kamwangamalu, N.M. (2006) South African Englishes. In B. Kachru, Y. Kachru and C. Nelson (eds) *The Handbook of World Englishes* (pp. 158–171). Oxford: Blackwell.

Krishnaswamy, N. and Burde, A.S. (2004) *The Politics of Indian's English* (2nd edn). Oxford: Oxford University Press.

Lourdes, M., Bautista, S. and Gonzalez, A.B. (2006) South Asian Englishes. In B. Kachru, Y. Kachru and C. Nelson (eds) *The Handbook of World Englishes* (pp. 130–144). New York: Blackwell.

Magnoli, D. (2004) A Conspiração [The conspiracy]. *Folha de São Paulo*, 16 December.

Magnoli, D. (2006) Esquerda e Direita [The Left and the Right]. *Folha de São Paulo*, 6 April.

Makoni, S. (1995) Linguistic imperialism; old wine in new bottles. *British Association of Applied Linguistics Newsletter* 50, 28–30.

Mallikarjun, B. (2001) Language according to census of India 2001. *Language in India* 1 (2). Available at http://www.languageinindia.com/april2001/indiancensus.html.

Mariani, B. (2004) *Colonização Lingüísica* [Linguistic Colonization]. Campinas: Pontes.

McArthur, T. (2002) *Oxford Guide to World English*. London: Oxford University Press.

Modiano, M. (2006) Euro-Englishes. In B. Kachru, Y. Kachru and C. Nelson (eds) *The Handbook of World Englishes* (pp. 223–239). New York: Blackwell.

Moita Lopes, Luiz Paulo da (1996) 'Yes, nós temos bananas' ou 'Paraíba não é Chicago, não': Um estudo sobre a alienação e o ensino de inglês como língua estrangeira no Brasil ['Yes, we have bananas' or 'Paraiba is not Chicago, by no means': A study of alienation and teaching of English as a foreign language in Brazil]. In: Lopes Moita, Luiz Paulo de (ed.) *Oficina de Lingüística Aplicada* [Workshop on Applied Linguistics] (pp. 37–62). Campinas, Brazil: Marcado de Letras.

Oliveira, G. Müller de (2000) Brasileiro fala português: Monolingüismo e Preconceito Lingüístico [A Brazilian speaks Portuguese: monolingualism and linguistic prejudice], http://www.ipol.org.br/

Oliveira, G. Müller de (2001) A língua entre os dentes [The tongue between the teeth]. *Jornal da Unicamp* http://www.unicamp.br/unicamp/unicamp_hoje/ju/ago2001/unihoje_tema165pag04.html (accessed on 5 January 2007).

Omoniyi, T. (2006) West African Englishes. In B. Kachru, Y. Kachru and C. Nelson (eds) *The Handbook of World Englishes* (pp. 172–187). New York: Blackwell.

Pennycook, A. (1994) *The Cultural Politics of English as an International Language*. London: Longman.

Pennycook, A. (1998) *English and the Discourses of Colonialism*. London: Routledge.

Phillipson, R. (1992) *Linguistic Imperialism*. Oxford: Oxford University Press.

Pinto, E.P. (1981) *O Português do Brasil: Textos Críticos e Literários* [Brazilian Portuguese: Critical and Literary Texts]. São Paulo: EDUSP.

Rajagopalan, K. (1997) Linguistics and the myth of nativity: Comments on the controversy over 'new/non-native' Englishes. *Journal of Pragmatics* 27, 225–231.

Rajagopalan, K. (1999a) Of EFL teachers, conscience, and cowardice. *ELT Journal* 53 (3), 200–206.

Rajagopalan, K. (1999b) A caveat or two on awareness and agency: A response to Canagarajah. *ELT Journal* 53 (3), 215–216.

Rajagopalan, K. (2001a) ELT classroom as an arena for identity clashes. In M. Grigoletto and A.M. Carmagnani (eds) *English as a Foreign Language: Identity, Practices, and Textuality* (pp. 23–29). São Paulo: Humanitas.

Rajagopalan, K. (2001b) Review of A. S. Canagarajah: Resisting linguistic imperialism in English teaching. *Word* 52 (3), 462–466.

Rajagopalan, K. (2002) National languages as flags of allegiance; or the linguistics that failed us: A close look at emergent linguistic chauvinism in Brazil. *Language & Politics* 1 (1), 115–147.

Rajagopalan, K. (2003a) The philosophy of applied linguistics. In A. Davies and C. Elder (eds) *Handbook of Applied Linguistics* (pp. 397–420). New York: Blackwell.

Rajagopalan, K. (2003b) The ambivalent role of English in Brazilian politics. *World Englishes* 22 (2), 91–101.

Rajagopalan, K. (2004) The concept of 'World English' and its implications for ELT. *ELT Journal* 58 (1), 111–117.

Rajagopalan, K. (2005a) Language politics in Latin America. *AILA Review* 18, 76–93.

Rajagopalan, K. (2005b) Non-native speaker teachers of English and their anxieties: Ingredients for an experiment in action research. In E. Llurda (ed.) *Non-Native Language Teachers: Perceptions, Challenges, and Contributions to the Profession* (pp. 283–303). Boston, MA: Springer.

Rajagopalan, K. (2005c) The language issue in Brazil: When local knowledge clashes with specialized knowledge. In S. Canagarajah (ed.) *Reclaiming the Local in Language Policy and Practice* (pp. 99–122). Mahwah, NJ: Lawrence Erlbaum.

Rajagopalan, K. (2005d) A geopolítica da lingual inglesa e seus reflexos no Brasil: Por uma política prudente e propositiva [The geopolitics of the English language in Brazil: Towards a politics of prudence and positive action]. In Y. Lacoste (ed.) *A Geopolítica do Ingles* [The Geopolitics of English] (pp. 135–159). São Paulo, Brazil: Parabola.

Rajagopalan, K. (2006) South American Englishes. In B. Kachru, Y. Kachru and C. Nelson (eds) *The Handbook of World Englishes* (pp. 145–157). Oxford: Blackwell.

Rajagopalan, K. (2007) Revisiting the nativity scene: Review article on Alan Davies' *The Native Speaker: Myth and Reality*. *Studies in Language* 31 (1), 193–205.

Rajagopalan, K. (2008) The role of geopolitics in language planning and language politics in Brazil. *Current Issues in Language Planning* 9 (2), 179–192.

Rajagopalan, K. and Rajagopalan, C. (2005) The English language in Brazil – a boon or a bane? In G. Braine (ed.) *Teaching English to the World* (pp. 1–10). Mahwah, NJ: Lawrence Erlbaum.

Silva, J.E. da and Gunnewiek, L.K. (1992) Portuguese and Brazilian efforts to spread Portuguese. *International Journal of the Sociology of Language* 95, 71–92.

Singh, K. (2001) Making English an Indian language. *The Tribune* (21 October). http://www.tribuneindia.com/2001/20011020/windows/above.htm (last accessed on 20 January 2007).

Skuttnab-Kangas, T. (2000) *Linguistic Genocide in Education – Or Worldwide Diversity and Human Rights?* Mahwah, NJ: Lawrence Erlbaum.

Sundaram, J.K. and Baudot, J. (2007) *Flat World, Big Gaps: Economic Liberalization, Globalization, Poverty and Inequality*. London: Zed Books.

Swan, M. (1985a) A critical look at the communicative approach-1. *ELT Journal* 39 (1), 2–12.

Swan, M. (1985b) A critical look at the communicative approach-2. *ELT Journal* 39 (2), 76–87.

Todd, L. (2008). Review of B.B. Kachru, Y. Kachru and C.L. Nelson (eds) *The Handbook of World Englishes*. *Journal of Linguistics* 44 (1), 248–253.

Velez-Rendon, G. (2003) English in Colombia: A sociolinguistic profile. *World Englishes* 22 (2), 185–198.

Webster, N. (1789) An essay on the necessity, advantages, and practicality of reforming the mode of spelling and of rendering the orthography of words correspondent to pronunciation. In *Dissertations on the English Language: With Notes, Historical and Critical, to Which Is Added, by Way of Appendix, an Essay on a Reformed Mode of Spelling, with Dr. Franklin's Arguments on That Subject* (pp. 391–406). Boston.

Wright, S. (2004) *Language Policy and Language Planning*. London: Palgrave Macmillan.

## Chapter 10
# Rethinking Origins and Localization in Global Englishes

ALASTAIR PENNYCOOK

## Introduction

Drawing analogies with issues of localization in hip-hop, this chapter argues that processes of localization are more complex than a notion of languages or cultures spreading and taking on local forms; rather, we have to understand ways in which they are already local. Recent debates over the inapplicability of a World Englishes (WE) framework to current conditions of globalization, or concerns that a focus on English as a Lingua Franca (ELF) presents a new form of homogenization, miss the point that what we need to react not only to new conditions of postmodernity but also to the postmodern imperative to rethink language. This suggests the need to articulate a new sense of history and location, avoiding narratives of spread, transition, development and origins, and thinking instead in terms of multiple, heterogeneous and simultaneous histories that the dominant historical narrative has overlooked. If we question the linearity at the heart of modernist narratives about language origins and spread, we can start to see that global Englishes do not have one point but rather multiple, co-present, global origins. Just as hip-hop has always been Aboriginal, so has English. Such an understanding of global Englishes radically reshapes the ways in which we can understand global and local cultural and linguistic formations, and takes us beyond the current debates between monocentric and pluricentric models of English.

## It's an Ancient Culture, with a New Name

Vulk Makedonski and Raceless of Melbourne-based hip-hop artists Curse ov Dialect suggest that the origins of hip-hop can be found in multiple cultural resources. According to Vulk Makedonski, 'hip hop is the culture of people that were oppressed at one stage, and a lot of cultures have songs about oppression in their folk tales. To me, that's hip hop. They're expressing themselves through song, through dance – which hip hop is – through graffiti, you know the old way when people used to write on rocks or whatever. That's hip hop.' Hip-hop, he suggests, has to be seen in relation to both diverse cultures and spaces and as having a long history: Hip-hop 'is too powerful to be modern, that's why I believe it's more ancient. It's an ancient culture, with a new name. And the new name is hip hop, that's the modern name, but the elements that come out of hip hop go back – way, way, back.' The elements of hip-hop, he suggests, should not be seen in terms of breaking, rapping and so forth, but rather as part of forms of music and dance that have been part of different cultures for centuries. Hip-hop, asserts Raceless, is about 'bringing back old things, and reappropriating it' (CoD Interview, 23 September 2006).[1]

These comments raise several quandaries: if hip-hop is an ancient culture with a new name, then it is not hip-hop itself that has spread but only the term. And if the elements of hip-hop have ancient origins, then it is not hip-hop that has taken on local characteristics but rather local practices that have taken on hip-hop. As we shall see in the later discussion, then, this is not merely a question of tracing back the origins of hip-hop to African or other antecedents, but rather of looking at local hip-hop as a long-term local practice with a new face. By analogy, therefore, instead of assuming that English has spread and taken on new characteristics (the core argument of WE), the argument would be that what we are looking at are, in fact, old cultural and linguistic practices with a new name. It is these questions that I shall pursue in this chapter. I shall look first of all, as do other chapters in this book, at the broader context of globalization that makes such flows of language and culture possible.

## Globalization and Worldliness

Vast amounts have been written about globalization. Here I shall focus on some very particular themes than have implications for notions of language and culture. Globalization is not only about economic processes but about political, technological and cultural as well. Globalization may be better understood as a compression of time and space, an intensification of social, economic, cultural and political relations, a series of global linkages that render events in one location of potential and immediate importance in other, quite distant locations. To suggest that globalization is only a US or Western domination of the world is to take a narrow and ultimately unproductive view of global relations. The very point about globalization is that it is global, and thus inevitably caught up in multiple influences.

Indian call centres, Indigenous education conferences, Japanese ani-
mated cartoons, anti-globalization networks, fast-moving fashions, gay
and lesbian travel organizations, the ubiquity and similarity of urban graffiti are all part of globalization. To view culture and language in terms
only of reflections of the economic is to miss the point that new technologies and communications are enabling immense and complex flows
of people, signs, sounds and images across multiple borders in multiple
directions. Education is a good example of this, with students moving in
increasing numbers to take up educational possibilities elsewhere (Singh
& Doherty, 2004), resulting in changing practices in the new 'educational contact zones' and new, appropriated knowledges travelling across
borders.

   Analyses that place the expansion of capital at their core, and argue
that globalization is nothing more than the logical next step of imperialism, have been critiqued for their failure to grasp that there is something
fundamentally different going on. As Hardt and Negri (2000: 146) argue,
most analyses fail to account for 'the novelty of the structures and logics
of power that order the contemporary world. Empire is not a weak echo of
modern imperialisms but a fundamentally new form of rule.' Unlike the
old imperialism(s), which were centred around the economic and political structures and exchanges of the nation state (indeed, the two were
in many ways mutually constitutive), and which may be best portrayed
in terms of world maps with different colours for different empires, the
new Empire is a system of national and supranational regulations that
control and produce new economies, cultures, politics and ways of living.
Mignolo (2000: 236), however, takes a different view, arguing that the 'current process of globalization is not a new phenomenon, although the way
in which it is taking place is without precedent. On a larger scale, globalization at the end of the twentieth century (mainly occurring through
transnational corporations, the media, and technology) is the most recent
configuration of a process that can be traced back to the 1500s, with the
beginning of transatlantic exploration and the consolidation of Western
hegemony.'

   It is quite possible, however, to reconcile these apparently divergent
views on globalization, the one arguing for historical continuity, the other
for a radical break with the past. On the one hand, if we lose sight of
the historical precedents of the current state of globalization, we lose a
crucial understanding of how current global conditions have come into
being; on the other, if we focus too much on continuity, we fail to see that
the forces of globalization demand new ways of thinking, new solutions
to new problems. A new era of Empire, as Hardt and Negri (2000: 46)
argue, requires new ways of thinking: 'We should be done once and for

all with the search for an outside, a standpoint that imagines a purity for our politics. It is better both theoretically and practically to enter the terrain of Empire and confront its homogenizing and heterogenizing flows in all their complexity, grounding our analysis in the power of the global multitude.' While imperialism was a territorial expansion of the nation state, globalization is decentred and deterritorialized. The modern nation state 'was structured in part by new capitalist productive processes on the one hand and old networks of absolutist administration on the other. This uneasy structural relationship was stabilized by the national identity: a cultural, integrating identity, founded on a biological continuity of blood relations, a spatial continuity of territory, and linguistic commonality' (Hardt & Negri, 2000: 95). What this suggests is the need to think about language and globalization outside the nationalist frameworks that gave rise to 20th-century models of the world. If we wish to deal historically, to understand the background to globalization, we of course need to take the role of the rise of the nation state and the notion of languages as national entities as crucial. But we also need at the same time both to see this history for the cultural artefact that it is and to view the modern world under globalization as offering new possibilities both materially and epistemologically.

Here, then, we need to make an important distinction between an understanding of globalization as a realist position that focuses on the state of the world under late capitalism, and an alternative position that focuses on the ways in which globalization undermines our modernist modes of thought. I shall call this position *worldliness* (cf. Mignolo, 2000; Pennycook, 2007), a term explained by Radhakrishnan (2007: 313) as acknowledging 'that the very one-ness of the world can only be understood on the basis of an irreducible perspectival heterogeneity,' or put another way, while globalization on the one hand pushes us towards a worldly oneness, on the other hand it obliges an understanding that must draw on the multiple worldly localities of its viewers. Like Radhakrishnan, therefore, I want this term to do several things, in particular to suggest both localization and epistemological alternatives. It is unfortunate that in much discussion of globalization, localization has been confined to various narrow options: nothing more than globalization on a small scale, traditional cultural practices or one pole of the dialectic pull between macro and micro forces (which are then sometimes elided in the rather trite 'glocal'). From the perspective I am raising here, however, localization is part of worldliness and is thus also a cultural, linguistic and epistemological challenge to globalization.

A focus centrally on globalization draws attention to changes to social structures, communication, culture and so forth as a result of new conditions of work, economy and political structure. Of principal concern here are the ways in which 'postfordist' work practices, 'new times,' flattened work hierarchies, new technologies and new media impact on issues such as literacy. From this point of view, a pluralization of literacies – multiliteracies – is needed in order to cope with more diverse demands (Cope & Kalantzis, 2000). In terms of language policy, the concern is about mapping language spread against changing economic and political conditions. What are the causes and effects, for example, of the spread and promotion of major languages, such as English? Similarly, in studies of global Englishes, various pluralization strategies – language rights, world Englishes – are invoked to counter the dominance of English or of centrist claims to control of the language.

This version of globalization, however, in which linguistic and cultural concerns are a reflection of political and economic forces, is to remain stuck within the same epistemology that produces those very notions of linguistic imperialism, language rights and so forth: language reflects society, and superstructural concerns are a reflection of infrastructural relations (language, culture, discourse or ideology are reflections or legitimations of more primal social, economic and political goals). It is precisely such materialism and realism that worldliness seeks to challenge, attempting either to invert this relationship or to collapse it altogether (making language, discourse, ideology and culture primary sites of how the world is organized and understood). Worldliness questions the assumptions of modernity, the so-called Enlightenment, the hegemony of Western thought in the world and the tools and concepts that have been used to understand the world. From an applied linguistic or language policy perspective, the principal concerns from this point of view have to do with questioning the very concepts of language, policy, mother tongues, language rights and the like that have been the staples of language policy up to now.

From this point of view, worldliness represents an intellectual, cultural and political crisis in the Euro-American project of modernity. The political and economic dominance of the world by certain regions is countered by intellectual inquiry that has started to turn back on itself, to question how we come to think as we do, why we construct particular visions of reality and in whose interests supposed norms, values and givens operate. Worldliness, then, produces a grounded, local philosophical questioning of many of the foundational concepts of received canons of knowledge, by anti-essentialist and anti-foundationalist challenges to grand narratives. Thus, it calls into question any claims to overarching truths such as human nature, enlightenment or emancipation; it makes us sceptical about talk of reality, truth or universality, rejecting unity, totalization, transcendental concepts or a belief in disinterested knowledge. At the same time that one side of globalization has brought about the domination of Euro-American culture and knowledge in some parts of the globe, worldliness has also led to 'European culture's awareness that it is no longer the unquestioned and dominant centre of the world' (Young, 1990: 19).

The view of worldliness that I have been trying to establish here, then, may be summarized as a relocation of central global themes within a different and sceptical epistemology. Taken-for-granted categories such as man, woman, class, race, ethnicity, nation, identity, awareness, emancipation or language are seen as contingent, shifting and produced in the particular, rather than having some prior ontological status. This view of worldliness suggests a number of significant concerns for language: first, it raises important questions about how power operates in relationship to the nation state, and in particular how governance is achieved through language; second, it urges us to rethink the ontology of language as a colonial/modernist construct; third, it raises questions about the grand narratives or sweeping epistemologies of imperialism, language rights, lingua francas or world Englishes; and fourth, it points towards local, situated, contextual and contingent ways of understanding languages and language policies. While it would be a mistake to ignore the historical antecedents of globalization, the different world that emerges through localization requires different tools. We cannot explore globalization and English through 20th-century tools.

## Hip-Hop Origins and Plurilithic English

Where, then, do Curse ov Dialect's comments fit into this picture? First, it is worth noting that this group of artists – from the name of their band to the clothes they wear – like to challenge received notions of language and ethnicity. They take issues of language, culture ethnicity and multiculturalism and twist, flaunt and change them. Second, their view that hip-hop is very old and links to other cultural trajectories presents us with a different sense of origins. Such a view is only possible within a conceptualization of the global and the local that I sketched out in the previous section. The processes of localization are more complex than global hip-hop or global English taking on local flavours. While an analogy with world Englishes may bring us pluralization, the shortcomings of a vision of English with local flavours are also evident. It is not so much the case that hip-hop merely takes on local characteristics, but rather that *it has always been local.* As Indigenous Australian Wire MC says, 'Hip hop is a part of Aboriginal culture, I think it always has been' (Interview). Not only have Indigenous styles of clothing, dance, vocal styles, stances and movements combined with hip-hop styles to form indigenized hybrids where US hip-hop is no longer the host culture, but hip-hop is seen as having a direct link back to traditional ways of singing, dancing and telling stories.

One way to view this, as Somali-Canadian hip-hop artist K'Naan explains, is that it is easy to see the connections between traditional African practices and hip-hop in the West African tradition of *griots* and the East African traditions of oral poetry.

> I'm certain that any country, any given country in Africa, you will find an ancient form of hip hop. It's just natural for someone from Africa to recite something over a drum and to recite it in a talking blues fashion, and then it becomes this thing called hip hop. (K'Naan interview)

This sits well with those Afrocentric arguments that draw strong connections between contemporary African American cultures and their African origins. But rather than viewing hip-hop as an American cultural form with African origins, K'Naan suggests that it is first and foremost an African form that has been Americanized. Senegalese hip-hop group Daara J likewise claim hip-hop as their own, not merely as an act of appropriation but rather as a claim to origins. According to their track 'Boomerang', 'Born in Africa, brought up in America, hip hop has come full circle.' As their MC Faada Freddy explains, the traditional Senegalese form of rhythmic poetry, *tasso*, is the original form of rap:

> So that's why we arrive at the statement where the American people brought out all that culture that was slumbering at the bottom of their soul . . . This was the beginning of rap music. This music went around the world because . . . it applied a certain influence over the world and all over. But now just realise that music is coming back home because it is about time that we join the traditional music, we join yesterday to today. (Daara J, 5 March 2005)

Here, then, we have a different possibility from the image of hip-hop emerging from US urban ghettoes and spreading across the world. Daara J take up the Afrocentric argument that traces all such movements back to African contexts. From this point of view, the arguments over the multiple influences of the Black Atlantic (Gilroy, 1993) or the Jamaican role in the development of hip-hop become subsumed under a wider argument that all are part of the wider influence of the African diaspora. The development of hip-hop in Africa from this point of view is merely a return to its roots. Thus while Perry (2004: 17) rightly critiques 'romantic Afro-Atlanticism' for overlooking the point that 'Black Americans as a community do not consume imported music from other cultures in large numbers' and thus ultimately the 'postcolonial Afro-Atlantic hip hop community is...a fantastic aspiration rather than a reality' (2004: 19), this in turn may overlook the point that African American hip-hop is only a part of a much wider circuit of musical and cultural influences.

Yet Daara J's image of the boomerang points to a problem with this story too. It brings us spinning in a circle back to Indigenous Australia and Wire MC:

> The reason I was attracted to it was the song and dance aspect to it, because the culture I come from, The Dreamtime, we always expressed our stories, our beliefs, our fears, our superstitions through song and dance. So being an Abo-digital in the 21st century, it was a natural evolution for me to move into hip hop and continue the corroboree, but with the modern day aspect. (Wire MC)

The point, then, is that this is not merely a question of whether hip-hop started in Africa and then returned but that hip-hop has always been Aboriginal Australian just as it has always been African. Hip-hop from this point of view is a continuation of Indigenous traditions; it draws people into a new relationship with cultural practices that have a history far longer than those of current popular music. Yet in doing so, it also changes those cultures and traditions, rendering them anew. From rappers in Berlin of Turkish background who draw on the traditions of medieval Turkish minstrels (*halk ozani*), acting as 'contemporary minstrels, or storytellers,... the spokespersons of the Turkish diaspora' (Kaya, 2001: 203), to Fijian Australian MC Trey's invocation of the connections between hip-hop and Pacific Islander cultures (Pennycook, 2007), hip-hop becomes not merely a cultural formation that has spread and been locally taken up, nor even one that has its origins in Africa and has returned, but rather one that has always been local. Put another way, rather than trying 'to sort out the autochthonous from the borrowed, we need to consider the uses musicians make of hip-hop, how they understand its relationship to their own condition, and what new meanings are generated by its use' (Urla, 2001: 185). And pushing this further in relation to English, rather than trying to sort out the local from the derived, or even trying to see how English has been appropriated locally, we can start to consider that English is only a name given to something that has always been local.

Such a view is of great significance for how we see varieties of English. The analogy I am trying to draw here between global Englishes and hip-hop suggests that common images of English or hip-hop as having spread around the world, with varying degrees of adaptation to local contexts, inadequately portray their local use. It is a far more dynamic and diverse process than this suggests, involving a constant struggle between identification, rejection, engagement with local cultural forms and uses of language that not only localize but also transform what it means to be local. Ultimately, therefore, whether we are dealing with the global spread of English or the global spread of hip-hop, we need to move beyond an image only of spread and adaptation, to include not only pluralization (global Englishes and global hip-hops) but also an understanding of the already local. If we take Wire's view seriously that hip-hop has always been Aboriginal, we are confronted by the need to articulate a new sense of history and location. The global locatedness of hip-hops demands that we rethink time and space, and adopt what Mignolo (2000: 205) refers to as a historiography that 'spatializes time and avoids narratives of transition, progress, development, and point of arrivals'. If we can allow for 'multiple, heterogeneous, and uneven temporalities and histories that the dominant historical narrative, often presenting itself as singular and linear, suppresses' (Inoue, 2004: 2), it becomes possible conceptually to question the linearity at the heart of modernist narratives about origins. Global Englishes do not have one point of origin but rather multiple, co-present, global origins. Global Englishes are not what they are because English has spread and been adapted but because they share different histories. Just as hip-hop has always been Aboriginal, so has English.

Such a view challenges the central myth of many current views on English, whether linguistic imperialism, world Englishes or English as a lingua franca. There has been much recent debate over the extent to which these models present different versions of diversity. Given the primary ideological focus on diversity in the world Englishes framework, it is not surprising that Braj Kachru (2005) is critical of the naming of English as a lingua franca, though this is largely on the grounds that this does not fit the original use of the term. Yamuna Kachru and Nelson (2006: 2) are clearer on this point, juxtaposing world Englishes with terms such as 'world English' (Brutt-Griffler, 2002), 'English as an International Language' (Jenkins, 2000) and 'English as a Lingua Franca' (Seidlhofer, 2001) on the grounds that they 'idealize a monolithic entity called

"English" and neglect the inclusive and plural character of the world-wide phenomenon'. Yet, in order to address such questions we need to get beyond simple questions of pluralization (English versus Englishes), since they leave unexamined both the question of relative scale and broader issues of epistemology.

While at one level, therefore, there is an important distinction here between a WE approach, with its centrifugal focus on local variation, and an ELF approach with its centripetal focus on the development of regional varieties (European and Asian English), at another level, this is only a matter of relative scale. While studies of Indian English, for example, would fall into the first camp, it is also clear that Indian English is more chimerical than this terminology allows. As Krishnaswamy and Burde observe, 'Like Indian nationalism, "Indian English" is "fundamentally insecure" since the notion "nation-India" is insecure' (1998: 63). Given the diversity of Indian languages and regions and the need to see India not so much as an imagined community but rather as an unimaginable community, it is unclear why Indian English itself is not a lingua franca. If we accept this obvious point, then it is unclear on what basis descriptions of Indian English differ from other descriptions of English as a lingua franca. And surely to discuss an entity called South Asian English, which comprises varieties across India, Sri Lanka, Pakistan and Bangladesh, is to talk in terms of a monolithic lingua franca English. At this level, surely world Englishes and ELF proponents are both describing regional varieties of English. While Kachru and others have long acknowledged the diversity within the supposed entities, this misses the point that the castigation of others for promoting supposedly monolithic English as a lingua franca rather than diversity has to be done in more complex ways than only pluralization. Thus, when Braj Kachru (2005: 39) focuses on 'educated South Asian English' rather than 'Broken English', he is surely open to the same critiques that he levels at the purveyors of ELF. Thus, as Parakrama (1995: 25–26) argues, 'The smoothing out of struggle within and without language is replicated in the homogenizing of the varieties of English on the basis of "upper-class" forms. Kachru is thus able to theorize on the nature of a monolithic Indian English.' Similarly, Canagarajah (1999: 180) observes that in Kachru's 'attempt to systematize the periphery variants, he has to standardize the language himself, leaving out many eccentric, hybrid forms of local Englishes as too unsystematic. In this, the Kachruvian paradigm follows the logic of the prescriptive and elitist tendencies of the center linguists.'

The point here, then, is despite apparent differences in the WE and ELF approaches, they largely share the same basic premises abut language, spread and variety. Just as a WE approach smooths out difference in favour of general description, so too do many approaches to ELF. If, on the other hand, ELF descriptions are trying to capture the pluricentricity of ongoing negotiated English – or, as we might call it, the *plurilithic* as opposed to monolithic character of English, since an ELF approach may posit no centres at all – it may be more pluricentric than WE. As Rubdy and Saraceni (2006: 13) put it,

> In the end, the validity of the EIL/ELF proposal will probably depend upon whether or not it chooses to embrace a polymodel approach to the teaching of English or a monolithic one, whether it leads to the establishing and promoting of a single (or a limited form of) Lingua Franca Core for common use among speakers in the Outer and Expanding Circles, possibly stripped of any cultural influences, or whether it will be flexible enough to manifest the cultural norms of all those who use it along with the rich tapestry of linguistic variation in which they are embedded.

In these struggles, then, over who has the most pluralist version of English, we are always left with various arguments over core and periphery, centre and variation, monocentric and pluricentric models. If we step outside this vision, however, and take up the challenge of the worldliness of English, we can start to see that English may only be a temporary name for a range of cultural and linguistic practices that have always been local.

## The Already Localness of English

Despite the significance of the work done under the WE banner, there has also been no small measure of criticism, particularly in relation to the inadequacy of the concentric model to deal with global linguistic realities (Bruthiaux, 2003; Jenkins, 2003). There have also been various, though not always convincing, defences of the circles as adequate to their task (Bolton, 2005; Kachru, 2005). I do not want to engage in this debate here since all charges that the concentric circles are inadequate for 21st-century language descriptions seem to be met by refutations that the circles can in fact incorporate any notions of diversity they need to. Of more relevance, however, is the need to take up the challenge posed by hip-hop's redrawing of origins, and questions of language ideology. When Bruthiaux (2003) quite rightly suggests that WE is a 20th-century framework inadequate to the task of 21st-century description, the issue is not therefore only one of changing global realities but also of the need to understand language ideologies.

We need to take one step back from these debates over who has the most pluralized version of English and instead question the ways in which a thing called English is considered to exist in the first place. It is assumed a priori that there is such a thing as English, a view reinforced by excluding those types of English, and, as Mufwene (2001) notes, those types of speakers, that don't fit what is deemed to be English, and by then employing the circular argument that if it doesn't fit, then it isn't English. For a world English to be such, it must adhere to the underlying grammar of central English, demonstrate enough variety to make it interestingly (sometimes exotically) different, but not diverge to the extent that it undermines the myth of English. If we acknowledge creole languages, however, if we refuse to draw a line down the middle of a creole continuum (exclaiming that one end is English while the other is not) and if we decide that those 'Other Englishes' may be part of English, then we are not dealing with a language held in place by a core structure but rather a notion of language status that is not definable by interior criteria. The dominant paradigms that have informed much of our discussion to date of the global spread of English – linguistic imperialism and world Englishes – are both mired in a linguistics and a politics of the last century, focusing inexorably on languages and nations as given entities, and ill-equipped to deal with current modes of globalization.

These frameworks do not have much to say to Aboriginal Australian Wire MC, when for him to perform in different parts of Australia is to perform internationally, since it means moving across the land of another Indigenous nation; or when he is urged to 'talk ocker',[2] to sound more Australian: 'I talk how I'm talkin'. I don't say "g'day". I don't say "g'day mate". I say, "how you going brother." That's what I say'; or when 'white boys' come up to him and say his rap should sound more 'Aussie': 'And I'm like "what?! Are you trying to colonise me again dude?! Stop it. Stop it" '; or when he sees hip-hop as a modern day corroboree (Interview, Wire MC). WE, ELF or linguistic imperialism have never been very good at dealing with this sort of mixture of global and worldly relations: A WE approach has always been uncomfortable with creoles, as Mufwene (2001) has repeatedly pointed out. It has also tended to relegate varieties such as Aboriginal English to the status of a sub-variety of Australian English – just as African American Vernacular English is classified as a 'sub-variety' of American English (Kachru & Nelson, 2006) – rather than dealing with their more complex status not as sub-varieties but as languages with long and complex creole histories (Malcolm, 2000). And when Wire claims this space of Aboriginal English, the global identification alongside the always local, WE may have little to offer unless it can shed its 20th-century assumptions about languages, nations, hierarchies and origins.

Rather than the model of language implied by a globalization-as-imperialism thesis, a position which suggests that the world is being homogenized through English, or the view of language suggested by a WE framework, which focuses on the heterogenization of varieties of English, I am arguing for an understanding of global Englishes that makes it possible to accept that varieties of English have always been local. This means on the one hand that we need to accept Harris' (1990: 45) argument that 'linguistics does not need to postulate the existence of languages as part of its theoretical apparatus.' The question here is whether 'the concept of a language, as defined by orthodox modern linguistics, corresponds to any determinate or determinable object of analysis at all, whether social or individual, whether institutional or psychological. If there is no such object, it would be difficult to evade the conclusion that modern linguistics has been based upon a myth' (1990: 45). And as I would suggest for global Englishes, paraphrasing Harris, the question is whether the concept of English or Englishes, as defined by linguistic imperialism, world Englishes or English as a lingua franca corresponds to any object of analysis at all, whether social or individual, whether institutional or psychological. This also means on the other hand that we should no longer be trapped by the necessity to account for something being 'in English'.

Returning to the comments by Curse ov Dialect with which I started this chapter, therefore, we might suggest that English, like hip-hop, is too powerful to be modern; it's more ancient. It's an ancient language, with a new name. And the new name is English, that's the modern name; but the elements that come out of English go back – way, way, back. Rather than seeing English in different parts of the world as all part of this thing called English that has been spread and locally adapted, we can start to see that this notion of English is only a confusing patina that obscures the local origins of language use. From this point of view we can transcend the arguments over pluralization – is WE more concerned with diversity than versions of ELF? – and engage instead with the possibility of multiple, co-present, local origins of English. This view of global Englishes radically reshapes the ways in which we can understand global and local cultural and linguistic formations, and suggests that plurilithic English has always been local.

## Notes

1. These interviews are drawn from the Local Noise project at University of Technology, Sydney (UTS). See localnoise.net.au.
2. Ocker is an Australian slang term for a (stereo)typical, white Australian male.

# References

Bolton, K. (2005) Symposium on World Englishes today (part II). Where WE stands: Approaches, issues, and debate in world Englishes. *World Englishes* 25 (1), 69–83.

Bruthiaux, P. (2003) Squaring the circles: Issues in modeling English worldwide. *International Journal of Applied Linguistics* 13 (2), 159–177.

Brutt-Griffler, J. (2002) *World English: A Study of Its Development*. Clevedon: Multilingual Matters.

Canagarajah, S. (1999) *Resisting Linguistic Imperialism in English Teaching*. Oxford: Oxford University Press.

Cope, B. and Kalantzis, M. (eds) (2000) *Multiliteracies: Literacy Learning and the Design of Social Futures*. London: Routledge.

Gilroy, P. (1993) *The Black Atlantic: Modernity and Double Consciousness*. London: Verso.

Hardt, M. and Antonio, N. (2000) *Empire*. Cambridge, MA: Harvard University Press.

Harris, R. (1990) On redefining linguistics. In H. Davis and T. Taylor (eds) *Redefining Linguistics* (pp. 18–52). London: Routledge.

Inoue, M. (2004) Introduction: Temporality and historicity in and through linguistic ideology. *Journal of Linguistic Anthropology* 14 (1), 1–5.

Jenkins, J. (2000) *The Phonology of English as an International Language*. Oxford: Oxford University Press.

Jenkins, J. (2003) *World Englishes: A Resource Book for Students*. London: Routledge.

Kachru, B. (2005) *Asian Englishes: Beyond the Canon*. Hong Kong: Hong Kong University Press.

Kachru, Y. and Nelson, C. (2006) *World Englishes in Asian Contexts*. Hong Kong: Hong Kong University Press.

Kaya, A. (2001) *'Sicher in Kreuzberg' Constructing Diasporas: Turkish Hip Hop Youth in Berlin*. Bielefeld: Transcript Verlag.

Krishnaswamy, N. and Archana, B. (1998) *The Politics of Indians' English: Linguistic Colonialism and the Expanding English Empire*. Delhi: Oxford University Press.

Malcolm, I.G. (2000) Aboriginal English: From contact variety to social dialect. In J. Siegel (ed.) *Processes of Language Contact: Studies from Australia and the South Pacific* (pp. 123–144). Montreal: Fides.

Mignolo, W. (2000) *Local Histories/Global Designs: Coloniality, Subaltern Knowledges and Border Thinking*. Princeton: Princeton University Press

Mufwene, S. (2001) *The Ecology of Language Evolution*. Cambridge: Cambridge University Press.

Parakrama, A. (1995) *De-hegemonizing Language Standards: Learning from (Post)Colonial Englishes About 'English'*. Basingstoke: Macmillan.

Pennycook, A. (2007) *Global Englishes and Transcultural Flows*. London: Routledge.

Perry, I. (2004) *Prophets of the Hood: Politics and Poetics in Hip Hop*. Durham, NC: Duke University Press.

Phillipson, R. (1992) *Linguistic Imperialism*. Oxford: Oxford University Press.

Radhakrishnan, R. (2007) Globality is not worldliness. In R. Radhakrishnan, K. Nayak, R. Shashidhar, R.R. Parinitha and D.R. Shashidhara (eds) *Theory as Variation* (pp. 313–328). New Delhi: Pencraft International.

Rubdy, R. and Saraceni, M. (2006) Introduction. In R. Rubdy and M. Saraceni (eds) *English in the World: Global Rules, Global Roles*. London: Continuum, pp. 5–16.

Singh, P. and Doherty, C. (2004) Global cultural flows and pedagogic dilemmas: Teaching in the global university contact zone. *TESOL Quarterly* 38 (1), 9–42.

Urla, J. (2001) 'We are all Malcolm X!' Negu Gorriak, Hip-Hop, and the Basque political imaginary. In T. Mitchell (ed.) *Global Noise: Rap and Hip-Hop Outside the USA* (pp. 171–193). Middletown, CT: Wesleyan University Press.

Young, R. (1990) *White Mythologies: Writing History and the West*. London: Routledge.

*Chapter 11*
# Final Reflections: Globalization and World Englishes

MUKUL SAXENA AND TOPE OMONIYI

## Introduction

The main objective of this volume has been to bring together diverse voices in the 'World Englishes' (WEs) research and see where the debate in WEs is in relation to globalization. In this concluding chapter, first, we look at how the WEs debate is located within different schools of thought in globalization debate. We revisit the contributions to this volume and analyze and synthesize the arguments relevant to this discussion. Each school of thought within WEs (Kachruvian WEs, EIL/ELF, Linguistic Imperialism) is much diffused in itself and complex in interaction with each other than can be captured fully in this chapter. Our main focus is on what we think are the salient features of their interaction with each other in response to globalization. In the later part of the chapter, we relate these features to the central conceptual issues within the theoretical debate of globalization, and explore the way forward by raising questions which will point to future direction of research in WEs. We present an agenda for WEs research which is decentred/deterritorialized and approaches language/English issue in a holistic way capturing the diversity and the unity that is seen in global multilingualism and changing world order.

## Globalization and World Englishes

We highlighted the complex nature of globalization in the introductory chapter and the multiplicity of ways that globalization is viewed and contested. The basic contentious points are centred on the nature, driving forces, the period of reference and outcomes of globalization. However, despite the disagreement as to how contemporary globalization is best conceptualized, it is essentially agreed upon that the processes

212 Contending with Globalization in World Englishes

of globalization fundamentally restructure the way commodities, ideas and people flow and interact, thereby problematizing the traditional notions of time and space. Looking at globalization only in terms of political, economic or technological imperatives would offer only partial understanding. There is also a general consensus on the view that scale, intensity, reach and instantaneity of current processes of globalization are unprecedented.

Nihalani (Chapter 2) writes, '... global infrastructures in English have become the bases for the emergence of an *inextricably interconnected world* – a world we describe by the cliché: the "global village".' There has been an expansion of the functional domains of English across socio-economic classes. Its linguistic and cultural capital has been produced and reproduced in the two 'waves of globalization' that Murray (2006: 88) describes as 'colonial globalization' (mercantilist phase and industrialist phase) and 'postcolonial globalization' (modernization phase and neoliberal phase). Bobda (Chapter 8), for example, in this volume, systematically charts the patterns of transplantation of English and modes of its diffusion throughout the history of the West African region since the 15th century up to the present; Rajagopalan surveys the scenario in Brazil, and in Latin America in general; Georgieva charts the growth of English in Bulgaria and Chew describes the situation in China.

As a paradigm of research in the study of English, WEs has been concerned with language variation and change over time and space. The global spread of English as ESL, EFL, EIL or *New* Englishes has been a focus of WEs research. Until recently, at the heart of WEs discourse, we have the 'diffusion model' wherein narratives of origin, spread, development and transition underpinned the explanations offered. But increasingly, we find that all three persuasions in the globalization debate, hyperglobalist, sceptic and transformationalist (Held *et al.*, 1999), and the allied debate on pro-globalization, anti-globalization and progressive globalization are relevant to our understanding of WEs research and our still emerging understanding of the way English is used as a means of intercultural and intracultural communication. Just as we observe that there are agreements and contradictions within all these different positions in theorizing globalization, similarly, we find agreements and contradictions are inherent in different schools of thought within WEs. However, there are salient features in each of the schools of thoughts within which we can situate the different strands of WEs research. The implications of all these viewpoints which are contributing to the development of a unified theory of globalization significantly format our understanding of the dialogue between language and culture.

## WEs and globalization theses of 'hyperglobalist', 'sceptic' and 'tranformationalist'

In general, we can say that the current arguments of WEs have adopted a 'transformationalist' worldview to the extent that WEs deal with the linguistic transformations that are occurring in the way English is being used and transformations that have taken place in the way English is conceived conceptually. The main point from this perspective is that English is currently the dominant language on a global scale, but it is constantly being refashioned by interaction between people and institutions on various scales in response to globalization wherein the core-periphery structures of colonial globalization no longer exist. Sharifian (Chapter 7) points to the 'glocalization' of English where 'speakers of World Englishes themselves have provided a strong response to the globalization of English by glocalizing it in varying degrees and in various ways'. Chew, Dewey and Jenkins and Georgieva (Chapters 3, 4 and 6) contribute to the transfomationalist WEs perspective of English as a Lingua Franca (ELF).

This current thinking contends with the 'sceptic' viewpoint inherent in the Kachruvian model of concentric circles which marks the earliest attempt at theorizing WEs. The model is seen as couched in the colonial globalization debate and, therefore, limited in dealing with the multilayered complex relationships between Englishes and the current wave of globalization.

While Kachru's model can be seen as positioned in the 'sceptic' thesis of the globalization debate, the arguments in favour of English as 'global' language or 'international' language (EIL) appear to take the 'hyperglobalist' (neoliberal) stance. In this stance, national boundaries are not seen as important, because international, supranational, regional and local bodies and markets are presumed to override the national governments and the world is a much more homogenized entity. Therefore, the EIL argument goes that in order to facilitate communication in this interconnected world, there is need for one language and English fits into this role neatly as it already has a 'global' reach in terms of books, methods of teaching and so on. The 'hyperglobalist' viewpoint may also be attributed to ELF research where the emphasis is on supranational/regional networks or where the role of nation-state has been increasingly taken over by the transnational flows between nations and governance by local, regional and supranational bodies. However, Dewey and Jenkins (Chapter 4) seek to clarify that the way ELF as a body of research approaches the use of English in lingua franca settings, whether these occur in inner, outer or expanding circle contexts, follows the 'transformationalist' narrative.

They explain that together with Kachruvian WEs, ELF attempts to offer a fuller description of cultural transformations occurring at global scale from 'transformationalist' perspective in the globalization debate and thereby 'seeks to legitimize and make sense of the way English is being transformed by speakers outside the ancestral contexts of the language'.

Notwithstanding above explanation of ELF being 'transformationalist', and not so distinct from the 'sceptic' position of the Kachruvian WEs (see Nihalani, Chapter 2), the proponents of the 'Linguistic Imperialism' position criticize EIL/ELF as promoting hegemonic aspirations of the Empire and bringing in from the back door the Inner Circle hegemony, thereby legitimizing Inner Circle variety. Their perception is shaped by the attempts of ELF scholars to research local situations in order to find regional standards. Regionalism and the neoliberal agenda according to them bring about neo-imperialism resulting in increasing marginalization of languages other than English and perpetuating the dominant position of English displacing local linguistic practices (Phillipson, 1992; Skutnabb-Kangas, 2000). There is also concern over differentiation of cultural identities and relativization along ethnic and racial lines. This thesis is also closely associated with the 'anti-globalization' viewpoint, as we will see below.

### WEs and the pro-globalization, anti-globalization and progressive globalization perspective

The 'pro-globalization' perspective (Mittelman, 2000) is present in the view which considers the spread of English as a progressive trend. Arguments in favour of English are parallel to those forwarded for the Capitalist agenda (i.e. the spread of market economics, competition, free trade and Western democracy), a type of view which may be associated with the British Council (parallel to the International Monetary Fund (IMF) and sister institutions, the World Bank and the World Trade Organization (WTO) at capitalism level). EIL or 'Global English' agenda seems to subscribe to this worldview, similar to the 'hyperglobalist' (neoliberal) viewpoint discussed above.

The 'anti-globalization' perspective finds its expression in the view that English as a concomitant to globalization is a threat to local/'indigenous' languages, just as globalization has a neo-colonial agenda endangering local social and natural environment (Adams, 2001). In a similar vein as argued in the context of globalization (Cowen & Shenton, 1996), English is seen as perpetuating inequality and increasing the unevenness of development in ways that are not necessarily reversible. Furthermore, this is made to *seem* inevitable because it protects the interests of those who promote it with adverse consequences for the marginalized groups/languages which get more marginalized. This echoes the 'sceptic' position that we have described above. However, while the Kachruvian WEs 'sceptic' position focuses on the neo-colonial agenda of EIL against the 'local varieties of Englishes', the 'sceptic' stance of the 'Linguistic Imperialism' school of thought has rallied against the endangerment of the 'local languages and practices' caused by English.

The 'progressive' globalization perspective (Mittelman, 2000) with its focus on human actions and the ability to make particular political choices as influencing the nature and outcome of globalization is seen in the 'transformationalist' viewpoint as described above. Within this perspective, importance is ascribed to the role of 'agency' wherein choices can be exercised in adoption, use and appropriation of English. There is no 'evolutionary' or 'pre-determined' path to follow.

## Future Directions: Conceptualizing WEs in 21st-Century Globalization

In this section we first summarize the contentious issues and controversies among different perspectives on WEs and then explore the ways in which the WEs field of inquiry may proceed in the globalized world of the 21st century.

It is argued that Kachruvian WEs is largely couched in processes shaped by colonial globalization, as it is a construction of that time (e.g. see Chew, Chapter 3). The salient units of categorization used in this enterprise were a combination of factors, like, 'colonialism and post-colonialism', English as 'native, second or foreign language', 'native and non-native varieties of Englishes', 'norm-providing and non-dependent', 'prestige of Englishes vis-à-vis other languages', 'motivation and purpose for learning Englishes', 'identity' and 'territory'. The core-periphery structure was a key guiding factor in the explanation offered. Kachru's concentric circle model is based on this structure. There are notable parallels between this model and another theory of its time, the Sociolinguistic of Periphery (SP), which took a critical perspective in describing unequal relationships between the majority and minority indigenous languages of Europe, starting around 1970s. The main agenda of the SP was to problematize Fishman's notion of diglossia. Likewise, the agenda of the concentric circle model, when proposed in the mid-1980s, was socio-political, that is, to contrast and legitimize the outer circle varieties of Englishes against the hegemony of 'native speaker'/'inner circle' varieties. The corollary of this, in terms of education, has been to contest the legitimacy of 'native speaker' variety and 'native speakers' as teachers of English.

With the rise of postmodernism, the distinction between the 'Circles' is seen as blurring and merging. The accelerated transnational flows of people, information/ideas and goods have opened up communication contexts which are rendering the distinctions between the 'Outer' and 'Expanding' circles inadequate and are giving rise to ELFs. The failure to deal with *new* global linguistic realities, say by the concentric circle model, has been pointed out by many (Bruthiaux, 2003; Jenkins, 2003; Nayar, 1997; Pennycook, 2003; Seidlhofer, 2001; see also Bhatt, Dewey and Jenkins, Pennycook and Chew, in this volume). In particular, it has been pointed out that people in Outer Circle and Expanding Circle are interacting with each other independent of the Inner Circle or Core. The implications this has had on language portfolios of these regions are significant.

The ELF scholars contend that even though they are in the early stages of development, the research findings of ELF corpora are leading to a theoretical understanding of the nature of ELF. The research is yielding understanding about the way large numbers of users in lingua franca settings can transform language. 'Core' linguistic features have been identified which characterize successful lingua franca communication leading to desired participatory mutual goals. It is argued that these 'Core' features are necessary to create 'a degree of common ground' for facilitating mutual intelligibility' (Dewey & Jenkins, Chapter 4). However, such attempts have led to the criticism of ELF research as 'promoting monocentricity'. For example, Nihalani (Chapter 2) argues that the segmental core features of Jenkins' Lingua Franca Core (LFC) are 'heavily grounded in RP' and display 'intolerance of diversity that has been unfortunately perceived as a threat to the Western cannon'. Instead, he offers an alternative for mutual intelligibility which preserves speakers' identity.

As Dewey and Jenkins (Chapter 4) put it, ELF has proved to be 'highly controversial among native and non-native speakers of English, World Englishes scholars, (applied) linguists, and English Language Teaching practitioners'. Using globalization discourses, one could say that while the 'sceptic' researchers criticize the ELF model for convergence and intolerance to sociolinguistic diversity, the 'hyperglobalist' ELT practitioners blame the model for divergence! So, on the one hand, ELF research has been seen as promoting monocentricity, and on the other hand, just the opposite, as promoting an 'unwieldy degree of diversity'. Dewey and Jenkins argue that this stems from misconceptions about ELF and address these criticisms by situating the model in the broader globalization debate.

The extent to which Kachruvian WEs (or even ELF) model presents different versions of diversity has been much debated (Canagarajah, 1999; Parakrama, 1995; Pennycook, Chapter 10). The 'standardized/homogenized' WEs (say 'Nigerian English', 'Indian English' and the International Corpus of English (ICE) project) with their focus on 'educated/elite' varieties can be readily subjected to the homogenizing/prescriptivist/elitist tendency that is so often ascribed to ELF or the criticism that is levelled against the reification of the 'native' or 'core' varieties of Englishes as 'International English'/'Global English'. The 'transformationalists' in the WEs debate highlight that these homogenized codes are a product of the nation-state taken as a territorial unit of analysis. They call for new theoretical perspectives which can describe evolving lingua francas (LFs) shaped by 21st-century globalization.

There are, therefore, a number of contentious issues and controversies in the theory and practice of WEs. Bhatt (Chapter 5) pins this down to 'a political logic of conformity – outside and within the field of World Englishes – that at once *en*ables discourses of strategic essentialism (via branding, policing labels, imposing boundaries, sanctioning legitimacy, etc) and *dis*ables discourses of transformation (of hybridity, heterogeneity, diversity)'.' He calls for a more general theory of the sociolinguistics of globalization to understand 'the various complexes of sociolinguistic nuances of the acquisition and use of Englishes'.

Pennycook (Chapter 10), on the other hand, argues that we need to 'rethink language' in reaction to postmodernist imperatives, rather than treating it as territorially bound as is the case with the other schools of thought in WEs. This implies that in order to explore globalization and Englishes in the 21st century there is a

> ... need to articulate a new sense of history and location, avoiding narratives of spread, transition, development, and origins, and thinking instead in terms of multiple, heterogeneous, and simultaneous histories that the dominant historical narrative has overlooked.

He calls this alternative position 'worldliness' that questions and decentres the prior ontological status of the analytical categories associated with language, demography (e.g. man, woman), affiliation (e.g. class, race and ethnicity), geography (e.g. nation, community) and so on.

It would appear then that the WEs enterprise is not fully unified and equipped to deal with *current processes* of globalization. What we propose, and which we outline in the next section, is that it has to come to grips with the emerging *interconnected* conceptual issues in globalization theories to revisit *existing* questions and raise *new* questions to understand, explain and develop a unified theory of WEs.

## Conceptual issues in globalization theories and emerging questions for WEs

So far we have analyzed and synthesized arguments in terms of different approaches in WEs and located them within different schools of thought in globalization debate. Our main focus was on what we think are the salient features of their interaction with each other in response to globalization. In this section, we relate these features to the central conceptual issues within the theoretical debate of globalization, and explore the way forward by raising questions which will point out the directions for future research in WEs.

### Local/global/scale

An important issue in the context of WEs research is that global and local cultural and linguistic formations have been understood in a very particular way. 'Localization' of Englishes is seen in terms of English taking on local forms in different socio-political-cultural contexts. Different schools of thought put differing emphasis on the 'global' and the 'local' forces which underpin the changes observed in the language domain. However, the boundary between what is local and what is global is increasingly seen as blurred (Gibson-Graham, 2002). In agreement with this position in the globalization theoretical debate and with those who take the 'transformationalist' stance in WEs, we see both 'globalizing' and 'localizing' forces simultaneously at work. In the cultural sphere for instance, on the one hand, we see a 'global' music industry, the predominance of 'global' brands and, on the other hand, we also have 'world' music scene with local musical styles. Therefore, attempting to separate the 'global' and the 'local' forces may be problematic, because they are not oppositional, but part of the same dialectical process. Massey (1991) draws on Giddens' (1990) concept of 'time-distanciation relationship' and calls this dialectical process as a 'global sense of the local' which we see increasing number of individuals experiencing in their daily lives in the 21st-century globalization.

The conceptualization of 'scale' in the discourse therefore assumes significance in offering explanations. In terms of their focus, Kachruvian WEs and ELF may be distinct, but at another level the difference lies on their conceptualization of 'scale'. As Pennycook (Chapter 10) puts it, though WEs approach has a 'centrifugal focus on local variation' and ELF approach has a 'centripetal focus on the development of regional varieties (European, South Asian English)', at another level, this is only a matter of relative scale.

So, the questions that must be raised are: *How relevant is this dichotomy of local/global in the context of WEs research? How is the issue of the 'scale' of localness and globalness to be addressed in this paradigm of research? How has this changed in the course of globalization?*

*Space, territoriality and deterritoriality*

The concept of space is important in shaping the way humans experience and interact with the world. In the context of globalization theories, Murray (2006) describes three views of space – absolute, relative and metaphorical. The first can be seen as referring to territoriality and the other two to deterritoriality. The distinction can be further categorized as 'spaces of places' (nations, territories and villages) and 'spaces of flows' (electronically based webs, networks) (Castells, 1996). In relation to time, the former can be articulated within the 'time-space convergence' relationship (Janelle, 1973), whereas the latter within the 'time-space distanciation' (Giddens, 1990) and 'time-space compression' (Harvey, 1989).

Pennycook (Chapter 10) argues that the theoretical debate in WEs is fundamentally territorially bound. Thus, the conception of 'borders' leads automatically to the idea of border for a language, for English and so on. The metaphor of the spatial border of a nation-state is extended to language, identity and so on. But, globalization is essentially a deterritorialized process, and this viewpoint has the potential to lead to a paradigm shift in WEs research. So, *how do we incorporate the notions of, for instance, 'scapes' (see below) and 'deterritorialized multilingualism' (see below) to take a fresh look at the theoretical debate in WEs?*

*Interconnectedness/network society/scapes*

Scholars have pointed to unprecedented interconnectedness/interaction/global connectivity as the most distinguishing feature of current processes of globalization. The contemporary world is 'best defined as a period of significant social, political and cultural transformations' (Dewey & Jenkins, Chapter 4). Notwithstanding the unevenness in accessibility to available resources, the expansion in telecommunications and transport sectors in particular that we have seen in late modernity is resulting in increased language and cultural contact at all levels, local, national, regional and international levels. The 'time-space compression and distanciation' of current globalization has rescaled interaction. We have moved from what Crang (1999) has described as world as 'mosaic', to world as 'system' and currently to world as 'network'. New networks of inclusion/exclusion which are more complex than the old patterns of differentiation have been forged or have emerged. The new 'spaces of flows' co-exist with old 'spaces of places' in network societies (Castells, 1996). And one of the distinguishing features of these 'new' connections is that they are quite substantially detached from territorial space, that is, they operate largely without regard to territorial distance, substantially bypassing territorial borders. So, the ramifications of these interactions/global conditions cannot be understood in terms of territoriality alone.

In order to understand the interconnectedness in the 'postnational' world order, Appadurai (1996) draws discourses from fractal geometry and chaos theory and elements from a range of other theories and suggests that global cultural flows occur in and through the disjunctures of five dimensions of 'scapes', namely, ethnoscapes, mediascapes, technoscapes, financescapes and ideoscapes. His book, *Modernity at Large*, provides a comprehensive hyperglobalist account of the shrinking deterritorialized world of global village.

Appadurai's work explores the interconnection between mass migration, transnational diaspora and electronic media, the essential processes of contemporary globalization, which fundamentally change the way 'here' and 'now' are experienced. The stability of the nation-state, family structure, global versus local and, therefore, *habitus* is fractured by the agency implied in transnational flows. The agency is seen as shaped by a complex interaction of flows of cultures, beliefs, values and movements filtered through the profusion of different kinds of electronic technologies and medias, destabilizing previous formations of nation imagined in identity, ethnicity and race. In the 'postnational' order of the world, the 'modernity' is 'at large' due to the ever emerging 'diasporic public spheres' and other 'yet unimagined social groups'.

The question for future WEs research, which we may pose, is *how it might apply Appadurai's discourses and analytical tools associated with scapes from the transformationalist point of view. How might one relate them in a systematic way with Pennycook's (Chapter 10) discussion of 'rethinking language' and Sharifian's (Chapter 7) notion of 'cultural conceptualization' (see below) and our notion of 'deterritorialized multilingualism' (see below)?*

### Homogeneity and heterogeneity

If we agree with the view that globalization entails processes bringing about unprecedented 'interconnectedness' (the 'transformationalist' viewpoint), then the main question is: Is globalization leading to 'homogenization' or 'heterogenization'? (Hülsemeyer, 2003).

Chew's Chapter 3 points to heterogeneity where 'historical and linguistic changes move from chaos to order: in the direction of increasing complexity and integration of more and more diverse elements'. As Dewey and Jenkins (Chapter 4) put it, 'heightened contact between communities results, in our view, not in a linguistic homogeneity, but in heterogeneity, as the English being spoken in these settings is not the English of the inner circle, but hybridized versions of the language that develop in situ as speakers accommodate towards the co-constructing of their discourse.' From the point of view of rethinking the nature of language, the heterogeneity and hybridized version of English referred to here, in Chapter 5 by Bhatt, and elsewhere in WEs literature (e.g. Canagarajah, 2007), has to be conceptualized, as discussed below, in the context of a broader theory of 'globalization and multilingualism' (see below).

Giddens (1990) argues that 'time-space distanciation' allows individuals to heterogenize global scale systems. Commenting on the debate on the related binary concepts of convergence and divergence under globalization, Cerny (2003) summarizes that they should be conceived as existing in a dialectical relationship. To the extent that globalization is brought about by processes and agendas which are dialectical, contentious and heterogenous, mapping the course of WEs is both a necessary and a challenging task for linguists.

*Globalization, governance and policymaking*

Kennett (2008: 3) argues that the current 'processes of globalization have disrupted the traditional analytical and conceptual frameworks through which policymaking and implementation have been understood'. The emphasis has changed from government to governance which involves not just the state but other terrains and actors involved in transnational, regional and subnational organizations. The future analysis of public policy in WEs, therefore, should take account of various interpretations and processes of governance. It faces a challenging task in sifting through and making sense of a diverse range of views and practices of language-in-education policymaking and practices associated with English in different contexts.

Empirical evidence across a spectrum of countries (from Iran, China and Bulgaria, for example, in this volume) points to attitudinal changes towards foreign languages in general and English in particular. Sharifian (Chapter 7) shows in her chapter how 'often sharply contrasting motives for learning English have led to just as many different attitudes and perceptions about what type of English to learn'. Georgieva (Chapter 6) in her Bulgarian study finds that people are no longer so vulnerable to assimilationist ideologies canonizing (or beautifying) Anglo-American socio-cultural values; rather, people are seen as shaping Englishes to cater to their own needs with a pragmatic attitude. Rajagopalan (Chapter 9) argues that in the years to come, English will cease to be a *foreign* language right across the world and that signals important consequences for the way the English language is taught. Chew's (Chapter 3) study from China points to the unevenness of impacts of globalization.

So, *what are the implications then for language planning and language policy in WEs?* Since language planning is intricately linked with history, politics and socio-cultural attitudes/aspirations of the people, the important questions which arise are: *Does it have a 'nationalistic' agenda? Or, does it have an 'internationalistic' agenda? Or, is there a shifting, fractured complex mix of the two under the impact of 21st-century globalization?*

A telling instance of the last scenario can be seen in the context of Malaysia's language policy. In the aftermath of post-independence nationalistic politics, English lost ground to Malay, until the current decade when imperatives of globalization reinstated its position as the international language. The latter has allowed 'workers without borders' (Stalker, 2000) to enter Malaysia. But just when skills in English were presumed to be a *passport* to borderless employment, in this case in Malaysia, the Malaysian government is currently in the process of making it compulsory for all foreign workers to know Malay before entering Malaysia, 'to ensure workers know the country's custom, culture, language and laws before getting a work visa' ('Introduction course for new foreign workers in Malaysia', *Borneo Bulletin*, 4 June 2008, p. 17). As much as English is deemed essential, evidently it is no longer a *sufficient* condition for entry into current globalized labour market. Furthermore, while English carries international cultural capital, Malay derives its symbolic power, not just as the national language of Malaysia, but also as a regional language used/understood widely in the South East Asia (Indonesia, Singapore and in parts of Thailand and the Philippines; it is also the national language of Indonesia and one of the national languages of Singapore). Such instances of policymaking practices are not peculiar to Malaysia. For example, academic appointments in Denmark also require competence in Danish if not from the outset, but definitely before any tenure is granted.

WEs, therefore, has to come to grips with the dialectical processes of English-related policies and practices in the broader contexts of national and global multilingualism. That would be necessary to fully appreciate the challenges involved in the learning and teaching of English in globalization context. A number of authors in this volume have problematized the issues of teaching and learning of English in the current debates of

WEs. In a broader discussion of 'comprehensibility', 'intelligibility' and 'identity', for example, Nihalani (Chapter 2) has asked whether the focus needs to be shifted from 'what is *convenient* for teachers to teach' to 'what is *effective* for learners to learn'.

### WEs, territorialized and deterritorialized multilingualism

Just as SP ignored the minority non-indigenous languages of Europe (e.g. Panjabi in Wales), Kachruvian WEs can be held accountable for being biased in overlooking their own hegemonic position in focusing only on the local elite/educated varieties of Englishes. Therefore, while this model takes a 'sceptic' position against the EIL/ELF, paradoxically, in this situation, it finds itself positioned in the 'hyperglobalist' school, *albeit* in relation to the territorial boundaries of the nation-state, rather than at the international level.

In fact, the majority of the debate on the interrelationship between WEs and globalization has treated 'English' almost autonomously, both structurally and contextually. References have been made to the broader spatial contexts of bilingualism and multilingualism in which 'Englishes' exist. However, the analyses and discussions have centred on the nature and function of Englishes in relation to other Englishes. Also, the contexts that give rise to variation and diversity are largely treated in a generally non-linguistic sense, undermining the role that multilingualism plays in the broader sociolinguistic ecology. For instance, in the context of 'plurilingual' Europe, Georgieva (Chapter 6) points to the fact that the more English has grown as a means of wider communication in the Bulgarian region, the more English seems to lose its hold as a marker of prestige and an instrument of professional advancement, and as a result, new opportunities have risen for *other languages* to find a proper place in people's language repertoire. The situation in the traditionally recognized multilingual regions of Asia, Africa and Latin America is much more fluid and complex.

It is important then that the theoretical and pedagogical debate in WEs and globalization situates itself in the broader debate of multilingualism and globalization. This will be a good starting point for making sense of the postmodernist imperative of understanding the nature of language that Pennycook (Chapter 10) has proposed. However, the nature of multilingualism has become far more complex than the traditional territorialized multilingualism that has been the main focus of study until recently. The 21st-century globalization is giving rise to diverse forms of, what we would like to call, 'deterritorialized multilingualism'. While the territorialized multilingualism is conceptualized within the 'absolute' spaces, the deterritorialized multilingualism needs to be conceived within the 'relative' and 'metaphorical' spaces. The former can be seen as located within the 'time-space convergence' relationship whereas the latter within the 'time-space distanciation' and 'time-space compression'.

WEs scholarship has to figure out *how the territorialized and deterritorialized multilingual spaces shape each other; how they shape and are shaped by emerging diasporic and non-diasporic groups and networks; what is their dialectical relationship with agency; how individuals traverse these spaces and 'scapes' in their daily interactional practices; and in these interactions, what 'Englishes' are produced and reproduced and what role they play.*

### Changing world order

A long-term historical perspective on various waves of globalization directs our understanding towards changing world orders and twists and turns in the fortunes of different economies, cultures, politics as well as language. The contemporary wave has arrived at a juncture where, depending on which side of the prism of globalization (hyperglobalist, sceptical and transformationalist) one looks at, the juggernaut of English seems unstoppable, and, on the other hand, it has to contend with the local forces of appropriation. The extreme position is that its survival, as we know it, may be at stake.

In the context of *current processes* of 21st-century globalization there is general consensus on the view that the emergence of China and India as potential 'superpowers' of this century signals a changing world order. But we need to ask, *does this merely imply a relocation of global central themes, or a more fundamental change in global realities of languages, nations, supranational organizations and hierarchies?*

During his visit to China in 2008, Manmohan Singh, the Prime Minister of India, signed a joint document named 'A Shared Vision for the 21st Century of the People's Republic of China and the Republic of India', which covered extensive bilateral and multilateral fields between China and India. He remarked in his speech to the Chinese Academy of Social Sciences in Beijing, 'We are at an exciting point in history when the centre of gravity of the world economy is moving towards Asia' (http://en.fondsk.ru/article.php?id=1165), and 'I look forward with optimism to the future and the role which India and China are destined to play in the transformation of Asia and the world' (http://www.china-embassy.org/eng/gyzg/t399827.htm). We anticipate this partnership will bring significant negotiation and alteration of the worldview shaped by the notion of linearity through 'cultural conceptualizations'. However, Sharifian (Chapter 7) talks about the production of 'cultural conceptualizations' from below through agency. This is in contrast to what the PM of India envisioned in his speech that the changing world order and changes in cultural conceptualization in China and India will be from the top, at the structural level. So, the question for WEs is *how such cultural conceptualization in the changing world order will change the way education is delivered, the kinds of Englishes that are delivered and the kinds of materials that are used for teaching English. Another question is whether this new world order would promote English to the extent that the WEs enterprise thinks it will.*

Just like the nation-state instruments of China and India, their transnational companies, riding on the current wave of globalization, would like to change the way the world thinks and behaves. For example, Bollywood moguls, through corporate mergers and takeovers of Hollywood interests in the United States and elsewhere, would like to dominate the world by telling their own ways of storytelling (Choo, 2008). Choo quotes the President of Reliance Big Entertainment (the entertainment arm of India's largest private company Reliance ADA Group) saying, '... We have the longest tradition of story-telling ... Now is the time to conquer the world ... We are the oldest civilization in the world ... Now we have to make our culture familiar to the world.' As the newspaper report further elaborates, the battle begins by conquering the Southeast Asia, the Middle East, Africa, Latin America and the UK, the regions comprising 'India's natural zone of influence', and then extends to Europe and China by casting actors from and producing films for these zones.

Changes brought about by such transnational companies and their corporate and cultural ambitions as well as diffusion of Indian, Chinese and other countries' interests beg question as to what implications they will have for the theory of WEs, multilingualism and globalization. At the heart of this question are the issues of 'linearity' and 'circularity'. Chew (Chapter 3) explores them in relation to the Western and Chinese worldviews. Similar to the Chinese, the Indian worldview is circular (Bagchi, 1981). It is in this context that *WEs scholars have to conceptualize what the leaders of these countries and transnational organizations may be alluding to when they talk about their 'own ways' of thinking, behaving, doing things and how they can potentially alter the future world order in negotiation and contestation with other worldviews within and beyond their geographical borders.* Such a conceptualization would not only help us in understanding better the argument Pennycook makes about rethinking the categories 'origin', 'spread' and 'English', including other related categories. But it also has implications for the broader linearity and non-linearity debate within which World Englishes and globalization theory needs to be situated.

*Worldviews: Linearity to non-linearity/circularity*

Linearity is at the heart of modernist narratives about language origins and spread. But globalization when conceptualized as a 'historical process which is "more contingent and open ended and which does not fit with orthodox linear models of social change" ' (Held *et al.*, 1999: 11) demands a closer look at the limitations of this linear perspective in our analyses. And if we abandon the linearity perspective, Pennycook (Chapter 10) says, 'we can start to see that global Englishes do not have one point but rather multiple, co-present, global origins.' He also points out that all these frameworks (Kachruvian WEs, ELF and EFL) are inherently incapable of 'describing in any comprehensive fashion the ongoing negotiation of language'.

## Conclusion

As stimulating as the discussions in some of the territorially anchored chapters in this volume are, we must still acknowledge differences between the macro- and micro-contexts of transnational engagements in which World Englishes are in contact. In those situations, contrasting and competing attitudes about the varieties that are present become manifest and consequently feed evaluations and, possibly, hierarchizations. For instance, if we carefully scrutinize the most fundamental practices of the academy as an institution, that is, conference presentations, plenary and keynote speeches, lectures and so forth, we find that within this global community of practice, varieties of the major languages of transaction, including English, do not have equal capital in the packaging of knowledge. Depending on the forum and purpose, some varieties command greater capital than others. We note, *albeit* cautiously, that this variation is often reflected in the list of preferred vendors of ESL and EFL programmes around the world. The British Council enterprise and satellite campuses of British and American universities in Outer and Expanding Circle countries also bear testimony.

Perhaps more than in any other areas of the globalization experience, the deterritorialization of business processes that entail collaboration and cooperation between service providers and clients who are located in different linguiscapes suggests the degree of complexity of non-linearity. In the course of a working day, one provider may service several clients each of whom may be associated with a different language variety. In each of these encounters, the provider makes and encounters client-determined adjustments in the communicative process to accommodate peculiar and intricate features of intercultural exchanges. Such micro-processes are likely to be impacted by factors in the structural relationship between these multiple locations some of which may be more salient than others. In her investigation of the role of interpreting in the multinational neighbourhood, Inagaki (2008) references Bourdieu's notions of field and capital in arguing that in community interpreting in the UK languages are measured by their potential commodity values and 'the values of linguistic capital changes according to the field.' The implication that this remark holds for World Englishes scholarship in a globalized economy is that researchers must be cognizant of dialect-cum-accent-level capital value variation and the contexts as well as politics of their occurrence (Blommaert, 2007).

Finally, in much of the literature on World Englishes, talk about transplantation has been about English as a language unit. Even its indigenization around the world has been discussed within the framework of the emergence of new Englishes. However, there is a relative paucity of literature on the adoption and reinterpretation of sublanguage forms. In other words, instead of the wholesale adoption of English across all functions and interactional regimes in specific national contexts, partial adoptions of the language might be incorporated into or accommodated within an emergent hybrid global dialect of English that includes forms from all three of Kachru's Circles. These forms may be evident at a microlevel, for instance, in marking politeness, in telephony practices and so on. The sociolinguistic research of popular culture, especially of hip-hop which has been growing recently, has provided invaluable insights into the transnational appeal of some elements of language use such as the tropes that are globally observed in rap performances. Similarly, 'call and response', code-switching and other discursive practices of the third space (cf. Bhatt, 2008), and 'deterritorial multilingualism' associated with globalization pose problems for old analytical frameworks. These consequences of what Pennycook (2007) calls transcultural flows require further exploration towards revising the World Englishes paradigm for more efficient analyses of the social realities of globalization. Such transcultural flows of Englishes need to be conceptualized, described and explained within some of the fundamental questions raised in this chapter and the central issues driving the emerging new world order of 21st-century globalization.

## References

Adams, W.M. (2001) *Green Development: Environment and Sustainability in the Third World* (2nd edn). London: Routledge.

Appadurai, A. (1996) *Modernity at Large: Cultural Dimensions of Globalization.* Minneapolis: University of Minnesota Press.
Bagchi, P.C. (1981) *India and China: A Thousand Years of Cultural Relations.* Calcutta: Saraswat Publishing.
Bhatt, R.M. (2008) In other words: Language mixing, identity representations, and third space. *Journal of Sociolinguistics* 12 (2), 177–200.
Blommaert, J. (2007) A market of accents. *Language Policy* 3 (9), 243–259.
Bruthiaux, P. (2003) Squaring the circles: Issues in modeling English worldwide. *International Journal of Applied Linguistics* 13 (2), 159–178.
Canagarajah, S.A. (1999) *Resisting Linguistic Imperialism in English Teaching.* Oxford: Oxford University Press.
Canagarajah, S.A. (2007) Lingua Franca English, multilingual communities, and language acquisition. *The Modern Language Journal* 91 (5), 921–937.
Castells, M. (1996) *The Rise of the Network Society.* Malden, MA, Oxford: Blackwell.
Cerny, P.G. (2003) The uneven pluralization of world politics. In A. Hülsemeyer (ed.) *Globaliztion in the Twenty-First Century: Convergence or Divergence?* (pp. 153–175). New York: Palgrave Macmillan.
Choo, S.T.P. (2008) Bollywood to conquer Hollywood: India plans world domination with movies. *Borneo Bulletin* 1 June 2008, p. 30.
Cowen, M.P. and Shenton, R.W. (1996) *Doctrines of Development.* London: Routledge.
Crang, P. (1999) Local-global. In P.J. Cloke, P. Crang and M. Goodwin (eds) *Introducing Human Geographies* (pp. 34–50). London: Arnold.
Gibson-Graham, J.K. (2002) Beyond global vs. local: Economic politics outside the binary frame. In A. Herod and M.W. Wright (eds) *Geographies of Power: Placing Scale.* Oxford: Blackwell.
Giddens, A. (1990) *The Consequences of Modernity.* Cambridge: Polity Press.
Harvey, D. (1989) *The Condition of Postmodernity: An Enquiry into the Origins of Cultural Change.* Oxford: Blackwell.
Held. D., McGrew, A.G., Goldblatt, D. and Perraton, J. (1999) *Global Transformations: Politics, Economics and Culture.* Cambridge: Polity Press.
Herod, A. (2003) Scale: The local and the global. In S. Holloway, S. Rice and G. Valentine (eds) *Key Concepts in Geography* (pp. 229–247). London: Sage.
Hülsemeyer, A. (ed.) (2003) *Globalization in the Twenty-First Century: Convergence or Divergence?.* New York: Palgrave Macmillan.
Inagaki, Noriko (2008) Reversing the curse of babel. Paper presented at the *Multilingual Transnational Neighbourhoods Workshop,* University of Southampton, 2–3 June 2008.
Janelle, D.G. (1973) Measuring human extensibility in a shrinking world. *Journal of Geography* 72, 8–15.
Jenkins, J. (2003) *World Englishes: A Resource Book for Students.* London: Routledge.
Kennett, P. (2008) Introduction: Governance, the state and policy making in a global age. In P. Kennett (ed.) *Governance, Globalization and Public Policy* (pp. 3–18). Cheltenham: Edward Elgar.
Massey, D.B. (1991) A global sense of place. *Marxism Today,* 24–29 June.
Mittelman, J.H. (2000) *The Globalization Syndrome: Transformation and Resistance.* Princeton, NJ: Princeton University Press.
Murray, W.E. (2006) *Geographies of Globalization.* London: Routledge.

Nayar, P.B. (1997) ESL/EFL dichotomy today: Language politics or pragmatics? *TESOL Quarterly* 31 (1), 9–37.

Parakrama, A. (1995) *De-hegemonizing Language Standards*. Basingstoke: Macmillan.

Pennycook, A. (2003) Global Englishes, Rip Slyme, and performativity. *Journal of Sociolinguistics* 7 (4), 513–533.

Pennycook, A. (2007) *Global Englishes and Transcultural Flows*. London: Routledge.

Phillipson, R. (1992) *Linguistic Imperialism*. Oxford: Oxford University Press.

Seidlhofer, B. (2001) Closing a conceptual gap: The case for a description of English as a lingua franca. *International Journal of Applied Linguistics* 11, 133–158.

Skutnabb-Kangas, T. (2000) *Linguistic Genocide in Education, or Worldwide Diversity and Human Rights*. Mahwah, NJ: Lawrence Erlbaum.

Stalker, P. (2000) *Workers without Frontiers: The Impact of Globalization on International Migration*. Boulder, CO: Lynne Rienner.

# Index